In Search of the Elusive Zimbabwean Dream

VOLUME I

VOLUME II: The Path to Power (2003–2008)
VOLUME III: The Deputy Prime Minister and Beyond (2009–2017)

In Search of the Elusive Zimbabwean Dream

AN AUTOBIOGRAPHY OF THOUGHT LEADERSHIP

VOLUME I

THE FORMATIVE YEARS AND THE BIG WIDE WORLD
(1983–2002)

Professor Arthur G.O. Mutambara

SAPES Books
Harare, Zimbabwe

Staging Post
The Stories We Tell

First published by Staging Post in 2017

10 Orange Street
Sunnyside
Auckland Park 2092
South Africa
+2711 628 3200
www.stagingpost.co.za

ISBN 978-0-9947079-2-5 (paperback)
ISBN 978-0-9947128-0-6 (hardcover)

Cover design by Shawn Paikin
Set in ITC Garamond 10/12pt
Printed by ABC Press, Cape Town
Job no. 002999

This book is dedicated to the heroic people of Zimbabwe as they strive for peace, equality, stability, inclusive democracy and shared economic prosperity
– The Elusive Zimbabwean Dream

Table of Contents

About the Author

Professor Arthur G.O. Mutambara is the former Deputy Prime Minister (DPM) of the Republic of Zimbabwe. He was one of the three Principals who created and led the Government of National Unity (GNU). The other two were Prime Minister Morgan Tsvangirai and President Robert Mugabe. As the Deputy Prime Minister, his key functions included assisting the Prime Minister in policy formulation by the Cabinet and supervision of policy implementation by the Council of Ministers. He also specifically supervised the Ministries which fell under the Infrastructure Cluster, such as Energy and Power Development, Transport and Infrastructure, Information Communication Technologies, Water Resources and Development, and Public Works. Professor Mutambara was also involved in coordinating regional policy formulation, within these sectors, across SADC and COMESA. Furthermore, DPM Mutambara was in charge of driving three key national efforts of the GNU: development of a *Shared National Vision*, *Rebranding Zimbabwe*, and formulating a *National Infrastructure Master Plan*.

Professor Mutambara is currently the President of the African News Agency (ANA), Africa's first syndicated, technology-driven multimedia news platform. His primary mandate includes media technology innovation, digital platform development, and harnessing social media tools. In particular, he is driving the use of Artificial Intelligence and deployment of Intelligent Algorithms in media, resulting in the development of new business models. An additional mandate involves the development of strategic media relationships and partnerships across the African continent. Prior to ANA, Professor Mutambara headed a team of consultants who provided high technology and strategic advisory services throughout Africa.

He is a Chartered Engineer, a Fellow of the Institute of Engineering and Technology (IET), a Professional Engineer, a Fellow of the Zimbabwe Institute of Engineers (ZIE), a Fellow of the Zimbabwe Academy of Sciences (ZAS), and a Senior Member of the Institute of Electrical and Electronic

Engineering (IEEE). He was Director of Electronic Payments at Standard Bank in South Africa. In the United States, he was a Research Scientist at the National Aeronautics and Space Administration (NASA), Visiting Professor at the Massachusetts Institute of Technology (MIT), Professor at the Florida Agricultural and Mechanical University – Florida State University (FAMU-FSU) College of Engineering, and a Management Consultant with McKinsey & Company. He has written two electrical engineering books that are widely used in engineering graduate schools in the US, Europe, China, Japan and Africa: *Decentralized Estimation and Control for Multisensor Systems*, and *Design and Analysis of Control Systems*.

Prof. Mutambara holds a PhD in Robotics and Mechatronics and an MSc in Computer Engineering, both from the University of Oxford where he was a Rhodes Scholar. He graduated in 1991 with a BSc (Honours) in Electrical and Electronic Engineering from the University of Zimbabwe, where he was Students' Union President from 1989 to 1990, and Secretary General from 1988 to 1989. In 2007, Mutambara was accorded the World Economic Forum's (WEF) Young Global Leader (YGL) status, and subsequently attended WEF events from 2007 to 2013 in Davos (Switzerland), China, India and Africa.

Acknowledgements

I would like to thank the following for reading various parts of the manuscript and providing useful comments: Dr Ibbo Mandaza, Dr Blessing-Miles Tendi, Prof. Lovemore Madhuku, Munyaradzi Gwisai, Prof. Paul Mavima, Dr Cyril Ruwende, Prof. Adekeye Adebajo, Andrea Bryce, Brendan Seery, Ryland Fisher, Shepherd Mukwekwezeke, Tsitsi Dangarembga, Josiah Sithole, Ignatius Mabveni and Moses Mudzwiti. The institutions that housed and nurtured me, as my thoughts developed, deserve special mention: Hartzell High School, University of Zimbabwe, UZ Students' Union, Wankie Colliery Company, University of Oxford, Merton College, Programming Research Group, Robotics Research Group, Massachusetts Institute of Technology (MIT), National Aeronautics and Space Administration (NASA), McKinsey & Company, and FAMU-FSU College of Engineering. I would also like to thank my family for their support: my wife Dr Jacqueline Mutambara; sons Gutsai and Kundai Mutambara; my sisters, Dr Audrey Mutambara (Mabveni), Prof. Tsitsi Mutambara and Dr Rosemary Mutambara (Chigwanda).

Preface

Since the dawn of independence on 18 April 1980, Zimbabweans have striven to achieve the 'Zimbabwean Dream' – peace, equality, stability, inclusive democracy and shared economic prosperity. This aspirational vision has remained largely elusive, notwithstanding the extensive efforts towards its achievement. These vigorous attempts have been rooted in unflinching determination by an active citizenry. *In Search of the Elusive Zimbabwean Dream: An Autobiography of Thought Leadership* is a series comprising three volumes based on my political interpretations, leadership opinions and philosophical disposition over a period of 35 years, from 1983 to 2017. This is an era in which my generation and the rest of the nation have sought to become the change they wish to occur in Zimbabwe. It is a period whose hallmark is a growing political consciousness and involvement of my generation in an effort towards political and socio-economic transformation and regeneration.

This series is a collection of three volumes of grounded reflections that I expressed over time, as I endeavoured to move, lead and inspire people. These reflections were informed by research, observation and experiences. The trilogy records my initiatives that sought to turn strategic thinking into reality through the speed of execution. The work is ostensibly the documentation of my participation in, and contributions to, thought leadership – *intellectual influence through innovative and pioneering thinking*. My ambition has always been to change the world by igniting citizen activism through ideas. The collection is a journey of ideas that created evolutionary, and even revolutionary, advancement of inclusive democratic values, institution building, social justice, empowerment, shared economic prosperity, people-centred governance, ethical leadership and efficacious statecraft. Events and circumstances leading to, and informing, the documented thoughts are presented and discussed. Thus, the three books consist of contextualised anthologies of speeches, statements and publications I have made over 35 years. Admittedly, over such a long expedition, from 1983 to 2017, there have been mistakes, failures, oversights, but there was intellectual growth and expansion, as my ideas distilled and in some cases changed, crystallised, broadened and deepened. In some instances, there have been radical shifts, as was the case with my position on the one-party state system. It is also of significance that some of the forthright speeches on social, political and economic matters presented in these books have led to my persecution, arrests, torture, detention and trial by the authorities in Zimbabwe.

The speeches in this anthology reveal unrelentingly consistent themes and ideological dispositions from 1983 through to 2017. These enduring themes include a belief in the legacy and values of the liberation struggle, anti-imperialism, servant leadership, egalitarianism, justice and equality. They also incorporate a nationalist outlook, people-centredness, Pan-Africanism, social and gender justice, meritocracy, fairness and equity, technology-driven leapfrogging and Afro-centricity. These foundational frameworks and ethos are what I believe inform and underpin an aspirational shared national socio-political-economic destination, which is yet to be achieved in Zimbabwe. Although the paradigms and prescriptions proffered in these books span a period of more than three decades, their intrinsic value and relevance are both enduring and timeless. This is particularly so for the postulations on value systems, redefining competitiveness, national vision, regional integration, nation branding, 21st-century Pan-Africanism, China–Africa relationships, unmined resource value, the sovereign wealth fund concept, the ICT revolution, womenomics, glocalisation, coopetition, green economy leverage, creating shared value, making sustainability profitable and talentism. In fact, these aspects of thought leadership and empowering statecraft have become even more relevant and applicable in our beloved Zimbabwe today than when they were first proffered. The redemptive and paradigmatic shift required in the country in order to achieve sustainable national development and shared economic prosperity requires the operationalisation of some of these thoughts.

While the views are primarily in pursuit of the Zimbabwean Dream, there is a strong Pan-Africanist thread pervading all the thoughts, particularly in the later years, which include my invaluable tenure as Deputy Prime Minister of the Republic of Zimbabwe. Hence, the material presented in the three books also lays the foundation for the ambitious vision of the African Dream, characterised by a peaceful, stable, integrated, democratic, technology-driven, industrial, and economically prosperous continent according all the associated social amenities to its citizenry. Under globalisation, the nation state is no longer a viable unit of analysis, political stability, economic growth or security, neither is it still the best platform for survival or prosperity. Instead, regional and continental initiatives, organisations and frameworks have since become the more efficacious platforms. It is precisely for this reason that Pan-Africanism is a recurring theme in the three books. The advent of Brexit (the United Kingdom's prospective withdrawal from the European Union) in 2016 and the election of Donald Trump as President of the United States, in the same year, while seeming to dent the perceived viability, assumed efficacy and global desirability of regional economics, only serve to increase rather than decrease the urgent need for regional and continental integration on the African continent. The value proposition of Kwame Nkrumah's vision – a united and integrated Africa – remains unassailable.

This anthology also attempts, in its own way, to resolve one of the African continent's tragedies, that its peoples generally do not have a strong reading culture, much less a vibrant writing culture. More specifically, African leaders, activists and changemakers do not adequately, if at all, document their experiences. This malaise needs to be addressed in order to enhance the collective repertoire of national and Pan-African institutional memory and value, as well as advance individual development. Successful civilisations flourished, and continue to do so, because they cherish reading and writing their own experiences. Documentation is divine, sacrosanct, instructive, durable and eternal. The three books constitute a modest and personal effort at addressing this challenge within the Zimbabwean context. My views and thoughts over the past 35 years which are documented in the three books are organised as follows: Volume I: *The Formative Years and the Big Wide World (1983–2002)*; Volume II: *The Path to Power (2003–2008)*; Volume III: *The Deputy Prime Minister and Beyond (2009–2017).*

This book, Volume I, deals with my formative years and early professional career during my sojourn in the big wide world. The starting point is engaging the thoughts and experiences that shaped my early consciousness and politics. The record of my reflections starts in 1983 as a 16-year-old Form 3 student at Hartzell High School in Manicaland, Zimbabwe. I was, at that time, clearly in awe of, and intrigued by, the grand narratives of the liberation struggle. I was a zealot of the new dispensation. When I was in Form 6 in 1986, I participated in an essay-writing competition organised by the Commonwealth Parliamentary Association. I won a national prize with a submission that defended the one-party state system as the necessary foundation for the development of socialism in Zimbabwe. Thereafter, I enrolled at the University of Zimbabwe (UZ) from 1987 to 1990, where I studied for a BSc (Honours) degree in Electrical and Electronic Engineering.

These were the glorious days of uncompromising student radicalism steeped in Marxist-Leninist thinking. I, together with other students, adopted communism as my political ideology and philosophy, while embracing socialism as the corresponding socio-economic system we sought to establish in Zimbabwe. I was elected Secretary General and then President of the UZ Students' Union. Writings and speeches from this period include relentless attacks on government corruption and challenging misguided government priorities, while voicing opposition to the one-party state, and pushing for academic freedom, democratic rights and social justice. The statement *'In defence of academic freedom',* which I released on 2 October 1989 in response to police brutality and interference on campus, led to the unprecedented and violent closure of UZ on 4 October 1989. Earlier on that fateful day, at around 3am, about 300 armed police and army units had invaded the UZ campus. They raided my university hall of residence and violently captured me. I was badly injured in the incident and subsequently detained without trial for six weeks. The university was later reopened and I was also eventually released. I completed my degree with outstanding performance and was awarded a Rhodes Scholarship and a place to pursue graduate studies at the prestigious University of Oxford.

It must be noted that our national political efforts, as the UZ Students' Union, were not in vain. They were complemented by those of an increasingly radicalised labour movement, vocal academics at UZ, nascent opposition groupings, and the reawakening churches. As a direct consequence of these mutually reinforcing activities, the ZANU-PF government's campaign for a one-party state was defeated, plural politics started to germinate, and the demand for a democratic culture grew louder. We inspired civil society and it blossomed. More importantly, the pivotal unity in struggle among the workers, students and academics, against neo-colonialism, was established, and continued to grow.

As I lurched and dived into the big wide world, the journey of ideas did not stop. It continued at Merton College, University of Oxford, in the United Kingdom, from 1991 to 1995. I was a Rhodes Scholar, studying for an MSc in Computer Engineering and a PhD in Robotics and Mechatronics. I was elected President of the Merton College Middle Common Room (Graduate Union) and President of the Oxford University Africa Society. Issues explored and articulated in this period included the Oxford experience, the collapse of Eastern Europe, Pan-Africanism and the Japanese economic miracle. From Oxford, the thought leadership odyssey moved across the Atlantic to the United States, from 1995 to 2002, where I was, among other roles, a Research Scientist at the National Aeronautics and Space Administration (NASA), Professor at the Massachusetts Institute of Technology (MIT), Management Consultant at McKinsey & Company, and Professor at the FAMU-FSU College of Engineering. Thought leadership engagement during this sojourn included African-American struggles, general US politics, the African agenda and the Zimbabwean governance crisis. Thereafter, in 2002, I headed back to the continent, to South Africa, with a renewed focus on redemptive narratives for the continent, SADC and Zimbabwe.

The book is organised into three sections: Section One – *A Naive but Vigorous Young Mind (1983–1986)*; Section Two – *No to the One-Party State! Yes to Socialism! (1987–1991)*; and Section Three – *Out into the Big Wide World (1991–2002)*. Each of these sections opens with a chapter in which I present the context in terms of the events and circumstances leading to, and informing, the documented thoughts and views. I also review some of the outcomes and analysis thereof. In this way, the context, circumstances and issues are discussed. All this is done in the present tense as the events unfold. Thereafter, in the subsequent chapters of each section, the speeches are also presented in the same tense. This book provides a story of ideas and thoughts as they develop.

SECTION ONE

A Naive but Vigorous Young Mind

1983–1986

The context, circumstances and issues

As a student at Hartzell High School, I have a naive, uncritical and romantic view of Zimbabwe's national liberation struggle, its participants and outcomes. That naivety, however, also contains a purity of thought about principles and ideas which are at the core of my political disposition. These values also constitute the essence of my thinking, to which I stay true through the ups and downs of my political life. My writings show the early euphoria of post-independence Zimbabwe, when the newly minted state is full of promise, and is the envy of many across Africa. It is also a time of significant hope and opportunity for young people like me. My imaginative portrayal of the heroic exploits of guerrilla fighters, in a winning national essay for the Ecumenical Arts Workshop creative writing competition in 1983, at the tender age of 16, shows my innate understanding of the redemptive nature of the revolutionary violence deployed by freedom fighters in the armed struggle for independence, the cruelty and savagery of the colonial regime, and the brutality of war in general. Respect for Zimbabwe's liberation struggle and its legacy is one of the enduring themes of my political disposition. While I later revolt and fight against the excesses of the Robert Mugabe regime, I am all too aware of the sacrifices made by the freedom fighters and ordinary Zimbabweans, in pursuit of our national independence. The ideals of those gallant armed guerrillas – freedom, democracy, non-racialism, equity and commitment to a struggle whatever the cost – remain with me throughout my life. Of course, I later challenge the Zimbabwe African National Union – Patriotic Front's (ZANU-PF) attempts to monopolise the liberation struggle, as it seeks to ring-fence patriotism, in a brazen strategy to defend its excesses.

Still in high school, as my education advances and my intellect grows, I then move on to tackling sensitive Zimbabwean and global issues through the prism of the youth, for whom I am one of its aspiring spokespersons. I believe the future lies in the hands of the youth of the world and serve notice that the new youthful wave will change the conservatism of the older generation. My ideas are beginning to form and take shape, with my recognition that the problems of young people are often social, and not always political, in nature. My belief that the youth are the drivers of change has its genesis in my early years and my suggestions for youth programmes still have resonance to this day, no matter what ideology holds sway in a particular country. This awakening about the role of young people is clearly manifest in my speech at the International Youth Year Conference on 12 December 1985 at the University of Zimbabwe in Harare. Also formed at this time are my strong beliefs that hard work, commitment, resilience, conviction, discipline and self-awareness are what are needed to drive any revolution.

My political beliefs are fluid and evolving, but I am clearly strongly influenced by socialist and communist revolutionaries such as Karl Marx, Vladimir Lenin and Mao Tse-tung. In fact, I slowly gravitate towards communism as my political ideology and philosophy, while envisaging socialism as the aspirational socio-economic system. It is essential to note that at this time, Zimbabwe is just five years into independence, young people are still radicalised from the recent war, socialist rhetoric dominates the national discourse, and the ruling party ZANU-PF is still viewed as the only vehicle for revolutionary transformation. As a result, I also embrace the idea of the one-party state as the best possible political system for Zimbabwe. I posit the idea that multi-party democracy is a Western concept. My ascriptions to a one-party state reflect my understanding and admiration of Lenin's philosophy, namely that a true socialist revolution can only be led by an elite 'vanguard party'. At the same time, my beliefs recognise that a redistribution of wealth has to occur to sustain peace in post-colonial Africa.

As the crowning act for this period in my intellectual growth, in September 1986, while I am in Form 6, I participate in an essay-writing competition organised by the Commonwealth Parliamentary Association (CPA) on the subject of the one-party state in Zimbabwe. I win a national prize for my submission that defends the one-party state system as the necessary foundation for the development of socialism in Zimbabwe. There I am, defending a ZANU-PF one-party state in Zimbabwe! I am not alone, though. Every one, without exception, of the other seven winners from the various provinces is vigorous in their support for a ZANU-PF one-party state as the vehicle to socialism. We all get together to receive our awards at the Parliament of Zimbabwe on 3 December 1986, where a lavish dinner is hosted for us by the Speakers of the Zimbabwean and Tanzanian Parliaments, Honourable Didymus Mutasa and Honourable Chief Adam Sapi Mkwawa, respectively. Among these seven other prizewinners are two later-to-be-avowed acerbic critics of ZANU-PF – Munyaradzi Gwisai (then Enock Chikweche), representing Chaplin High School, and the late Lovemore (Briggs) Zano, representing Allan Wilson High School. ZANU-PF, the one-party state and socialism are in vogue. They define the national mood. This is particularly so among the young, who are still in awe of, and heavily inspired by, the liberation war. This is in addition to being continuously subjected to the intoxicating ZANU-PF socialist rhetoric and narratives about a glorious revolution. It is important to note that in the period 1982 to 1987, the Gukurahundi massacres are taking place in the southern provinces of Zimbabwe. However, there is a total media blackout on the severity of the situation and culpability of the Zimbabwean state. As a young and impressionable high school student in Manicaland, all I grasp is that there are disturbances and strife in Matabeleland, without sufficiently questioning the role of the ZANU-PF government.

One source of immense inspiration to us, as young people in high school, is Samora Moisés Machel, the first President of Mozambique who led the country to independence in 1975. When he is killed on Sunday, 19 October 1986, after his presidential aircraft crashes near the border of Mozambique and South Africa, we are gutted. We are inconsolable. Our great hero, the venerated Mozambican military commander, distinguished politician and avowed Marxist-Leninist is gone. We have to do something. On Tuesday, 21 October 1986, we decide to march from Hartzell High School to the city of Mutare, a journey of some 17 kilometres, going through the mountainous Christmas Pass highway. Along the way, we sing liberation struggle songs and chant revolutionary slogans. When we get into Mutare, we go straight to the ZANU-PF offices where Edgar Tekere, former ZANU-PF Secretary General and the current chairman of the party in Manicaland, speaks to our group. Before his address, I am asked to speak on behalf of the students. I am brief and, in part, say the following:

> *Cde Edgar Tekere, the Chairman of ZANU-PF in Manicaland, Fellow Students, and the People of Zimbabwe;*
>
> *Allow me to say a few words on this sad day. A dark cloud has engulfed the African continent. A gallant son of the soil has been uprooted from us: a freedom fighter, a distinguished commander, a liberation hero, a revolutionary socialist, and a Pan-Africanist. Without Samora Machel, there would be no ZANLA, there would be no ZANU-PF, and there would be neither independence nor freedom in Zimbabwe. Samora Machel was the creator of the Zimbabwean state. Without Samora Machel, there would be neither Cde Edgar Tekere nor Cde Robert Mugabe.*
>
> *The apartheid regime in South Africa has killed the founding father of armed and revolutionary struggles in Southern Africa. That cowardly racist, P.W. Botha, must pay. Cde Edgar Tekere, fellow students, and the people of Zimbabwe, we must keep the legacy and spirit of Samora Machel alive. Anyway, we can para-phrase General Douglas MacArthur and say, "Revolutionaries never die, they just fade away."*
>
> *Viva Samora Machel. Abasha P.W. Botha.*

This is my first national political speech! I am just 20 years old, and give it while sharing the platform with the great freedom fighter, distinguished nationalist, and liberation war hero, Cde Edgar Tekere.

Already formed, or developing, at this stage in my life, are beliefs in social justice, equality and the need for Africans to take charge of their own future. It may be easy to consider these early outputs of my questioning mind to be naive, but in their innocence, they show my early-in-life commitment to the Mahatma Gandhi doctrine of 'being the change you want to see in the world'. I pledge total allegiance to the service of my people and country.

While I am politically conscious and active, I maintain a stunning and outstanding record of academic excellence throughout my years in high school. I am consistently, without variation, number one out of about 130 students, during my entire six years at Hartzell High School. At the end of Form 4, in 1984, with eight distinctions (A grades) in the Cambridge Ordinary Level Examinations, I am the top student in the school and one of the best in the country. I am the top student in Manicaland Province. In 1986, in Form 6, I am the top student in all my five Advanced Level subjects: Mathematics, Physics, Chemistry, Further Mathematics and General Paper. At a colourful prize-giving ceremony I receive the five A Level Book Prizes, an unprecedented feat at Hartzell High School. In fact, in three out of four of the Mid-Year Examination papers I sit for, in preparation for the Mathematics and Further Mathematics final examinations, I achieve the perfect score of 100 per cent. When the final A Level results are out, once again, I have some of the top results in the country, and certainly the best in Manicaland Province. That same year, while in Form 6, I also win the Silver Medal in the National Mathematics Olympiad, organised by Old Mutual and the Department of Mathematics at the University of Zimbabwe. I am number two in the whole of Zimbabwe. On 6 August 1986, there is a Mathematics Olympiad Lunch and Award Ceremony, organised by Old Mutual in Harare, for the top three national winners. Prof. Phineas Makhurane, the Pro Vice Chancellor at the University of Zimbabwe, is the Guest of Honour. Kevin van Breda of St George's College is number one, I come in second, and Divya Sundaram of Peterhouse Boys' School takes the third position.

After the sterling Mathematics Olympiad performance, back at my school, the Headmaster, Mr Shepherd Mukwekwezeke, asks me to address the whole school. I do not say much. I am used to speeches of a political nature, and certainly not ones where one is receiving an award or accolades. Among my few words were the following:

> *The Headmaster, Members of Staff, Fellow Students*
> *Lend me your ears.*
>
> *I would like to thank the Headmaster, Mr Shepherd Mukwekwezeke, for affording me this opportunity to speak before you all. I feel honoured. I would also like to extend my gratitude to Old Mutual and*

> *the UZ Department of Mathematics for organising the Mathematics Olympiad. My Mathematics teachers, Mr Christopher Mvere and Mr Frederick Fee, are the real winners today. I thank them profusely. As students, we must study hard. We must have both ambition and discipline, while staying focused. Without hard work and dedication, there is no victory. In fact, success is 99 per cent perspiration and 1 per cent God!*
>
> *I thank you.*

The students are ecstatic. They are cheering in uncontrollable applause. That last bit about perspiration is what my fellow students find most memorable and humorous. Do they realise I am quite serious, I wonder? Will they internalise the philosophy behind the dictum? I do not know. I am only 20, yet I am very convinced about the immortality and unassailability of my argument. Owing to my Mathematics Olympiad performance, Old Mutual offers me a scholarship to pursue Actuarial Science, but I turn them down. I want to pursue Electrical and Electronic Engineering at the University of Zimbabwe.

(Gandhi, 1927) (Fanon, 1963)

1 A day in the life of a freedom fighter

This is an essay I write for the National Ecumenical Arts Workshop's creative writing competition. I participate as a Hartzell High School Form 3 student and win the national prize. The programme is run by prominent authors, Chenjerai Hove and Charles Mungoshi, at St Patrick's Secondary School in Gweru on 24 April 1983. The essay demonstrates the extent of the influence of the liberation struggle narratives on a young man with a romantic view of guerrilla warfare.

It was not a dream, neither was it mere imagination. As if I could not believe my five senses I pinched my arm. 'Well, no dreaming this time, boy,' my sixth sense whispered into my literally unconscious brain.

Above my head, a bird was hovering. It was a bird which laid poisoned eggs, explosive eggs which split apart body and soul. It was growling in the clouds, tilting now and then to deposit them – the yolks of death. Others were coming bursting with fury in the far-off distance.

My AK-47 was dangling at my side as I lay flat as a pancaked lizard in a crack. I felt it was a toy. It was useless in contrast to the jet bombers above. These enemy planes started to lay live chicks with big balloon-like wings. These started to dangle with deadly weaponry in their wings. They meant to finish off the remaining bits of life forms. I was one of those.

It was then that my body systems started to work at an accelerated rate. My heart began to pound up as if there were women pounding sorghum in my chest. 'But what has happened to my comrades?' I asked myself. I didn't know. As if in reply, I just set my eyes on one of them. There he was – Chimurengaihondo, with his toothless gums biting the dust. He was gone. Dead.

Hate and anger seized me and all the chicken-heartedness disappeared. I clutched my gun and crawled towards them – the parachutes. My blood was steaming. I had to take revenge.

After crawling for about five minutes I felt my hair stand on end. But there was no going back. I remembered my uncle's words: 'My son, fear is the traitor within.' These words strengthened me. I put off the safety catch and tensed my body for action.

I could see a moving figure disentangling himself from the parachute about 30 metres away. Well, that was that. I closed my eyes to pity, and I ripped his belly open with my AK. I saw the man hold his intestines in his hands before collapsing in a heap. The last thing I remember was a piece of metal piercing my wrist then my hand dancing in the sand. Then I blacked out.

2 The role of young people: Participation, development and peace

This is the speech I give at the 1985 International Youth Year Conference at the University of Zimbabwe in Harare on 12 December 1985. I am the selected student delegate from Hartzell High School. The Conference is officially opened by Deputy Prime Minister Simon Muzenda. It involves all key youth organisations in the country. It is my first big meeting away from my high school, and my first opportunity to mix and mingle with the UZ Students' Union leadership. As a Form 5 student, I am overly impressed by the eloquence of outgoing SRC President Edward Musabayana, and the sophistication of incoming SRC President, Kingdom Mabhena.

Since the beginning of the 20th century, the youth throughout the world have witnessed the dawning of a new era where the platform for them to contribute to shaping and designing the future of humanity has started to materialise. This is of paramount importance because the youth have 'strong backs' on which the economies of the international world are hinged. They constitute the most sensitive and dynamic component of society. If educated and well equipped with the necessary skills and disciplines, they are the forerunners and the vanguard of development. As scholars, young people provide progressive revolutionary intellectuals who are both the theoreticians and practitioners of revolutionary change and democratisation against a background of general conservatism and domination by the older generations. The youth should therefore participate in deciding what was good for them yesterday, what is good for them today and what will be good for them tomorrow. This is of undoubted necessity, for one cannot learn to swim by walking on the edge of a swimming pool.

For the past four to five years, Zimbabwe has done a commendable job in terms of addressing the affairs of young people. More schools have been built, both primary and secondary, to cater for the otherwise underprivileged and unschooled victims of colonialism. The unemployed and non-schoolgoing young people have been organised into youth brigades and cooperatives. In this way, they have been armed with different skills in such areas as agriculture, mechanics and building. Building brigades have been effective in constructing social amenities like schools and hospitals. Encouragement has also been given to the youth to organise themselves into cooperatives and joint ventures, all this being geared towards self-reliance. Technical colleges have been opened to absorb and accommodate Zimbabwean youth. These are institutions such as Kushinga Phikelela, the Nyabara School of Forestry and Magamba Agricultural Training Centre.

Historically, churches throughout the world have produced disciplined youth. Zimbabwe is no exception. Zimbabwean churches have played a positive role through youth fellowships and conferences where ideas on how best to serve society are discussed and adopted. This has been consolidated by efforts to raise funds for charitable organisations such as orphanages, adult literacy schools and hospitals through youth activities. Through the Ministry of Education, Sport and Culture, Zimbabwean youth have tried to bring about the promotion of sport and raised money for charity through events such as sponsored walks and charity matches. The UZ, through its TIRA (teaching in the rural areas) programme, has helped to alleviate the problem of the shortage of teaching staff in rural areas. It has provided medical students to rural hospitals for service.

The position of the youth has not always been rosy in Zimbabwe. Young people have been prone to a range of vices. There has been rising juvenile delinquency in the form of drug abuse, uncontrolled drunkenness of underage youth and sex abuse, leading to social cancers such as prostitution and baby dumping. As if this were not enough, the schools are producing learned youth but not educated youth. They are learned because they have acquired good grades at high school, but they are uneducated because they do not possess any appropriate skills, and lack the disciplined moral values called for by society. There seems to exist the unpalatable mentality of book education geared towards paper degrees. As a result, there is a high aspiration for white-collar jobs among the youth. This is retrogressive, not to mention counter-productive and counter-revolutionary.

Zimbabwean people need to own the means of production, that is, land, labour and capital. This calls for disciplined and skilled youth. Zimbabwe desires to bring about equitable distribution of wealth through a socialist revolution. How are they (the youth) going to bring about this democratisation at grass-roots level when they are victims of such vices outlined above? However, in Zimbabwe the struggle is not lost. This stage of the revolution is deceptively easy and this is why there are these deviations from the norm.

The above problems are not ideal or unique to Zimbabwe. They are problems of developing countries in general. Zimbabwe is simply an example. These are problems that threaten young and developing nations. Further disastrous setbacks that compound the difficulties are poverty, desertification, deforestation and political destabilisation. These problems cannot be wished away by academic or ideological incantations in the same way curses are dispensed with by incense burning. These challenges require both qualitative and quantitative analysis. That is primarily why we are here, ladies and gentlemen.

Where goest thou, youth? The youth should be absorbed into the economic and political mainstream. They should be taken into the National Service Programme. This may be after high school, just before joining a university or training institution. This could be done for a period of four to 12 months in the form of military service, health or helping in organisations like the local Red Cross. Service in the agricultural or industrial sectors would also be ideal. These activities would be for no personal gain to the youth, but simply in accordance with the theme of development.

Another more dramatic operation would be a 'Take a School to a Rural Area' programme, where pupils would spend six months sharing their agrarian expertise, industrial skills and scientific theories with those living in the rural areas. University students could do the same. In this way, the youth could fight Third World problems by spreading the gospel about the evils of cutting trees. They could bring reforestation by planting trees and conservation. Similarly, they could help fight desertification and poverty by advocating good agricultural practices. The studying of ecology and its balance can bring about the conservation and stability of ecosystems. This is the practical mode of learning.

University students could be assimilated into different ministries on their long vacations; for example, economists into the Ministry of Manpower Planning and Development, and physicists and engineers into the Ministry of Industry and Technology. Here they would carry out research and work as part of their studies for no financial gain. In the process, they would be able to take part in policymaking, thus conscientising the masses about government policy and ideology. Moreover, by meeting the people and reporting back to the respective ministries, it would be ensured that the umbilical cord between the people and the government would not be broken. The scholars and intellectuals having taken part in policymaking would undoubtedly approve of government policies and this would bring about harmony between agents of production.

On the theme of peace, the youth have a considerable role to play. The youth should form pressure groups and organisations which would discuss ideas against government involvement in nuclear arms production and deployment. They could boldly carry out mass demonstrations against nuclear deployment in their regions. As scholars of history and politics, being physicists and research scientists, they should write on the evils of nuclear weapons and conscientise the masses of their predicament in the event of a nuclear holocaust. They should talk about the amount of energy wasted in efforts leading to the extinction of mankind, when industries are starved of power.

Through sheer solidarity between youth organisations, international peace could be promoted. This solidarity could be manifested in the form of cultural exchanges, sharing of arts, literature, film and interaction in sport and technology. Ladies and gentlemen, no posh meeting on disarmament between Ronald Reagan and Mikhail Gorbachev could bring about world peace better than a simple charity soccer or basketball match between a youth team from the United States and their Soviet counterparts to raise funds for underprivileged Southern African youth!

Regional peace could be achieved through cooperation and interaction. In addition to military service and participation in the youth brigade, vigilance by the youth to infiltration by destabilisation forces is complementary. However, there is a danger that the effective role of youth in bringing peace could be minimised, because of rigid policies most governments have concerning military affairs. It seems the military is the cornerstone of power and politicians are less flexible in this area and, hence, they give the youth a secondary role. This militates against the establishment of peace.

Sometimes governments have to be cruel in order to be kind. This is what is called for on the issue of discipline. There should be direct government restriction concerning such facilities as night clubs, public drinking places, brothels and the type of films screened to the youth. These restrictions should be accepted to constitute the rule of thumb for young people. The exposure of the youth to certain drugs and narcotics should be limited if drug abuse is to be curbed. All the societal regulatory restrictions should be in accordance with the level of development of the concerned country. There is no need to expose schoolkids to films with sex scenes unless the government is prepared to legalise prostitution and brothels. This is not pragmatic for Africa. Throughout the world and on a global basis, governments should protect the young from sexual abuse. Social ills such as sex for jobs and 'sugar daddyism', which are characteristic of developing countries, should be nipped in the bud. Controversial issues like the use of contraceptives and abortion should be looked at through analytical spectacles and not oversimplified.

The general trend among developing countries is to shun the use of contraceptives, saying they are contrary to cultural and traditional practices. This is a suicidal blunder, for it ignores the very fact that culture is dynamic and not static. It is simply a characteristic of what is called the 'ostrich philosophy'. Ladies and gentlemen, do you know what any ostrich does when it is in great danger from a hungry hunter? It ducks its head and buries it in the sand while the bulk of its body is exposed. The idea being that it does not see the danger. This is ostrich philosophy, swimming in an ocean of fantasy in total disregard of reality. It is unrealistic because with the raging winds of change, it is almost inevitable that contraceptives will soon be part of our culture.

When all is said and done, all the above suggested ideas would not be worth the scroll they were scribbled on unless the youth achieved and acquired certain values and qualities demanded of them. The youth should be vigilant, resilient, patriotic and not spineless, reactionary and submissive. They should resist disruptive, subversive and destabilising attractions which can only lead to their demise. These forces could be in the form of warmongers, latter-day freedom fighters, diehard reactionaries, opportunistic political agitators and psychopathic leaders who bring endless wars for self-aggrandisement. It should be noted that it is the youth who fight and die in wars.

There is a lot of fighting worldwide: Nicaragua, San Salvador, Afghanistan, Namibia, South Africa, Iran, Iraq and Lebanon, to name a few. On top of that, the whole of Africa, from Cape to Cairo, is riddled with bandits and counter-revolutionaries. It is all fuss and fighting. But do the youth in all these cases see the nobility and justification of the causes of the struggles? Yes, the youths must fight in liberation struggles as they are doing with South West Africa People's Organisation (SWAPO), uMkhonto we Sizwe (MK) and the Azanian People's Liberation Army (APLA). However, there is the need to resist working with the destabilisation forces in Mozambique and Angola. Young people must not join rebels and bandits. This is in line with the theme of peace.

The youth should be gallant and fearless. Young people with freedom of speech say statements as a measure of that which is factual. They should be bold enough to stick their necks out and point out areas of corruption, weakness or maladministration. Contrasting ideas, revision of opinions, points of correction and alternative viewpoints are characteristics of a healthy state of affairs. They are signs of growth, maturity and responsibility. They are priceless! Young people globally should try to avoid and reduce East-West polarisation among themselves. United we stand, divided we fall. We need more cooperation than competition. This is in keeping with the theme of peaceful coexistence between nations irrespective of ideological differences.

In the final analysis, ladies and gentlemen, the dynamism, sensitivity, intellectualism and revolutionary radicalism of the youth cannot be overemphasised. The youth's struggle for self-determination drives socio-geopolitical progress and democratisation. This follows from the fact that the true determinant of democracy is the extent to which there is participation by ordinary people, including the youth. Young people are the agents of revolution. Mr Chairman, change, forever change, for to resist change is to resist life itself. We are the creators of our own future. Yes, we the youth of Zimbabwe shall make history, if not invert and reinvent it. Thank you.

(Chung, 1985) (Marx, 1969)

3 In defence of the one-party system as the foundation for socialism

In September 1986, the Commonwealth Parliamentary Association organises an essay competition on the efficacy and relevance of the one-party state system in Zimbabwe. The topic is as follows:
'The one-party parliamentary system, rather than the multiparty system, is more conducive and relevant to Zimbabwe's thrust towards socialist development. Do you agree? Give a reasoned reply.'
Below is my response affirming the proposition, which I pen as a Form 6 student at Hartzell High School. I win a national prize. I am in good company in my defence of the one-party system. All seven other winners from the various provinces are of the same disposition. As young people, we are still heavily inspired by ZANU-PF's liberation war credentials and we are oblivious to its excesses. Hence, we give the party unconditional and uncritical support. We are also convinced about the value proposition of socialism as the ideal socio-economic system for our country. This is because we are continuously subjected to the seductive ZANU-PF socialist rhetoric, which is backed by a popular ZTV programme called The Road to Socialism, *featuring prominent revolutionary intellectuals like Kempton Makamure and Shadrack Gutto.*

As political, social and economic conditions vary considerably from country to country, so does the form of power. In fact, there is conflict between the character of political power in contemporary Africa and the idea of an opposition party as known in Western democracies. It is within this context that there is room for honest debate and discussion as to whether 'the one-party state system, rather than the multiparty system, is more conducive ...'

Fundamentally, a one-party state democracy constitutes a political situation whereby there is one authentic vanguard party in a country. This is an umbrella organisation covering a wide spectrum of diversified opinions. The non-existence of other political parties is obvious, but the methods of eradicating them differ. These range from integrating them into the one-party political mainstream, to elimination by any means appropriate, relegating them by destroying their impetus for existence and, finally, by making them join the ruling party after round-table negotiations or out of free will.

The alternative to the one-party system is the multiparty system. In essence, this depicts the proliferation and spread of political parties, ranging from diehard right-wing conservatives to extreme leftists. In between are sandwiched democrats, republicans and liberal democrats ... the list is endless! Elections are held, usually after five years, and the party with the majority forms a government, or if there is no majority a coalition government is formed. Thus, the multiparty democracy. Where goest thou, Zimbabwe?

Zimbabwe is a newborn nation crawling out of colonialism, imperialism and subjugation, and still intertwined and mingled with neo-colonialism within a capitalist economic structure. Zimbabwean politicians are emerging from nationalism to internationalism; they are moving from being theoreticians to being practitioners of revolutionary change. In short, we have a revolutionary government trying to transform society into an egalitarian socialist state. But apparently not everyone who fought against colonial rule and its evils is a socialist! In fact, there are some petit bourgeoisie, comprador bourgeoisie and motivated anti-colonial agitators whose middle-class mentality compelled them to fight the oppressive Smith regime. Thus, the Zimbabwean socio-geopolitical atmosphere that confronts this debate is complex.

Sticking to political exactitude, the Zimbabwean political climate is composed of ZANU-PF as the dominating popular front. Its popularity and sovereignty are manifested by its overwhelming victory in two consecutive elections. This is a mass party with worker and peasant interests at heart. Minority opposition parties are in the form of the Zimbabwe African People's Union (ZAPU), United African National Council (UANC), Zimbabwe African National Union (ZANU) (Sithole), Conservative Alliance of Zimbabwe (CAZ) and Independent Zimbabwe Group (IZG). These, except for ZAPU, which claims socialist ideals, have generally conservative, reactionary and particularly anti-socialist tendencies. These are the political dynamics in Zimbabwe today.

With the Zimbabwean socio-economic political arena portrayed, unwrapped and depicted as above, it is not surprising that the question of whether a one-party democracy is more conducive to Zimbabwe should arise. Within the given framework, it is abundantly clear that not only is the one-party system conducive to Zimbabwe, it is the best solution to Zimbabwe's socio-economic problems and the only guarantee for political stability.

Schools of thought against the above stance have centred on such concepts as: sacrifice of democracy; regimentation of society; national self-glorification; illusory ideological mongering and bickering; dictatorship and corruption; incompetence due to lack of an active opposition; and the likelihood of coups d'état. These reactions and concerns are born out of sheer oversimplification, lack of proper conceptualisation, basing ideas on pure romanticisation and mystification, while neglecting the Zimbabwean objective reality. As French philosopher Jean-Jacques Rousseau once said: 'Never confuse the reality that exists in your mind and the reality that prevails in your surroundings.' It can be portrayed, although with stress and strain, how a Zimbabwean one-party democracy answers to an intellectually reasonable extent the above-stated obstacles and criticisms.

The proliferation of political parties works against a healthy democracy for Zimbabwe, which does not lie essentially in a mass of conflicting opinions, but in the possibility for each group of people to satisfy its most noble national ambitions while respecting the equality of citizens without discrimination on the basis of birth, race or religion. This is evident of Zimbabwean society. One should dismiss the temptation to equate democracy to multiplicity of parties, for this multiplicity has been capable of making parties instruments of authoritarianism, fascism and, in some cases, dictatorship, much as a one-party system does.

Our position as a Third World country should be taken seriously, as well as our political, social and economic background. Yes, we can appreciate and emulate Western democracy, but can we afford it? Apparently not.

Zimbabwe is still building, restructuring, rehabilitating and resettling what was misshaped by colonial rule. Economic resources and political attention should go towards this re-establishment. Consequently, numerous political associations will militate against the policy of national cohesion and unity.

In any case, what is the origin of the multiparty system? Suggested opinions include the persistence of deep cleavages in a political society caused by differences in nationality or religion, irreconcilable elements within the nation, and social transformation whereby groups differ on both the goals and means of implementation. Now, do we have such a situation in Zimbabwe? It might be debatable but certain factors and concepts are easily discernible – pure and simple. We are one nation, basically a people of one nationality, we have the same problems of a post-independent nation and our goal is distinct and clear – to fight neo-colonialism and establish socialism. Then why should we be divided by a concept which is alien to Zimbabwe?

Scientific socialism is based on the theory and practice of the teachings of Marxism-Leninism as a world outlook, not on idealism and sentimentalism but on the use of dialectical materialism as the study of natural and social phenomena. In the study of human history and development, scientific socialism recognises class contradictions between the development of productive forces and relations of production as the motive force for social revolutions and human advancement. This is an applicable recipe for contemporary Zimbabwe.

The Zimbabwean economy at independence, in 1980, was – and to a large extent today is – capitalistic, exploitative and driven by the bourgeoisie and multinationals. They control and own the mining, manufacturing and even the agrarian sectors. The workers were, and continue to be, oppressed and have very little say in production. The profits generated are not ploughed back into the Zimbabwean economy, nor do the workers have any shares. In fact, the multinationals can be said to own the means of production. That's the economic problem of contemporary Zimbabwe.

To solve such a complex economic and social dilemma, it is imperative that revolutionary intellectuals conscientise, spearhead and champion scientific transformation in a bid to create a new economic order. This can only be achieved by a progressive worker-peasant class, well indoctrinated, conscientised, reoriented and hence ideologically clear-minded. Effectively, therefore, this calls for a well-organised vanguard party at the forefront of socialist change. A united front of revolutionaries is the only solution to the Zimbabwean economic situation of destabilising capitalism and its bourgeois morality, bringing about equitable distribution of resources, collective ownership of the means of production and general socio-political-economic democratisation. In fact, creating an egalitarian society should be our mission. This can only be possible under an umbrella organisation, the one party.

Of necessity, the party has to be a vanguard party and within the context of an underdeveloped society like Zimbabwe, an alliance between the workers, the peasantry and the revolutionary wing of the intelligentsia should form a combined force within it. This fits Zimbabwe's social strata. ZANU-PF is still a loose amalgamated mass party, but its adherence to socialism as an economic policy is distinct and definite. Back at the 1964 ZANU Congress, it declared socialism as its policy. In 1977, at Chimoio, Mozambique, the reality of the armed and ideological struggles led the party to further define its ideological direction in more scientific terms and it adopted Marxism-Leninism as its ideological stance. Hence, now in power the party is geared towards evolving into a vanguard organisation. Principles like the 'Leadership Code' go a long way to illustrate this process. Thus, if other progressive forces within the nation would unite under ZANU-PF in a bid towards socialism, this would become more of a reality than a pipe dream.

Bearing in mind that socialism is a historically determined phase in the development of society, unnecessary division is an unaffordable luxury. We have a historical opportunity as a united Zimbabwe to destroy the bourgeois state and, in its place, create a socialist society.

Another prerequisite for socialist transformation is peace. Zimbabwe's security situation is a sensitive area of attention. Inside Zimbabwe there are strife and disturbances in Matabeleland, while down south the 'Boer Republic' of South Africa threatens our existence as an independent nation. In such a time of threats from external aggression, unity under an umbrella party is a necessity.

Just as there is no perfect system, so there are weaknesses and demerits of a one-party system, as already stated. Most of these have had their validity and authenticity eroded in the preceding arguments. The major challenges, such as lack of democratic opposition, fears of dictatorship, incompetence, inefficiency and corruption, should not be oversimplified or rationalised. However, democratic centralism within a single party can reduce their severity. Under this system of structured and democratic communication, ideas, complaints, sentiments and suggestions move from cell to village, branch, district, province and then to the national forum. Similarly, instructions, ideas and solutions take the reverse direction down the channel. Thus, centralism institutes democracy from the grass-roots level up the hierarchy to the top leadership. Effectively, this shows that there can be opposition within the single party, thus enabling and providing for constructive criticism. Such a two-way feedback system in turn facilitates efficiency, honesty and growth. It provides checks and balances among politicians. Those incompetent and corrupt can be censored or removed democratically.

When all is said and done, the merits of a Zimbabwe one-party system outweigh the demerits. Resolving the problems of our nation's underdevelopment is not compatible with Western democracy. True democracy for Zimbabwe is social democracy, which is expressed not in the quarrels and squabbles of parties, but in the concord of people. Hence, the one-party parliamentary system is more conducive and relevant to Zimbabwe's thrust towards socialist development.

(Anderson, 1976) (Marx, 1969) (Lenin, 1961) (Chung, 1985)

SECTION TWO

No to the One-Party State! Yes to Socialism!

1987–1991

The context, circumstances and issues

Enrolling at the University of Zimbabwe (UZ) in 1987, to study for a BSc (Honours) degree in Electrical and Electronic Engineering, is a turning point in my young life. The intellectual ferment of university life stimulates the growth of my ideas and ideology, and facilitates their maturation, but at the same time, it starts to open my eyes to the reality of life around me in Zimbabwe. I remain true to both scientific socialism and to ZANU-PF as the agent for bringing about that revolutionary change, where the generality of the people own the commanding heights of the economy, land, labour and capital. However, I realise the struggle is increasingly being betrayed and forgotten by those in the ruling party who are hell-bent on enriching themselves at the expense of their fellow citizens. It is prudent to note that during these UZ days I do not just suddenly change my worldview and disposition. I discern that, tragically, the Zimbabwean leaders are not living up to the high ideals to which I aspire. More specifically, they desecrate the sacrosanct revolutionary values of the liberation struggle. My coming of age, politically, is to show that I understand that my generation has to become that voice of conscience, that voice of reason, that voice of hope, both for my country and for the African continent as a whole. We have to be the voice of the voiceless – that unrelenting and indefatigable voice of the voiceless.

My first foray into the field of active politics is as a student leader, attacking corruption and demanding that the ZANU-PF leadership acts to end the betrayal of the heroes of the struggle and the enduring values that inspired and drove it. In this, I and the other student leaders are associating with critics within ZANU-PF in what is the country's first nascent political opposition, although the importance of the movement is not recognised as such at the time by many, even though the ruling party knows only too well that student activists are both the moral and ideological conscience of Zimbabwe's revolution. This is the heyday of uncompromising student radicalism steeped in Marxist-Leninist thinking. However, in addition to Karl Marx, Vladimir Lenin and Mao Tse-tung, the sources of inspiration expand to include Leon Trotsky, Che Guevara, Malcolm X, Thomas Sankara, Kwame Nkrumah and Patrice Lumumba. It is also important to note my active involvement in prominent Marxist and Pan-Africanist student groups, such as the Society for Modern Scientific Thought (SMST) and the Society for African Studies (SAS). UZ Marxist academics such as the indomitable law lecturers Shadrack Gutto, Kempton Makamure and Issa Shivji heavily influence my evolving political beliefs, paradigms and worldview.

On 18 August 1988, I am elected Secretary General of the UZ Students' Union and the UZ Student Representative Council (SRC). The following year, on 15 August 1989, I am elected President of the Students' Union, and also become Chairman of the SRC. What is striking, unique and unprecedented, is that I become a leader of the Students' Union from a natural sciences background, specifically, Electrical and Electronic Engineering. Most of my contemporary student leaders and activists such as Tererai Mhungu (President 1987–1988), Tendai Biti (Secretary General 1987–1988), Edgar Mbwembwe (President 1988–1989), Thulani Ndebele (Vice President 1989–1990), Munyaradzi Gwisai (Secretary General 1989–1990) and Christopher Giwa (President 1990–1991), are drawn from the Faculties of Law and Humanities. My writings and speeches during this period include relentless attacks against government corruption, challenging misguided government priorities, opposing the one-party state, and pushing for inclusive democratic rights, social justice, and academic freedom, as well as a spirited defence of student rights and the promotion of their welfare. My leadership activities are not limited to the Students' Union, I am also elected Chairman of SMST and the Debate Forum, in addition to serving as an Executive Committee Member of SAS.

As Secretary General, with Edgar Mbwembwe as President of the Students' Union, our most significant action is the Anti-Corruption Demonstration of 29 September 1988. We need a statement that articulates the issues, and contextualises our demands and action. I author the radical and militant Anti-Corruption Document, with the assistance of the SRC Secretary for Information and Publicity, Tendai Kufa. Though hard-hitting, the statement is measured in its critique of Mugabe as a leader, and ZANU-PF as an institution. The historic and hugely successful Students' Union demonstration leads to the arrest and detention of the 15 SRC leaders and UZ lecturers, Kempton Makamure and Eliphas Mukonoweshuro. Shadrack Gutto is summarily deported from Zimbabwe. He is accused of writing the Anti-Corruption Document that we have, in fact, authored. As a foreigner, a Kenyan, the regime is merciless with him. He is given 48 hours to leave the country. The university government-funded grants and loans for 14 out of the 15 student leaders are withdrawn. They cannot touch my funding, because, unlike the others, I am on an Anglo American Scholarship, awarded on the basis of outstanding academic merit and achievement. The Mugabe regime is livid. It tries to pressurise Anglo American executives to withdraw my scholarship. They refuse. I surmise that the imperialists and capitalists have ways of making a positive contribution to the revolution! The struggle has friends in the most unusual of places.

Two government ministers – Moven Mahachi, Minister of Home Affairs, and Dzingai Mutumbuka, Minister of Higher Education – are particularly virulent and draconian in their persecution of students and lecturers. From the content of the Anti-Corruption Document, it is clear that we still consider ZANU-PF as our party, and Robert Mugabe as our leader. We are actually appealing to Mugabe, our upright and incorruptible revolutionary, to take drastic steps against corruption. How wrong we are. Mugabe is out of the country when we go into the streets. Upon his return, he is incensed by our Anti-Corruption Demonstration and its document. He denounces us as desperadoes without better things to do with our time. We are gutted, despondent and totally disillusioned. This is it. We are done with these running dogs of imperialism. We sever links with Robert Mugabe and his ZANU-PF. The divorce is final. This is October 1988.

I am well aware of the threat posed by neo-colonialism to real transformation. In my ideas and thoughts there is an emerging awareness of the Pan-Africanist tradition of revolutionary solidarity across the continent, along with a deep appreciation of the depredations of colonialism, both physical and psychological. On 28 March 1989, as Secretary General of the Students' Union, I deliver an outspoken speech attacking and denouncing British Prime Minister Margaret Thatcher – who is on a visit to Zimbabwe – for her government's continued support for the apartheid government in South Africa, showing a recognition of the common struggles of Africans and solidarity with those to the south.

As I participate in the rough and tumble of UZ student politics, I do not for a moment neglect my academic studies. I believe in both academic excellence and revolutionary confrontation. I dominate my Electrical Engineering classes from 1987 to 1990, with outstanding performance. There is stiff competition, but I thrive. In the first and second years, Engineering Mathematics is my favourite subject. In examinations that are meant to be two hours long, I finish in 45 minutes, and still score the highest mark among all Engineering students across all disciplines. Usually I score above 95 per cent. In a couple of examinations, I actually get a perfect score, 100 per cent. This is normal and routine for me in the first and second year at UZ. Electrical Principles, Digital Electronics, Electrical Measurements and Power Systems are fascinating subjects and I excel. At the end of 1988 after the Second Year Examinations, I receive the coveted UZ Book Prize for the best results in Electrical and Electronic Engineering. My third year project is titled '*The Smith Predictor Controller*', and my supervisor is Prof. Robert Appiah, an expert in Control Systems Engineering. For my fourth and final year project, which is graded First Class, I design and implement a '*Switched Mode Power Supply*'. Dr Engelbert Kapuya, who specialises in Electronic Circuit Design, is my main supervisor, and I also receive further guidance from the Power Electronics expert and UZ Dean of Engineering, Prof. Richard Harlen. This is the academic side. However, this story is about thought leadership of a political nature. Let us continue with the journey of such ideas.

The articulate criticism of the Zimbabwean government's policy failures and indiscretions disturbs the ZANU-PF hierarchy because they recognise the threat students pose to their corrupt way of life and dictatorial governance. When we demonstrate or boycott classes after raising national concerns, it is clear that we are starting to speak on behalf of the many disenchanted Zimbabweans. Even though we are university students, we have become the voice of the voiceless. It is important to note that at this juncture in the history of Zimbabwe, there is really no viable opposition party in the country. The Unity Accord between ZANU-PF and ZAPU is signed on 22 December 1987, combining the two into one party, the united ZANU-PF. At the same time, the Executive Presidency is introduced into the Zimbabwean Constitution. This means that Mugabe has consolidated his power as the President of the united ZANU-PF Party and Executive President of the country. Zimbabwe is now a de facto one-party state! In fact, strictly speaking, it is a dictatorship by one man. We have to fight this regime. The students and the workers under the leadership of the Zimbabwe Congress of Trade Unions (ZCTU) are providing the alternative narratives. However, the students are more radical and critical of the government, because the ZCTU is compromised by its direct historical links with ZANU-PF.

As students, we do not have that baggage. We are determined and undeterred. In fact, we posit that students have a de facto social role imposed upon them by material conditions and history. The majority of the students come from under-privileged classes of peasants and workers. They are thus quite cognisant of the problems, aspirations and conditions of the toiling masses. This enables students to constitute an effective barometer of social consciousness. The students are in this way an integral and vibrant component of society. With this solid ideological foundation and intellectual clarity we confront and engage the state. We do not relent. There is no retreat or surrender. In response, the Mugabe regime unleashes violence, cracks down on the students, and accuses them of being fronts for various foreign and domestic anti-state plotters. All these experiences make us question the essence and meaning of national independence. How can we say a country is independent when its people have no freedom? It is clearly not yet Uhuru! That is our message, on 14 April 1989, as we approach Zimbabwe's ninth Independence Day.

In September 1989, a year after the historic Anti-Corruption Demonstration of 29 September 1988, we decide to hold a revolutionary gala on campus to commemorate this event. The government of Zimbabwe decides to violently disrupt and stop this celebration. In response to this police brutality and unwarranted interference, I release the statement '*In defence of academic freedom*' on 2 October 1989. This leads to the unprecedented and violent closure of UZ on 4 October 1989. Earlier on that fateful day, at around 3 am, about 300 armed police and army units invade the UZ campus. They raid my university hall of residence and violently capture me. I am badly injured and, subsequently, detained without trial for six weeks. The violent nature of my arrest and the extent of my injuries lead to rumours that I have died! Consequently, the Mugabe regime, on 11 October 1989, through its mouthpiece – The *Herald* newspaper – produces a picture of me in a front page article whose headline reads 'Mutambara alive and in good health'. Also arrested and detained with me on 4 October 1989 is the Secretary General of the Students' Union, Enock Chikweche, my erstwhile fellow defender of the ZANU-PF one-party state in prior years. I guess we are now paying back for that lavish and sumptuous dinner!

In sync with radicalising student voices is an awakening, and increasingly critical, Zimbabwe Congress of Trade Unions (ZCTU) under Morgan Tsvangirai, Jeffrey Mutandare and Gibson Sibanda. As a result, after our arrest, Tsvangirai, as Secretary General of the ZCTU, issues a strong solidarity statement. He, in turn, is detained. This is the first time he is arrested as an activist in Zimbabwe. We are the revolutionaries – the bona fide post-independence freedom fighters. Tsvangirai is one of our supporters. A mere cheerleader.

After the closure of the university, a UZ advisory committee chaired by prominent lawyer Honour Mkushi is established to investigate the causes of the instability and recommend remedial actions. While they recommend the reopening of UZ, and the return and readmission of all students (after each student is forced to sign a non-aggression pact), they seek to dissolve our SRC. They propose fresh elections, arguing that since the university is starting afresh, it has to re-elect a new student leadership at the beginning of the academic year. In the Zimbabwean courts, charges are dropped against the student leaders under the pretext of wanting to create a conducive learning environment on campus, yet four ordinary members of the Students' Union still have pending cases of public violence. As the student leadership, we are not amused at all by these shenanigans. In fact, we are extremely disenchanted and seething with venomous and vicious outrage. The stage is set for a major showdown with the Vice Chancellor, Prof. Walter Kamba. Traditionally, as part of UZ established practice, at the end of Orientation Week, during the beginning of each academic year, the Vice Chancellor and SRC President jointly address the new students. This year, as the Students' Union, this is a perfect opportunity for us to robustly and unequivocally state our case to the UZ authorities, the ZANU-PF regime and the generality of the people of Zimbabwe.

It is a cool and breezy Friday morning of 27 April 1990 as I take to the podium in front of the UZ Great Hall. The atmosphere is electric and pregnant with great, but conflicting, expectations. The students are already psyched up, and cheering even before I get busy on the microphone. On the other hand, the university bureaucrats look timid, anxious and are shaking with fear of the unknown. Professor Walter Kamba himself is a miserable sight. He is a nervous wreck, shifting continuously in his seat. I take a menacing glance at him. Discomfort and anguish are all over his bearded face. Part of me feels sorry for him, but this is not time for mercy. It is time for slaughter. I get down to work. Well, I do not disappoint. It is a classic unrestrained massacre. A no-retreat, no-surrender and no-prisoners-taken verbal assault. In some parts of the delivery, I can hardly proceed, as my boisterous voice is drowned out by the cheering, whistling, ululating students. They are so excited and agitated. They want mob justice there and then. 'Surely Kamba deserves a thorough hiding, right now.' I can see their demands in their ecstatic faces. In part, some of my arguments are as follows:

> *We do not apologise for the closure of the university. Our activities that led to the crisis are bona fide. They are part of our fundamental democratic rights. In future, we will make the UZ ungovernable again, if we deem it necessary. We are totally opposed to the incompetence and excesses of the ZANU-PF regime. This dishonourable government must resign. If Robert Mugabe, the lucky coward of the liberation struggle, has any guts, he must come and speak directly to the students. As the voice of the voiceless, we will continue to be a barometer of social consciousness, while fighting for the improvement of the material conditions of the people of Zimbabwe. As a union of students, we violently and vehemently dismiss the idea of a one-party state, or a one-man dictatorship. This is not an issue for negotiation or compromise. It should be thrown out with the contempt that it deserves.*
>
> *We reject the false claim that the Zimbabwean state withdrew charges against the student leaders in order to create a conducive environment at UZ. The impression being created is that of magnanimity and mercy by the state towards the students. We are very angry. We are very apprehensive about these distortions. The state withdrew charges because they had no case. They could not prosecute. This must be publicly acknowledged. End of discussion. Since when does the Attorney General's job description include creating a conducive environment of peace and tranquility at UZ? Why are we very angry? Four of our members are still being prosecuted for public violence. They will appear in court on 17 May. What kind of magnanimity and mercy is that?*
>
> *We reject, and will viciously fight, any attempts to dissolve our SRC. The Students' Union is set up by an Act of Parliament. It has a separate existence from both the UZ administration and the government of Zimbabwe. Neither the Vice Chancellor nor the University Council has the power to dissolve the SRC. Consequently, an attempt to dissolve*

> *the SRC is ultra vires. It contravenes the law. This SRC you see here on the platform is the bona fide and legitimate representative organ of the UZ students. It is functional. We condemn you, Kamba, for your ambivalence on this nonsensical subject of dissolution. As a lawyer, we expect you to know the law. While we are on you, we want a full-time Vice Chancellor. This rubbish of you chairing the Boards of ZBC, Kingston's, or the Electoral Supervisory Commission, must come to an end. Spend more time at the university. Concentrate on the university. We want a Vice Chancellor who will never close this university again.*
>
> *There is a lot of inefficiency and bureaucratic reactionarism within the UZ administration. This must change. There must be speed and effectiveness in the resolution of student welfare matters.*

I say more, but this captures the essence of my remarks. After I am done, Kamba gives his timid speech. He underwhelms. What could he do? I have just put him, and his friend Robert, in their rightful places, before the entire nation, in the open glare of the local and international media.

Through these trials and tribulations at UZ and in the country, my generation comes to the conclusion that a one-party state or, more accurately, a 'one-man, one-party state', is a governance framework to be opposed. It becomes the principle around which the growing opposition voices coalesce. It is also around this time, in late 1989, that as students we become fully aware of the scale and full extent of the Gukurahundi massacres that had taken place in the southern provinces of Zimbabwe from 1982 to 1987. While the rest of the country enjoys relative peace and stability, as well as hope for a better future in the aftermath of the liberation war, the Midlands and south-western regions of the country are in turmoil. Patriotic Front – Zimbabwe African People's Union (PF-ZAPU) supporters, nationalist leaders and liberation struggle heroes are under siege by the ZANU-PF government, under the guise of fighting dissidents.

The height of it all is the forced exile of the distinguished nationalist leader, Joshua Nkomo, from 1983 to 1985; the arrest, in 1982, of outstanding liberation war hero Dumiso Dabengwa and the exceptional war commander Lookout Masuku; and the illegal detention of the two for four years, after their acquittal in 1983. In fact, Masuku dies in detention in 1986. In doing all this, Mugabe and his ZANU-PF party seek to crush all opposition forces, in particular PF-ZAPU, in order to consolidate power in line with their one-party state ambitions. An estimated 20 000 people lose their lives. As students we are not fully aware of these tragic events as they occur. In 1989, when we exhaustively discover and intimately understand this genocidal chapter of Zimbabwe's history, ZANU-PF and PF-ZAPU have already united, on 22 December 1987, into one political party, ZANU-PF. Still, we are shocked, apprehensive and completely disillusioned. How can our heroic ZANU-PF freedom fighters do this to their fellow citizens? How can they deal with a sister liberation movement in such a vicious, callous and murderous way?

We are appalled.

For me, there is the dawning realisation that the guarantors and protectors of a revolution, democracy, freedom and radical economic transformation are competing multiple political parties, a vibrant civic society, and a politically empowered citizenry. We cannot depend on one political party. Yet, my politics are still Marxist and socialist in orientation. No to the one-party state! Yes to socialism! That is the new mantra and formulation. Consequently, on 15 May 1990, I present a Students' Union position paper in total opposition to ZANU-PF's desire to establish a one-party state in Zimbabwe. In just four years the tide has turned. I have come full circle.

It does not end there. A direct confrontation with Mugabe over the one-party state ensues. Friday, 13 July 1990 is graduation day for the student groups that finished their studies in December 1989. As the President of the Students' Union, traditionally and by convention, I am part of the graduation process, which includes Mugabe as the Chancellor of the university. I was in detention for six weeks in October and November 1989, and we are meeting for the first time since that ugly episode. Moreover, as a union we have now taken an official position against the one-party system in Zimbabwe. After the main ceremony in the Great Hall, we all troop to the 'College Green' where graduates and their guests are served food and beverages. This is where it all happens.

Vice Chancellor Walter Kamba introduces me to Mugabe, and the armed and menacing Central Intelligence Organisation (CIO) operatives quickly encircle the three of us. Mugabe tries small talk, 'How many new Engineering graduates were there today? When I graduated from Fort Hare in 1951, there were nine graduates in the whole country.' I am not having any of that meaningless talk. I know I only have this man for a minute, if not seconds. I have to attack with stealth and vigour. I unexpectedly and aggressively barge in, completely out of the blue, saying, 'We do not want to talk about any of that. We are completely against the one-party state by any means necessary. We do not want a one-party state in Zimbabwe!'

Mugabe is stunned. He looks dazed, but soon gathers his composure, and tries to shoot back, 'If you take such extreme views we will be dismissive of your views.' I was ready for him. 'We have already dismissed your thinking, so it is not consequential whether you dismiss our views or not!' Mugabe is visibly livid. His face is awash with discomfort. He is beside himself with rage. However, he cannot find his tongue. Kamba then moves with alacrity and dexterity in a rescue bid to calm the raging waters. 'We need rational disputation ... we must have collegial dialogue.' It is too late. I am not even listening. The mission is accomplished. The numerous security details who had completely encircled the three of us quickly whisk away the wounded and verbally incapacitated Mugabe.

His Ministers Sydney Sekeramayi, David Karimanzira and a couple of others remain behind and begin to harangue, terrorise and intimidate me, saying, 'Why are you not being respectful to the President?' I just laugh at them and retort, 'Robert Mugabe is just another sheer mortal, a human being like all of us. There is nothing special about him. We as students can and will insult him, as and when we want to. It is our fundamental democratic right.' Such is the beauty and purity of youth, principles and fearlessness.

Our national political endeavours as the UZ Students' Union are not without impact. They are enhanced and complemented by those of an increasingly radicalised labour movement, outspoken intellectuals at UZ, nascent opposition groupings and an emerging civic society. In particular, Edgar Tekere and his Zimbabwe Unity Movement (ZUM); academics such as Kempton Makamure, Shadrack Gutto, Masipula Sithole, Ibbo Mandaza and Jonathan Moyo; and labour leaders, such as Morgan Tsvangirai and Gibson Sibanda, play a pivotal role. As a direct consequence of all these complementary and mutually reinforcing efforts, the ZANU-PF government's campaign for a one-party state is defeated, plural politics starts to emerge, the demand for a democratic culture becomes emboldened and civic society blossoms. Of particular significance is the essential camaraderie and unity in struggle among the workers, students and academics against neo-colonialism, which takes root. Future UZ student leaders such as Christopher Giwa, Paul Chimhosva, Tawanda Mutasah, Brian Kagoro, Learnmore Jongwe and Job Sikhala continue with this tradition of struggle and solidarity.

Even while I attack those who betray the revolution, my understanding of the economic forces at play in the country is deepening. I start to tackle the issues of unemployment and underemployment among graduates and the mis-deployment of those graduates, which has effectively hamstrung the economy and worsened the effects of political misrule.

After my outstanding A Level results in 1986, I won an Anglo American Scholarship with attachment to their subsidiary Wankie Colliery Company (WCC) in Hwange. The scholarship obligated me to work for WCC after graduation. Hence armed with a BSc (Honours) in Electrical and Electronic Engineering, I move into industry in Zimbabwe to do the Engineering Pupillage Programme. This is my first job as a graduate trainee. Now at WCC I face new challenges. I am frustrated by the racism of virtually illiterate white supervisors, as well as the rampant corruption and abuse of authority in the company. I defend myself and the workers, while challenging the status quo in a manner which shows I will not be put down without a fight. There will be neither retreat nor surrender. I stand up to abuse. That is what I do. On 6 May 1991, I issue an angry rebuttal to a subjective industrial performance appraisal by an illiterate and racist 'Engineer' at WCC.

Friday, 12 July 1991 is my graduation day in Harare, at the University of Zimbabwe, a BSc (Honours) in Electrical and Electronic Engineering, award of a Rhodes Scholarship, and a place at the University of Oxford. It is a joyous day indeed. An occasion to focus on self-accomplishments. But as my nature would have it, I still find time for protest. The issue of the escalating unemployment of graduates remains unaddressed by the government. Hence, as I arrive in Harare from Hwange, I make a huge fuss at the Students' Union building and give an impromptu address to current students who are present:

> *'Comrades, what is the meaning of graduation, when our fellow graduates have no jobs? Graduating from what to what, when you are unemployed? About 40 per cent of our colleagues have no jobs. The graduation ceremony is a national manifestation of hypocrisy. Mugabe and his ZANU-PF government have failed. Where are the jobs? I am not going to bend on my knees before Mugabe so that he can cap me. (The practice was and remains that every graduating student at UZ goes on their knees and Mugabe touches their head with the cap of knowledge, thus signifying the graduating act.) He can go to hell! I will not shake his hand. When my name is called, I will walk across the stage, grab my certificate and walk back to my seat.'*

This is my protest plan as I walk into the UZ Great Hall on that day. Word has already gone around the university establishment and the government system about my plans. Mugabe is sitting right in front looking pensive. I can see nervousness in the eyes of his security aides, and I notice curious but anxious glances directed at me, intermittently, by university bureaucrats. However, most of my fellow graduating students do not know of my plans. They are too excited about the ceremony that I do not even bother to seek recruits or solidarity. When it is time for our department to be conferred with degrees, and it is my turn, Professor Richard Harlen, the UZ Dean of Engineering, who is also one of my lecturers and project supervisors, calls out my name, and indicates my outstanding academic achievements, UZ Book Prize for Electrical Engineering Part II Results, Distinction for the Final Year Project, the Rhodes Scholarship Award, and a place for Graduate Studies at the University of Oxford. The Great Hall erupts in a sustained standing ovation that lasts for at least a minute. I cannot believe it! I am stunned and humbled at the same time. I am in a state of confusion. I am not even sure whether the ovation is for my academic achievements or my notoriety as a student leader or perhaps both. If I go ahead with my plan, some would say the ovation has gone to my head. What do I do? I change tack and decide to at least shake his hand, but I am still averse to the idea of going on my knees for him. To me this smacks of subordination to him when all that I want to do is rebel against his authority.

First, I bow to the cheering crowd, and then I approach him while I am on my feet. He stands up, we shake hands, chat for a while and he eventually caps me. It is quite a scene. The next day, Saturday, 13 July 1991, *The Herald* newspaper runs a story that says: 'When the former SRC President, Arthur Mutambara, walked onto the stage the whole hall went wild. Moved by the crowds, he bowed to it, and after nearly a minute when the noise had died down, walked up to President Mugabe. Unlike the others who were capped once, the controversial student leader was capped three times.' A myth is then generated that I was awarded three degrees in one ceremony, after only spending four years at UZ! What a legend. Anyway, this is how my UZ history of disagreeable and conflictual interactions with Mugabe ends. Our paths will cross again in the future.

Back in Hwange at WCC, the incompetent and unqualified white racists will not let up. In addition to the challenges they create by undermining young black professionals, they are also involved in endemic corruption and abuse of company assets. To protect themselves, they involve senior black WCC managers in their corrupt activities. They take the bulk of the loot, and give the senior black managers crumbs. That is enough to compromise senior black officials into inaction. On 26 July 1991, I dispatch another highly charged salvo meant to expose industrial corruption and abuse of authority at WCC. All these activities lead to a vicious confrontation with the Managing Director of WCC, Kudzanayi Bwerinofa. He is defending incompetent, corrupt and racist white managers, because he has been compromised. They have given him crumbs, while they loot the company's major assets. He organises a dramatically ugly but memorable altercation, the final showdown against me, involving himself as MD, the WCC Human Resources Director Rugare Gumbo (later a ZANU-PF government minister and now an opposition politician), and WCC Chief Engineer, John Dudman. It is quite a verbal punch-up. I give as much as I get. I must have won, since it is three corporate giants versus one lowly graduate learner. Needless to say, we part ways on very disagreeable and unpleasant terms. The only saving grace for me is that they have paid for my UZ fees for the four-year Engineering programme; they get no refund after the bare-knuckle confrontation, and I leave them with their moribund WCC while I embark on my sojourn in the big wide world. I am off to Oxford – the City of Dreaming Spires, the citadel of knowledge. I do not miss that wretched company. I am doing just fine.

(Lenin, 1961) (Marx, 1969)

4 The Anti-Corruption Document

This is the Students' Union declaration we write and circulate as part of the Anti-Corruption Demonstration on 29 September 1988. It becomes famous as the Anti-Corruption Document. The massively successful demonstration is violently crushed by the government of Zimbabwe. This leads to the arrest and detention in Chikurubi of all 15 SRC members. Lecturers Kempton Makamure and Eliphas Mukonoweshuro are also briefly arrested, while law lecturer Shadrack Gutto, a Kenyan national, is deported. Gutto is in fact accused of authoring the Anti-Corruption Document. He is given 48 hours to leave the country. This is a travesty of justice because he has had absolutely no input or involvement. I am the one who gives him a copy of the completed document to read. The statement is a product of the union, and the union alone.

We, the students of Zimbabwe, are alarmed and concerned at the growing number of cases of corruption, scandals and crimes that are committed by the national leadership at both party and government level. The problem of corruption and looting of national coffers in Zimbabwe has become virtually a daily topic for debate in so many places, including the media and Parliament. Consequently, today, 29 September 1988, we the students of Zimbabwe have decided to turn the tables against these evils. We review the situation from a progressive outlook as a reflection of the political and ideological bankruptcy of some of our petit bourgeois leadership. It is therefore imperative that we as students do not allow such a leadership to lead our party, ZANU-PF, especially after the unity talks. Comrades, our aspirations have been betrayed by the ideologically bankrupt leaders. It is high time we, as students, say enough is enough! We therefore call upon the President, Robert Mugabe, to act now; and we repeat now. Nothing other than now is acceptable.

The student body is concerned with the betrayal of our heroes, the workers, peasants and indeed all progressive people. Our cherished national goals of transforming and harmonising the means of production for the interests of the working class and peasants have been turned into an illusionary dream while some leaders of our party have gone on a looting and plundering spree without concern for the common people. We cannot afford to pretend or to be blind to these evils. We declare that the rot must stop.

Even our President, on his recent trip to London, embarrassed himself when he admitted that some of our leaders have ignored the Leadership Code. He admitted that the government is corrupt and those 'creatures' have to be weeded out. It is therefore in support of our President that we take to the street in order to demonstrate our solidarity with the revolutionary classes of Zimbabwe, that is, the workers, peasants and progressive intellectuals. We once again call upon the President to act now. Nothing other than now is acceptable.

The same views expressed by our President were also highly elaborated and elucidated by Comrade Edgar Tekere when he said, 'The Leadership Code must be enforced by the party leadership and the leadership is corrupt and rotten. It is the leadership that has chewed up its own Leadership Code.'

The corrupt, rotten and ideologically bankrupt mentality that has crept into the rank and file of our party, ZANU-PF, has become so embarrassing that the Politburo had to intervene in such issues as local government elections and party leadership squabbles. The progressive voice of the students says, 'The petit bourgeois element must go and be replaced by a vanguard consisting of progressive leadership.'

Even our Vice President, Comrade Simon Muzenda, expressed the same sentiments a week ago when he stated that our press had to play a major role in exposing corruption. 'While exposing these evils, developmental journalists have a duty to inject hope, self-reliance, creativity and resourcefulness in our people.' His remarks were right on target.

It is our submission that just as we condemn bureaucratic squandering and looting of the national coffers, we also do not condone the distortive and misinformative role that *The Herald* daily newspaper has assumed. We challenge it to stand up and be counted as the voice of the workers, peasants and revolutionary intellectuals.

In order to make our objectives clear, we will quote examples of high-level corruption that have graced our private and public media.

1. a. The case of a minister who was involved in an alleged embezzlement of funds and who was never brought before the courts. He was simply transferred to another ministry (the Paweni case)
   b. The case of a deputy minister who was involved in a multimillion-dollar scandal and embezzlement of funds. It was reported that the witness had suddenly turned hostile.

2. The case of party leaders chewing the Leadership Code and some going to the extent of buying nearly the whole of Bindura and Shamva and nothing has been done except for rhetoric sentiments.
3. The case of a certain party official who appeared in court for alleged assault. His defence was that, 'I am being framed by my political foes who want to dethrone me.'
4. The case of a certain deputy minister involved in arson, but the major issue is the character of the minister involved rather than the court case itself. His integrity is highly questionable, if not dubious. The revelations of sexual promiscuity in that case leave students with doubt whether justice exists in Zimbabwe. How can the government account for the rounding up of alleged prostitutes when it cannot put its own house in order, on the same matter?
5. The swindling case in the Ministry of Education which did not even grace our court rooms. Whatever happened to the so-called investigation? There was neither a report nor action.
6. The contradictions that exist in the Ministry of Labour and Social Welfare. Instead of it being the custodian of workers' interests, it has turned into a ministry for international capital. We as progressive intellectuals deplore and find the unwarranted criticism of the ZCTU unacceptable.
7. a. The violation of democratic debate and constructive criticism in which ordinary MPs have become targets for cheap 'politicking'. The so-called disciplinary actions are nothing other than ways in which the petit bourgeois class wants to protect the status quo. Surely this is constructive criticism.
   b. The criticism levelled against the purchasing of planes while workers spend more than three hours waiting for a bus both to and from work. That criticism was surely warranted.
   c. The criticism levelled against the size of the Cabinet especially considering the benefits entitled to each minister. We cannot afford to waste the precious foreign currency on unnecessary bureaucratic machinery.
8. The suspension of the resettlement programme while in the newspaper the word 'squatter' appears more than 14 times a week. For every so-called squatter, there must be land somewhere.
9. The validity of building white elephants in the form of the new party headquarters, civic centre, Sheraton Hotel, National Sports Stadium and the proposed new Parliament building while people have no accommodation.
10. The validity of petit bourgeois representation and continual co-option of some heavyweights of capital into Parliament and the ranks and files of ZANU-PF.

After taking into consideration the aforementioned points, one will surely agree with Comrades Mugabe, Tekere, Angeline Tongogara and Oppah Muchinguri that the heroes have been betrayed. It is now high time we flushed out the rotten elements and let the revolutionary momentum begin again.

On the basis of the above sentiments, the following resolutions are brought before the Government of Zimbabwe and the Zimbabwean people:

1. We take cognisance of the fact that to implement scientific socialism, a vanguard party is a fundamental prerequisite. Effectively, therefore, we call upon ZANU-PF to swiftly move from being a loose amalgamatory mass party towards a vanguard party. We are completely against a ZANU-PF one-party state, for it will only be a one-party state of a corrupt petit bourgeoisie against the workers and peasants. Our slogan therefore is 'A vanguard party first, socialism first and one-party state later'.
2. It is our contention that the land question has not been solved in Zimbabwe. People fought for land and for every so-called squatter there must be land somewhere. To this end, we call upon the Government of Zimbabwe to retract and repeal Section 16 of the Constitution of Zimbabwe and redistribute land.
3. The material conditions of workers and the fundamental ownership of the means of production have not changed in this country. We call upon the government to radically address the issue of foreign capital in the form of multi-national corporations who own more than 80 per cent of the economy. It is our submission that the grand programme of gradualism with its social reforms such as the minimum wage and the Labour Relations Act has failed because of the co-option into the capitalist system at personal, party and government levels.
4. We humbly call for openness, grass-roots democracy, accountability and press freedom. The mass media has become a banal censored organisation whose sole responsibility has been to misrepresent students and workers and in some instances even glorify gross national irregularities. We call upon the government to relax this entrenchment.
5. We strongly subscribe to the view that the ZCTU is the only legitimate and fundamental representative of the worker in this country. Hence, any attempts to underplay their role in favour of international capital are completely deplorable. We call upon the government to take prime cognisance of this and henceforth support and sponsor this organisation's attempts to link up the progressive activities of the workers nationally. The democratic right to strike should be restored without any absurd limitations.

In conclusion, we call upon the people of Zimbabwe to keep the spirit of this 29 September 1988 anti-corruption demonstration ablaze. As students with the interest of the workers, peasants and the general public at heart, we wish to say it loud and clear that the struggle against corruption and to establish a true socialist state is on and will continue until final victory.

(Fanon, 1963) (Marx, 1969) (Chung, 1985) (Lenin, 1961)

5 The importance of political activism among students

When new students arrive on campus, they go through an official week of exposure and adjustment to the university system. This is called Orientation Week. During this period as the UZ student leadership we take it upon ourselves to subject the fresh arrivals to extensive political education and revolutionary theory. Presented here is the political orientation address that I give them on 14 March 1989, as Secretary General of the Students' Union and Chairman of the Orientation Week Committee. It provides the ideological justification and rationale for political activism among students. It answers the question: 'Why should students participate in national politics?' The key message to the students, the country, and our detractors is: 'Students have a de facto social role imposed upon them by material conditions and history.' I also outline some of the national grievances and campus concerns, while emphasising that the right to demonstrate is an inalienable right. I also articulate and defend the union's scientific socialist ideological disposition. The ideas in this speech represent our manifesto and rationale for action – a call to arms.

Comrades, in order to analyse and concretely establish the significant role played by students in Zimbabwe, it is a fundamental prerequisite that a thorough analysis of the anatomy of the political economy of Zimbabwe be carried out as well as a substantial address of the concept of education. Pedagogy was a tool with which the colonial state of Rhodesia undertook the subtle task of mental colonisation with a view to control the mind of the colonised. Thus, cultural imperialism was established.

With the attainment of independence in 1980, Zimbabwe became a neo-colonial state and still is. Neo-colonialism is the final and most dangerous stage of imperialism. A state subjected to neo-colonialism is, in theory, independent and has all the outward trappings of international sovereignty. In reality, its economic system and thus its political policy is directed from outside. However, the internal contradictions and conflicts of neo-colonialism make it certain that it cannot endure as a permanent socio-political-economic dispensation. Comrades, it is only objective reality to say that Zimbabwe directly faces this confrontational and contradictory affront.

1. Problems of a neo-colony

- The land question remains unresolved;
- Because the problem is Section 16 of the Zimbabwe Lancaster House Constitution which provides protection from deprivation of property;
- Only 10 per cent of means of production is owned by the people;
- Unemployment, wage freezes, price hikes;
- National housing crisis, transport crisis;
- Mistaken priorities, white elephants;
- Corruption, looting, profiteering, outright bourgeois reactionism;
- Threat to the right to education.

2. Root causes

- Racial monopoly capitalism (not even indigenous);
- Neo-colonial and imperialist network;
- Growing radical aspirations of the peasant mass and expectant worker as contradictions continue to sharpen.

3. Education

- Education is part of the superstructure;
- The superstructure supports the economic base;
- In turn the economic base acts on the superstructure;
- There is a dialectical relationship between the two;
- Education is not neutral;
- Education for whom, by who, for what purpose.

Any consideration of the anatomy of social classes in a neo-colonial state must take into account the part played, or which can be played, by the students in the socio-economic political dynamics of the state. Students have a de facto social role imposed upon them by the material conditions and history.

4. Why students can play the de facto social role

- The origin of majority of students;
- They come from underprivileged classes of peasants and workers;
- A few from native indigenous bourgeoisie and comprador bourgeoisie;
- Thus, students are an integral vibrant component of society;
- Quite cognisant of the problems, aspirations and conditions of the toiling masses;
- They are a barometer of social consciousness;

- Hence, they have a duty and obligation to be the voice of the voiceless.

In fact, available historical evidence shows that students in neo-colonies constitute a potential radical force capable of making a considerable contribution to the struggles of the working people. Within the context of the aforementioned analysis, it is imperative that students be politically active. Even liberals agree with Marxist-Leninist scholars that man is a political animal. Consequently, we expect all UZ students to be both politically conscious and active. We must fight apathy among students in the following academic disciplines: Science, Engineering, Medicine, Pharmacy and Veterinary Science. A disproportionately high percentage of the female students do not participate in Students' Union activities. We must encourage and motivate them. The idea is to make sure that all students are ideologically conscious when they graduate and go into the socio-political economic system of work and employment. They must arm themselves with tools of analysis, in particular dialectical analysis and historical materialism.

5. Forms of political activism

The main platforms for political activism are the Students' Union itself, and student societies. The key societies are: the Society for Modern Scientific Thought (SMST), Society for African Studies (SAS), and Political Science Students (POSSA). These organise seminars, symposia, and public lectures.

6. General meetings

The General Meeting is the supreme platform and authority for all Students' Union decisions. It is therefore imperative for members to protect their interests, views and aspirations by attending such meetings.

7. The demonstration

This is an inalienable and fundamental democratic right of every union member. We reserve the right to demonstrate, and we will continue to demonstrate in this country. The right to demonstrate is not subject to being taken away from, or given away by, members of this union. The Students' Union is a corporate body set up by an Act of Parliament, University Act 27/1982, and run presently by the 1984 Students' Union Constitution. The fact that the union is set up by an Act of Parliament gives it a separate and autonomous existence outside the university administration. The relationship between the Students' Union and the UZ authorities has been that of a continuous class struggle.

As you will soon realise or have already envisaged there are quite a number of problems that constitute student demands:

- Unparalleled accommodation crisis;
- Shortage of academic facilities;
- Censorship of student publications;
- Lack of democratic say in UZ decision-making.

These constitute student trade union demands. On the other hand, the administration has been very reactionary, bureaucratic and outright conservative. In some instances, it has acted as if it is an extension of the government of Zimbabwe. In the running of the university, committee democracy is farcical, with the result that student representatives' role is to simply rubber-stamp decisions made by university bureaucrats. The UZ authorities use the Student Affairs Committee as a buffer between themselves and students. There is no genuine interest in student inputs, opinions and views. The struggle to press for student demands will continue unabated and we call for *glasnost* and *perestroika* in university administration.

8. The Students' Union's ideological standpoint

The preamble of the Students' Union constitution says, *'A scientific socialist stand shall be the guide to all the activities, aims, objectives and endeavours.'* Hence, within the confines of this ideological standpoint I will outline the revolutionary tasks of the union and its affiliated clubs and societies, in order for them to accomplish their duty to society:

- To translate socialist debate into socialist revolutionary action.
- To disseminate Marxist-Leninist ideas among students and to raise ideological consciousness and enthusiasm in the university.
- To identify the students with the cause of the toiling masses in Zimbabwe, Africa and the generality of the whole world.
- To contribute positively to the ideals of the African Revolution and people's struggles elsewhere and hence effectively support liberation struggles in Southern Africa.
- To help to stimulate revolutionary spirit and activism among the students and provide a positive contrast between scientific socialist thought and bourgeois thought. The latter being the dominant school of thought here at the UZ.
- To combat reactionary or imperialist supported activities which enhance an idealist outlook of society.
- Complete destruction of the bourgeoisie's traditions, style of work and syllabus, for we cannot see the rationale of training bourgeois economists, political scientist and lawyers, and at the end of the day, expect to have a socialist political and economic system in Zimbabwe.

In conclusion, comrades, it is imperative that we realise that recent events at this university have marked the ideological crystallisation of student radicalism in Zimbabwe. The revolutionary zeal and momentum have dramatically escalated. We cannot back down and we should never ever compromise on matters of principle. In terms of conviction and commitment, we stand where we stood and stood where we stand!

A luta continua – the struggle continues!

(Guevara, 1961) (Marx, 1969) (Gandhi, 1927) (Fanon, 1963)

6 The role of culture in the revolutionary struggle

This is the opening speech I give at the UZ Students' Union Cultural Gala during Orientation Week in Harare on 16 March 1989, as Secretary General of the Students' Union and Chairman of the Orientation Week Committee. We continue with ideological indoctrination of the new students. They must know that culture is not neutral, and they must avoid bourgeois decadence and lumpen tendencies.

The grandeur of a people's society in the eyes of the world depends in great measure on the form and quality of its artistic creations. The weapon of culture helped to crystallise a national consciousness that led to the adoption and execution of the armed struggle in Zimbabwe. In fact, the armed struggle for liberation is a demonstrable and veritable march along the road to cultural progress. In the world today, all culture, all literature and art belong to definite classes and these are geared towards definite political endeavours. In fact, there is no such thing as art for art's sake, art that stands above classes or art that is detached from, or independent of, politics. Proletarian traditional dances, music and other artistic activities are part of the whole proletarian revolutionary cause. They are cogs and wheels in the struggle. Revolutionary culture is a powerful class struggle weapon for the broad masses of the people. It prepares the ground ideologically before the revolution comes and is indeed an essential fighting front in the generality of any class struggle.

During the colonial era, our culture was downtrodden and stifled but did not die. It went into hibernation but it was still there. The infiltration of an alienating culture did not reach the majority of the population. The confrontation between the two cultures occurred in the cities where colonial alienation, assimilation and the imposition of cultural values of imperialism took place.

From the time of national independence, there was a great outburst of cultural activity as all over Zimbabwe came the emergence of groups devoted to dance, theatre, music, choral singing, literature and sculpture. The outburst was accompanied by a renewed interest in the nation's history, languages, traditions and the vast range of other interests that form part of our cultural heritage.

Comrades, let us take cognisance of the imperative nature of our agenda. Our duty and obligation are to ensure that our traditional and cultural practices fit well into the revolutionary machinery as a vibrant and integral component, that operates as a powerful weapon for uniting and educating the people by attacking and destroying the capitalist bourgeois system. In fact, a revolutionary culture is a dynamic locomotive of change.

Abasha cultural imperialism! Forward with a revolutionary culture!

I declare this dynamic gala open.

(Fanon, 1963) (Guevara, 1961) (Lenin, 1961)

7 Go right back home, British lady

We are irritated and dismayed by British Prime Minister Margaret Thatcher's policy of constructive engagement towards the apartheid regime in South Africa. When she visits Zimbabwe, we are livid. This is the speech I deliver during that visit, on 28 March 1989. As a union, we are concerned about national, regional and continental struggles. Our sectional interests as students are the least of our concerns. It is in this context that we give primacy to the anti-apartheid efforts in South Africa.

When is war not war? It seems when it is waged by a stronger nation against a weaker one as a pre-emptive strike. When is terrorism not terrorism? Apparently when it is carried out by a more powerful government against those at home and abroad who are weaker than it and whom it regards as a potential threat or even as insufficiently supportive of its own objectives. The above assertions can be established by analysing the ability of South Africa to attack neighbouring countries with impunity and to organise murder, kidnapping and massive destruction with the support of some permanent members of United Nations Security Council, in particular Britain.

The people of South Africa have been fighting against racial oppression for most of the 20th century. Their petitions, peaceful processions, demonstrations and even their campaigns of civil disobedience have been met with ever-increasing repression and violence. Yet, on the other hand, Margaret Thatcher has made it abundantly clear, and in no uncertain terms, that Britain will not support economic sanctions against South Africa, arguing that such measures will hurt the South African blacks more. Since when has Thatcher been speaking for the black majority? What are the real British interests in South Africa? The South African black population is spontaneously rejecting the laws and instruments of apartheid by the sheer force of its will and numbers. The daily death toll and torture which they suffer under detention and imprisonment do not deter them from fighting. They are challenging the guns of apartheid with their own blood and with the stones picked from the streets.

The question here then is: What suffering is Thatcher talking about? The people of South Africa have already jumped from the pan into the fire as we have just commemorated Sharpeville Day on 21 March 1989. We dedicated our solid solidarity with those on extensive hunger strikes and those sentenced to death, awaiting execution in South Africa.

We do not see the rationale behind tolerating and entertaining Thatcher with her absurd stance on sanctions against apartheid South Africa. In any case, a thorough analysis of the political economy of the apartheid regime will manifest and illustrate the irrationality, inconsistency and outright confusionism behind the Thatcher stance.

The rising cost of apartheid has created an economic crisis in SA. The SA economy consists of institutionalised economic barriers to the rights of the black population to freely sell their labour, gain access to world capital accumulation or even own land and other assets freely. These barriers are neither by accident nor by the spontaneous evolution of the economy. They are the outcome of a consciously designed socio-economic system. The objective of this system has been and remains the production of a unique rate of surplus extraction. Its essential function is to sustain the costly superstructure of white minority privilege, the high rate of return on investments and the consolidation of the power of capitalism in the racist economy.

In the context of the above analysis, with all due respect, can the British lady tell us what blacks will lose in the destruction of the above system? In any case, what does the black majority have to gain from a cheap labour system of moribund and racial monopoly capitalism which stands at the centre of the apartheid economy? It is our contention that as long as the black population remained subdued or cowed down into accepting their miserable existence, the apartheid system flourished at an incredible rate. However, this advancement did not include black aspirations socially, economically or politically. It is within this context that we expose the political and economic bankruptcy of Thatcher's stance on sanctions.

There is neither humanitarianism nor altruism in this stance; just sheer selfish aspirations to protect British interests in South Africa. In fact, it is a sincere realisation and conceptualisation of the need to perpetuate British imperialism today. It is our submission that, yes, there are costs to the region of economic sanctions against SA, but with the present annual costs of South African aggression and economic destabilisation already at US$6 million a year and rising with no end in sight, it serves no practical purpose to talk of the costs of sanctions to Southern Africa. The costs of coexisting with apartheid are immeasurably higher.

To this end, we in the region would like to say loud and clear that we believe that the imposition of comprehensive mandatory international sanctions would mark a critical and necessary stage in the battle against apartheid in particular and the struggle for regional economic liberation in general. Apartheid cannot be reformed. In fact, it should be totally destroyed and no amount of Western aid, including British military assistance, will save it. The weapon of economic sanctions is an essential part of the strategy to annihilate the shamelessly racist system in SA. Furthermore, we as the Students' Union not only agree to disagree with Thatcher, but we completely disassociate ourselves from her. We unreservedly say: 'Go back home, Maggie, and rethink and reflect on the issue of sanctions. You are not only unwelcome but irrelevant to our struggles in Southern Africa. We will triumph with or without you.'

A luta continua!

(Biko, 1979) (Nkrumah, 1965)

8 Independence Day Commemoration Seminar: Not yet Uhuru!

The day, 18 April, on which we attained our independence is approaching. We are thoroughly disillusioned by the nationalists' failure to deliver on the promise of freedom. This is a note I send out to the student body, on 14 April 1989, laying out plans to commemorate Zimbabwe's ninth Independence Day. I attempt to explain what has gone wrong, and proffer some strategic insights for the way forward. I then introduce a comprehensive seminar programme, with distinguished speakers, to delve into a broad range of matters, in pursuit of real freedom, meaningful independence, inclusive democracy and shared economic prosperity.

Comrades, 18 April 1989 marks the ninth anniversary of the Independence of Zimbabwe. What was ushered in in 1980 was the transition from colonialism to neo-colonialism, and this was characterised by a change in the class content of the state, forging of new class alliances within the country and a realignment of relations with imperialism. It meant the transition of the petit bourgeoisie, which formerly was part of the ruled class, to a ruling class. Bound by its own limitations, economic weaknesses and political bankruptcy, the petit bourgeoisie, as a class, became transformed into a client class in service of imperialism, the comprador bourgeoisie. The state of Zimbabwe, like any other state, is an institution of the society which arises out of the development, in society, of irreconcilable antagonisms among social classes with conflicting economic interests, thus enabling the dominant class to establish, protect and enhance their economic, political and cultural interests. The question with regards to Zimbabwe is: Which is this dominant class?

The protracted armed struggle for Independence in Zimbabwe had a clear class nature. Its prime objective was to dismantle not only the colonial socio-political system but the economic infrastructure and superstructure that constitute imperialism. The whole fundamental motive was to uplift the material conditions of the generality of the masses of Zimbabwe, the working class and the peasantry, by solving the long-standing land question and by establishing democratisation of the ownership of the means of production, labour, land and capital.

But confrontational objective reality demands a submission that this has not been attained at all! In fact, the Lancaster House Agreement reflects a compromise in the balance of forces that characterised the Zimbabwean political arena, thus it has pervaded the process and structures through which the new state has sought both to consolidate and provide a basis for genuine economic and social change. A crisis of expectation has thus been created with the land question unresolved, capitalism entrenched, and the material conditions of the workers unimproved, within a state characterised by petit bourgeois looting and profiteering, mistaken government priorities (white elephants), and threats to the basic fabric of democracy. Press freedom and the student voices are emasculated, while unrestrained political and ideological bankruptcy haunts the country.

The land question remains largely unresolved in spite of the government's attempt to do so through the establishment of a resettlement programme, and this is compounded by the development of a black agrarian bourgeoisie and the pervasive capitalist policies on land utilisation. Nine years after independence we ask ourselves: To what extent has land deprivation (quantitatively and qualitatively) been alleviated? What forms of social organisation and relations of production have been promoted in attempts to resolve the land question? What are the contradictions between long-term agrarian policy objectives and the further entrenchment of capitalism?

It is only when these questions are analysed that a historical contextualisation of the land question is established and postulations for the future made.

Focusing on the entrenching of capitalism, it is imperative to realise that the Zimbabwean political economic problems are fundamentally caused by this moribund monopoly capitalism. It is common cause that more than 80 per cent of the Zimbabwean economy is owned by foreign multi-national corporations. The grand programme of 'gradual ownership of the means of production' has completely failed as cooptation into the system flourishes. Coming to corruption, the recent revelations of the Sandura Commission show the outright decadence that has crept into the petit bourgeois leadership.

This is embarrassing primitive accumulation that even defies bourgeois ethics and morals. What baffles us is that they are busy looting titbits and crumbs from the capitalist's table while the capitalist gets away with millions from the exploitative economic system. Another serious observation is that Willowgate is but the tip of the iceberg – there is more looting to be unearthed! Absurdly, adding insult to injury, the looter stands up to defend capitalism!

The threat to democracy is very real as we commemorate this ninth anniversary of Independence. The state response to the student Anti-Corruption Demonstration of 29 September 1988, police brutality, trials of lecturers and students and removal of grants and loans, harassment of editors and journalists – and yet the very corruption the press and the students were attacking has now been profoundly proven!

Comrades, these are the challenges that face Zimbabwe today, nine years after independence. As students it is our duty and obligation to critically and scientifically analyse them and answer these questions: (a) Whither Zimbabwe? (b) What should be done?

Abasha the political economy of state robbery! Forward with scientific socialist orientation!

Now Comrades, to commemorate this year's Independence anniversary there will be a revolutionary seminar on Saturday, 15 April 1989, from 8.30am to 4pm, in the Great Hall.

Presentations:

1. The struggle for Independence in Zimbabwe, its class nature and prospects of an economic revolution in 1980 – Cde Ibbo Mandaza.
2. Economic and land reforms in Zimbabwe 1980–1989 and their effect on the underprivileged classes, the working class and the peasantry – Cde Tendai Biti.
3. Trade unions in Zimbabwe and the mobilisation of Zimbabwean workers: Problems and prospects – Cde Morgan Tsvangirai (ZCTU).
4. The state and the freedom of press in post-independent Zimbabwe – Cde Willie Musarurwa.
5. Student struggles and the state in post-independent Zimbabwe – Cde Thomas Deve.
6. Merits and demerits of the Executive Presidency in a one-party-state Zimbabwe – Cde Kempton Makamure.
7. The political economy of state robbery and its popular democratic negation: Open discussion.
8. The budget and socio-economic prospects for Zimbabwe – Cde Ben Hlatshwayo.

After every presentation, the debate will be taken to the floor for discussion. Please, let's all attend and effect a thorough commemoration of the ninth anniversary of Zimbabwe's Independence Day.

A luta continua!

(Fanon, 1963) (Lenin, 1961) (Marx, 1969) (Guevara, 1961)

9 Kadungure, a victim of mischievous disinformation

Government ministers routinely attack students, associating and linking them to enemies of the Zimbabwean state, reactionary forces or counter-revolutionaries across the region. The motivation is to delegitimise the critical and questioning voices of students. On 22 May 1989, I release this press statement in response to such denigrating remarks by Minister Ernest Kadungure.

As the Students' Union, we feel the views of the Minister of State (National Service) and ZANU-PF Secretary for Youth Comrade Ernest Kadungure on Saturday, 20 May 1989, as reported in *The Sunday Mail* of 21 May 1989 when addressing a joint ZANU-PF and PF-ZAPU youth league leaders meeting in Harare, cannot go unchallenged. Kadungure said: 'The country's enemies were more likely to infiltrate the youths, particularly our students at the local university ... Rumour has it that the MNR might infiltrate the country ...'

The minister's views were tantamount to equating students to the notorious counter-revolutionaries, the Mozambique National Resistance (MNR), thus discrediting the genuine national role played by students. With all due respect being accorded, we declare Kadungure a victim of mischievous disinformation, who is incompetent of intellectual and objective analysis of student struggles. Hence, we question his credibility as a minister. What infuriates the union is the fact that this is not the first time that he has addressed youths and condemned UZ students. The same thing happened after the great demo of 29 September 1988. As students, we feel compelled to state our case very clearly.

As the Students' Union, we are completely opposed to corruption of any kind, bureaucratic squandering, looting of national coffers, bourgeois profiteering and the prolific engagement in the futile establishment of white elephants.

We completely condemn the so-called New Investment Code as a clear blueprint and sign of the entrenchment of capitalism, a sell-out move that has heavily compromised the ideological standpoint of the government. To us, this signals the complete shelving of the socialist agenda. We reject this total incapacity to carry out revolutionary demands of the masses on the question of land, nationalisation and the building of a strong national economy. We completely deplore the total economic dependency on big international capital represented by the multinational corporations. This has led to corrupt tendencies and actions among the nationalists.

On democracy, we strongly condemn the attempts by the government to stifle and absurdly interfere with people's democratic rights. As the Students' Union, it is our unequivocal democratic right to demonstrate and the government cannot, and not at all, take away that fundamental democratic right from the union. As we fight to sustain and maintain this democracy for the union, we see the essence of extending this to the national framework. We do not see the rationale of establishing a petit bourgeois one-party state. In this vein, we unreservedly condemn the refusal by the police to grant permission to ZUM to hold their political rallies on Sunday. We want to make it abundantly clear that our condemnation of the police decision is based on principled grounds of maintaining national democratic rights and not out of allegiance to ZUM. This position is intended to ensure the existence of national democracy in the country, a necessary precondition for the mobilisation of the working class. As the Students' Union, we cannot join a political party as an institution. Joining a political party is an individual's decision and this does not lie in the confines of the policies and obligations of the union. Nonetheless, the Students' Union demands national recognition of fundamental and inalienable democratic rights of assembly, association and expression. It is an immutable right for students to listen to whomever they want so that they can condemn or support that person from the viewpoint of information and not disinformation.

To that end, the refusal to grant permission for the rallies 'in the interest of public order' characterises fascist policies and the very same tactics will be applied to students when they apply for permission to demonstrate. On public order, our question is, 'Who determines this so-called interest of public order or disorder and how impartial is their thinking?'

As the Students' Union, we should never betray the working class and the peasantry. We should continue to fight and combat bourgeois ideology and hegemony over the working class. We should continue to work more closely with the working class to strengthen its ideological independence and strengthen its radical trade union demands. As a Students' Union, we would also want to reiterate our completely autonomous existence from the UZ administration and the Government of Zimbabwe. No one in these two institutions can control or monitor our union activities and this includes the Vice Chancellor and the State President, who is also our Chancellor. We have a completely separate existence and we will fight tooth and claw to sustain this healthy democratic environment of academic and intellectual freedom. In a nutshell, these are the underlying principles that constitute the cogs and wheels of our union and they will be jealously guarded by every member of the union.

If the view of Minister Kadungure is that anyone who upholds the above ideals is being used by the MNR, then we not only agree to disagree with him, but also vehemently declare that the lines of battle have been drawn and defined. We will never ever compromise on matters of principle. Anyway, since the minister is not a product of an institution of higher education himself and is not likely to achieve such a status any time soon, the union will seek to educate him. Thorough and concerted efforts will be made to have him explain his weird thinking before a General Meeting of the UZ Students' Union.

A luta continua!

10 Students' Union mass action: The basis of our revolt

As students, we consider ourselves the voice of ordinary Zimbabweans. We speak and act in opposition to any transgressions against the people. Of late there have been draconian price increases, violations of democratic rights, and as the Mugabe regime moves to the right, it adopts sell-out programmes such as the Investment Code. We are not amused. We express our displeasure through a boycott of classes on 30 June 1989.

We, the Students' Union, have once again taken it upon ourselves, as our patriotic duty, to stage this mass action, protesting against the gross injustices that now prevail and promise to persist against the masses of this country.

The substantive reasons for our mass action are provided here in order of sequence:

1. We categorically and unequivocally deplore and denounce the astronomically high price increases recently announced by the government. We view this as an insensitive, callous and capitalist stance, designed to maximise the profits for a few financial magnates in our society. This is to the detriment of our marginalised popular masses, the workers and the dear peasants, and hence a perpetuation of class differences in our society. In essence, what this rise in prices of basic commodities means is that the cost of living for the masses has skyrocketed. It is again unrealistic for the government to think that the so-called collective bargaining by the workers will offset these rises. Basing on real, empirical, statistical and historical evidence and given the nature of the capitalist mode of production, is it plausible to expect the capitalist to raise the wages by 30 per cent? We submit that this unwarranted and unwise decision is a total annihilation of the marginalised masses and a condemnation of the unemployed to untold pangs of misery, hunger

and disease and consequently to their graves!

2. Recently the government announced the notorious Investment Code. What this code does, in essence, is to encourage foreign investors to invest in our country. Despite the various ideological justifications which the government provides for the Code, we, the patriotic and revolutionary intellectuals, view this code as a further entrenchment of capitalism in Zimbabwe. We further argue that the Code is evidence of acquiescence to the International Monetary Fund (IMF) and World Bank (WB) sponsored programmes. Thus, there has been a gradual tendency towards the removal of subsidies on basic essential commodities such as bread and mealie meal, and a trend to remove price and wage controls. We reject the tendency of going all over the world looking for financial handouts in the form of aid without realising the strings attached to the assistance. To all intents and purposes, the Code is incompatible with the doctrine of socialism and hence for that reason we completely deplore and reject it. We demand the government to reconsider soberly the implication of this heinous piece of paperwork. Which Third World country has ever developed on aid? How can foreign investment solve unemployment when its own success is dependent on the existence of reservoirs of cheap labour?
3. We further demand total academic freedom and our inalienable right both to be informed and to inform. We are totally opposed to the unwarranted, unjustified and malicious detention and the psychological harassment of university staff, in particular the Acting Dean of the Faculty of Law, Cde Kempton Makamure. Again, we will forever deplore the deportation of Cde Shadrack Gutto. To all intents and purposes, this is a threat to academic freedom, freedom of expression and above all freedom of conscience. We demand that the UZ administration lift its tacit and cowardly ban on the student magazine *Focus*. As students, we are entitled to freedom of expression and conscience, and it is utterly unconscionable for the administration and the government to deprive us of this right.
4. We want *Focus* back!
5. As per the Constitution of Zimbabwe, freedom of political association should be guaranteed for every citizen. Without implying support for ZUM, we denounce the unwarranted, unexplained and unlawful detention of its members. Our people are entitled to various political opinions and the denial to ZUM of a platform to express its political views is a derogation of this right. Is it not common cause that those African countries who declared one-party states have been characterised by scenes of murder, decapitations, mutilations, bloody deliriums, deportations, crude derogations of human rights and indeed endless coups d'état?
6. The use of force exercised on doctors while they were airing their clear, legitimate grievances is really an authoritarian and neo-fascist tendency and hence it has to be condemned. Better conditions of service for our doctors mean better medical attention and hence more efficiency on the

part of the doctors, leading to more direct benefits for the masses. Again, better conditions of service will curb the doctors' tendency to leave government hospitals for private practice, thereby depriving our masses of their service. The government must attend to the needs and problems of our medical professionals. We rally behind our doctors!

7. We hereby wish to remind the government that there remain hundreds of thousands of dispossessed and landless peasants. The land question remains unresolved while most of our peasants are declared squatters. We request the government to honour its obligations to provide land for the masses by 1990 and repeal the lethal, heinous and immoral section 16 of the Lancaster House Constitution.
8. We denounce the partiality and biased reporting by *The Herald* and request it to stop acting as a partisan paper or rather as an organ of misinformation. Numerous statements have been submitted to this paper by both students and staff of the university but they have been shamefully and cowardly suppressed. We challenge *The Herald to* stand up and declare to the whole world that it represents the under-provided workers and dispossessed peasants. Our masses have the right to be informed. We demand that our voice be heard.
9. The state apparatus through the Central Intelligence Organisation (CIO) has unleashed a campaign of psychological harassment against students on this campus. We have covertly been labelled as enemies of this country. Let the nation and the whole world know that we remain loyal and committed first and foremost to this country and its downtrodden masses. We are therefore by the same token ideological enemies of that class which is in alliance with international capital which seeks to keep the pauperised masses of Zimbabwe under perpetual subordination and suppression. We refuse to be turned into an ivory tower and we are committed to taking the university out to the people and turning it into an ally of the masses in the battle for economic and political emancipation.

In conclusion, the Students' Union would like to categorically emphasise its national obligation and duty. Because the majority of students are of worker and peasant background, they are quite cognisant of the problems, aspirations and conditions of the toiling masses. Therefore, students in Zimbabwe have a de facto social role imposed upon them by material conditions and history. Hence, on the basis of the above submissions we demand an audience with the government.

A luta continua!

(NB: The initial mode of the mass action was meant to be a massive student demonstration and an application was lawfully launched with the Zimbabwe Republic Police, but a political decision was made refusing to grant us the permission to march, hence we resorted to this class boycott.)

(Lenin, 1961)

11 An agenda for the Students' Union

After serving as Secretary General of the Students' Union from August 1988 to June 1989, there is a general consensus that I have done a fairly good job. I am under pressure from fellow students to run for the union presidency. I succumb and decide to give it a go. Previous candidates have presented themselves to the electorate without detailed plans, specific objectives and clear strategies. I choose a different path. This is my UZ Students' Union presidential election manifesto which I release on 4 July 1989, for the 15 August 1989 polls. It leads to a thunderous victory, marked by an unprecedented and historic margin.

Preamble

Applying dialectical materialism to the cognition of social phenomena, the Students' Union is envisaged as a front for the presentation and resolution of student demands. Put differently, it is a trade union for students characterised by a platform for collective representation of student problems, interests, rights and aspirations. Having been set up by an Act of Parliament, the University Act 27/82 of 1982, it is a body corporate with a separate autonomous existence from the university administration and the Government of Zimbabwe. Effectively, for all intents and purposes the establishment of the Students' Union provides the theoretically ideal operational framework for strong resolution of student demands. It becomes incumbent upon union members, and it is indeed the demand of objective reality, that they provide a consistent, ideologically clear and uncompromisingly committed leadership which has a duty and obligation to sustain an independent and strong union bent on resolving student problems and presenting a comprehensive representation of their aspirations. It is on these principled grounds that I present my candidacy for the Students' Union presidency (1989–1990).

1. Accommodation

This remains a major perennial problem as the university student population continues to increase without a corresponding infrastructural expansion. The problem is most critical at the beginning of each year in March. The SRC should pressurise the Department of Accommodation and Catering Services (DACS) to ensure an efficient and maximum utilisation of the available limited accommodation on campus. To illustrate the urgency of this role, for 1989, at the end of the first term, there were 216 vacant rooms and, presently, 28 rooms are vacant. Whatever flimsy excuse given is completely unacceptable. This outright negligence and inefficiency, when students are sleeping in semi-habitable quarters all over Harare, defies logic and rationality. Prior to March, the SRC and the Student Affairs Department should intensify efforts to procure additional accommodation in and around Harare for students at reasonable rates. A subsidy should be demanded from the UZ administration and the government. Inefficient bureaucrats should be forced, in no uncertain terms, to speed up and expedite the completion of housing projects such as the New Hall of Residence. The SRC should champion the Students' Union pressure on the government to cut down on unnecessary reactionary bureaucratic delays in the establishment of the second national university, the National University of Science and Technology (NUST), in Bulawayo. Our stance should be, 'We do not want that campus tomorrow. Neither do we want it today. We demand it yesterday!' Government bureaucrats and technocrats should be made aware of our disenchantment. Government involvement in the construction of white elephants such as the National Sports Stadium, proposed new civic centre and a new Parliament building should be challenged in the context of the need for student accommodation and the urgency of the second university campus in Bulawayo.

2. Transport

This is a critical problem for non-resident students daily and also a problem over the weekends for the residents. The SRC should increase the number of the contracted buses with Harare United Omnibus Company (HUOC) and carry out thorough research into the timetables to ensure that the major student peak hours are serviced with more buses. The provision of a 10:30pm bus for those non-residents using the library is a fundamental prerequisite. The SRC should subsidise and hence make viable bus services from outskirt suburbs like Chitungwiza and Seke. A long-term programme of procurement of minibuses to operate as emergency taxis (ETs) from the UZ into town should be pursued with the Ministry of Higher Education and Willowvale Motor Industries. Over weekends, UZ buses from the Site and Transport Department should be hired to ferry students to and from town at the critical peak hours.

3. The clinic and CIMAS

It is common cause that the clinic facilities and staff have become completely inadequate for the swelling student numbers. Adding insult to injury, this inadequacy is compounded by the inhuman, inconsiderate and downright insensitively unethical reception meted out by the clinic staff to the students. The lack of drugs and the non-availability of the doctor when urgently required worsen the situation. The SRC should blast this social and professional bankruptcy and demand the provision of adequate medical facilities, drugs, resident doctors and an increased number of committed nurses. Plans are under way to establish an expanded clinic but because of the reactionary technocrats within the UZ administration these efforts have not taken off. The CIMAS facility remains an unchecked abuse of student money. Each student pays $85 annually which implies a total of more than $765 000 annually and yet some drugs are not available in the clinic. Furthermore, when you get them elsewhere the CIMAS scheme does not cover most of the drugs. In addition most clinics and hospitals in town have resorted to denying treatment to UZ students on the CIMAS scheme. They refer them back to the mismanaged UZ clinic. The SRC should call for a revamp of CIMAS conditions by holding a direct meeting with CIMAS officials and the university bureaucrats. A comprehensive accountability of all the money should be given. In case of failure to come to favourable agreeable terms, the whole CIMAS facility should be abrogated and students refunded all their money forthwith.

4. Sports

Sporting activities are an integral component of varsity life. Hence there is a need for an extensive and comprehensive expansion of sporting facilities embracing all the different types of sport activities. The sports budget money is presently not enough. The SRC must increase its present contribution of $15 000 to at least $20 000 and pressurise the UZ administration to also beef up their contribution to meet the sport requirements. The administration of these funds should be heavily monitored to ensure proper management to avoid situations whereby students taking part in national games or any such activities live in appalling conditions as witnessed recently in the Mutare saga.

5. Food

Recent trends have manifested a general denigration of the quality, quantity and variety of our food. There have been reported allegations of abuses and misappropriation of our food by high-placed DACS officials. This is crowned by general looting and consumerist tendencies among the ordinary workers in the dining halls. All these activities coupled with gross inefficiency and negligence have led to the complete collapse of the quality and quantity of the food in all halls of residence. Monotony has become the rule and order of the day, not the exception. All these problems need radical redress. DACS should be instructed by the SRC to overhaul their cooking efficiency and quality production capacity. Those involved in looting student food (among the senior DACS officers) should be kicked out. The SRC should demand an immediate end to the hoarding of students' food in packs and bags by the dining workers on buses on their way home. This should not be misconstrued as a negation of our unflinching support for the working class. The Students' Union should actually fight for the improvement of the working conditions of these employees and demand increments to their meagre salaries. Paying the workers a living wage will reduce pilfering and petty theft.

6. Hooliganism and general social integration

It is imperative for the union to realise that these are internal contradictions and that they should be resolved internally and amicably. We should never allow the state hooligan, Tommy Sithole, and his notorious vanguard paper of disinformation, *The Herald*, to take advantage of these isolated and unfortunate incidents to further his partisan political struggle against the students. What this political malcontent Tommy and his government masters are at pains to say is, 'Look, these students are morally and socially decadent. Do not listen to whatever political thinking they expound.' It would be very naive of the Students' Union to fall for this ploy. Ours should be an independent and systematic combating of hooliganism by applying a comprehensive disciplinary code and a re-enunciation of Ordinance 30 (the UZ framework for student conduct). As background to this, a thorough scientific analysis should be carried out to establish the fundamental socio-economic causes of this phenomenon of hooliganism. Consultations should be carried out among members of the union to come up with rational punitive measures. All members of the union should be made aware of the established disciplinary penalties. This will act as a deterrent but we should never hesitate to implement the measures when duly necessary.

Still on this issue of discipline, the SRC should never be an ally of the UZ administration or the government. These two institutions have proven to be reactionary class enemies of the students and hence their desire to discipline students will be purely for political and not social reasons. Nonetheless, the Students' Union should not only denounce but strongly combat the victimisation of female students residing in Complex IV and Swinton by this monster, hooliganism. An immediate end should be put to the general molestation and abuse of women in and around the SU facilities. The SU building should be a free and accessible place for both sexes. Lastly, members of the union should, however, realise that all these social problems are not major antagonistic contradictions. They are non-antagonistic, hence a Maoist approach should be adopted in their resolution: Unity – Contradictions – Unity.

7. Religion

We cherish the freedom to believe or not to believe. However, we acknowledge that a significant majority of our union members is of a religious disposition. Hence, to this end, the SRC should take an all-embracing stance to accommodate all the diverse religious factions. Thus, projects like the extension of the chapel, which has a shortfall of $41 000, after $160 000 has been secured from donors through the offices of the Chaplain, should be boosted by the various religious denominations with the backing of the SRC through a variety of fundraising activities. With as many as 61 denominations the SRC will try to discourage the tendency towards fragmentation and encourage more ecumenical cooperation among students.

8. Representation on UZ administration committees

The university bureaucracy is run on a farcical committee democracy. This is because on most important committees such as the Finance Committee and the Executive Committee of the UZ Council (the engine of the UZ), there is absolutely no student representation. On other platforms, students sit in an ex-officio status and hence they are always outvoted by the government and university bureaucrats who sit on these committees. The SRC should demand increased and more effective representation on these university committees for it is in these forums that decisions that affect students are made. A radical long-term programme should also be embarked on. This should envisage a total abrogation of the University Act 27/82 and liquidation of the current farcical administrative structure, leading to the establishment of a tripartite representative and democratic structure involving students, lecturers and the government. In this set-up, chief officers such as the Chancellor and Vice Chancellor will be democratically elected. Yes, let democracy prevail.

9. Loans/grants

In the wake of the astronomical price increases, the Students' Union should demand an increment in student support finances. This is of urgent prominence to the non-resident students. The grant-to-loan ratio should be adjusted to 80 per cent grant to 20 per cent loan. Hence, the SRC should draft a document stating from a purely social, economic and legal viewpoint the arguments for this ratio to convince the Ministry of Higher Education and the Minister of Finance, Dr Bernard Chidzero. The SRC should also press for an exemption of the loan amount from the student graduate's gross income when paying tax, so as to reduce the financial pressure on the lowly paid, heavily taxed and loan-repaying graduate.

10. The political front

It is common cause that over the past one and a half years, this Students' Union has positively taken a dramatic upsurge out of its history of docility and passivity. Student political activism during this period has marked the ideological crystallisation of student radicalism in Zimbabwe. The revolutionary momentum and general political consciousness has escalated dramatically. This has led to the effective and dynamic contributions by the students to the current socio-geopolitical economic debates raging on in the country and thus impacting or setting changes into motion.

However, one might ask: Why political activism? Why by students? Any considerations of the anatomy of social classes in a neo-colonial state such as ours must take into account the part played or which can be played by the students in the socio-economic political dynamics of the state. Students have a de facto social role imposed upon them by material conditions and history. The generality of the students are of worker and peasant background. In fact, the student community is a reflection of the existing social classes. As such, it is my submission that the students are an integral vibrant component of society, quite cognisant of the problems, material conditions and aspirations of the toiling masses. Hence, the Students' Union has to act as a barometer of socio-political consciousness. In this vein, the union has a duty and obligation to provide a platform and a forum for the voiceless and disorganised masses by vehemently declaring and venting their problems and aspirations.

This forum takes different modes, including seminars, symposia, conferences, press statements and the demo. The demonstration is an inalienable democratic right to the Students' Union. Admittedly, it is the most effective means of communicating with the generality of the masses of Zimbabwe but it must be used with caution and as the last resort. In such an eventuality, thorough consultation should be carried out to ensure maximum student support. This can be ensured by an elaborate publicity campaign for General Meetings. Members should be conscientised on the uncompromising need and necessity of attending General Meetings and making decisions for themselves. I would like to reiterate that it is only a General Meeting which decides on any student mass action and not individuals in or out of the SRC. Section 16.4.4 of the Students' Union Constitution (1984) clearly states that the SRC is subordinate to the SU General Meeting. Hence the SRC cannot veto a decision of such a gathering.

However, imperative and incumbent on the SRC, as a further safeguard, after a major General Meeting decision, the result should be communicated to the entire Students' Union as early as possible and, if necessary, a referendum should be held to register other students' views. In the event of serious apprehension or disagreements, the SRC should reconvene the General Meeting and have students reconsider the matter at hand. All those who would not have attended the initial General Meeting will be encouraged to attend and express their views. Thus, under this presidency there is an absolute guarantee that any mass action will be in concurrence with the thinking of the entirety of the Students' Union.

Nonetheless, we should never, ever compromise on our principled national revolutionary role. A committed Marxist-Leninist stance should be maintained against corruption of any kind and level, bureaucratic squandering, downright looting, and petit bourgeois profiteering. We need a complete rejection of a corrupt petit bourgeois one-party state, a rejection of the total incapacity to carry out the revolutionary demands and a protracted denunciation of the shelving of the socialist agenda (as evidenced by adoption of the notorious Investment Code). A stance to sustain national democratic rights – of association, assembly and expression and a fearless defiant demand for ultimate academic and intellectual freedom – should be upheld. In all these endeavours, our long-term objective should be to blast and smash the moribund and racial monopoly capitalism which characterises neo-colonial Zimbabwe today and fight for the establishment of an egalitarian socialist Zimbabwe. In fact, our role has become more than necessary with the advent of the expiration next year of the 10-year reform constraint on the Lancaster House Constitution. We have to push for revolutionary constitutional change. Hence, the struggle continues unabated with neither retreat nor surrender.

In a nutshell, these are the principles that constitute the agenda for the Students' Union and it is within this context that I define the essence of thorough objective analysis in the forthcoming elections and hence a consideration of my candidacy for the Students' Union presidency for the 1989 to 1990 period.

A luta continua!

Arthur G.O. Mutambara, UZ SRC Presidential Candidate; Outgoing UZ SRC Secretary General (1988–1989)

(Lenin, 1961) (Fanon, 1963) (Chung, 1985)

12 In defence of academic freedom

I am successfully elected President of the Students' Union and Chairman of the SRC in July 1989. Exactly a year after the historic Anti-Corruption Demonstration of 29 September 1988, we decide to hold a revolutionary gala on campus to commemorate this great event. The Zimbabwe government has different thoughts. Through the police, they decide to disrupt and stop this celebration by deploying gratuitous violence. There is chaos on campus. The union is incensed. I quickly draft an angry and uncompromising response released on 2 October 1989. This statement leads to my violent arrest and the unprecedented closure of UZ on 4 October 1989. I am severely injured and detained without trial for six weeks.

Comrades, on Friday, 29 September 1989, we witnessed yet another violation of our legitimate inalienable democratic rights. The Students' Union organised a gala (seminar) to commemorate the great Anti-Corruption Demonstration of 29 September 1988. This was an entirely student affair with student speakers in the local Great Hall. The Government of Zimbabwe through the ZRP invoked the notorious emergency powers and declared the seminar illegal and cancelled. To enforce their decision, a 200-strong battalion of the riot squad was deployed and sealed off the Great Hall. They were armed with automatic rifle power, tear gas, rubber batons and other forms of live ammunition. They harassed and terrorised students indiscriminately throughout the campus, randomly tear-gassing halls of residents, wantonly clobbering and brutalising students and threatening to use gunfire when necessary. This continued to 3am on 30 September from 7pm the previous day.

Comrades, this is state terrorism at its worst! Yes, we did not apply for permission and we will never apply for permission from anyone in this country to hold a seminar at this university. The charter that establishes any university enshrines academic and intellectual freedom as constituting the fundamental fabrics of such an autonomous institution. We envisage a university as a demonstrable melting pot of ideas.

To them, the running dogs of imperialism, academic freedom involves the narrow acquisition of knowledge, domination of knowledge and who should be taught and by whom. Our conception of academic freedom involves the acquisition and dissemination of knowledge for the advancement of humankind, to eliminate poverty, disease and hunger, and to realise the best in human beings. We demand ultimate academic freedom to freely participate in the socio-geo-economic and political debates raging on in Zimbabwe using the tools of analysis we have acquired through education.

Comrades, is it a legitimate government that uses its state machinery of violence – the police force and army – to crush a student internal gathering in a university hall? Is it a self-respecting government that displays brute and neo-fascist force, only comparable to that of SA, against its own unarmed and defenceless students? It is our strong submission that the institution of government has thus been rendered completely disreputable and hence the incumbents have completely lost legitimacy. Who in this government can have the audacity and credibility to criticise the De Klerk regime in South Africa? Or are we even worse than De Klerk? Ian Smith never banned political seminars at this university. In this country emergency powers are being used against Zimbabwean workers and professionals (doctors, National Railways of Zimbabwe (NRZ), Posts and Telecommunications Corporation (PTC)), lecturers and students. The manifestation of excesses of neo-colonialism in this country is even defying bourgeois ethics and morals. We cannot even respect the bourgeois democratic rights of assembly, association, press and speech provided for by the reactionary Lancaster House Constitution.

Comrades, what is at stake today affects the entirety of the university, that is, the students, lecturers, academics, non-academic staff and the generality of the community in which the university is situated. Consequently, what has happened is a vicious attack on the dignity and foundation of the Zimbabwean nation. The question is whether this academic institution is still a university, or worse, does it even qualify to be labelled a high school? Are we going to have to apply for permission to attend certain lectures or tutorials, apply for permission to have student General Meetings, apply for permission to have Workers' Union meetings, and apply for permission to show politically inclined films? This is completely unsustainable and unacceptable.

Comrades, are we going to apply for permission to live from the Minister of Home Affairs, Moven Mahachi? We must be under no illusions. The Friday tragedy sets a terribly regrettable precedent and has serious implications for the university. It is the most serious and direct threat to our autonomy and credibility as a university. There is now a greater need than ever for this university to act as a community. Administration, teaching staff, students and workers should have a common interest in the protection of this institution.

It is deplorable that certain sections of the UZ administration have decided to sit on the fence. By not condemning the recent and ongoing unjustifiable, manipulated and malicious campaign against students, they have actually taken a position against students. We demand that they now join the rest of the university in fighting for what a university is essentially all about, academic freedom.

We demand an immediate end to the misguided, naive and outright bankrupt onslaught being launched against students at both social and political public forums. We unreservedly condemn the attitude that students are young and hence confused and ignorant about the history and future aspirations of this country. There is nothing young about our analysis and conceptualisation of national issues. That one fought for this country does not justify that person to loot, plunder and wreck the economy of Zimbabwe, let alone stifle people's democratic rights. The Students' Union does not believe in the notion of a personality cult, but rather in principles and principles only. We completely denounce in the strongest terms anyone who takes advantage of public platforms to attack students. We challenge them to rationally and objectively discuss issues with the students, if at all they have any political spine strong enough for them to intellectually engage the students.

The ugly scenes of Friday should be understood in their definite class context. The political thought of the various social classes and groupings throughout civilisation is above all characterised by their attitude towards the state and their definition of its essential nature. The state is an institution born out of the existence of irreconcilable contradictions in society. Hence, it is not neutral but rather has a definite class nature. What is critical is identifying the class interests it is serving. Every state is the organised political expression and an instrument of the decisive class in the economy. The violence, brutality and coercion exercised by the Zimbabwean state were the ultimate resort applied to maintain the material interests of the exploiters – the bourgeoisie. The corrupt leadership are being just a client class of imperialism, the comprador bourgeoisie.

With immediate effect, the Students' Union is demanding immediate urgent meetings with UZ Vice Chancellor, Walter Kamba and President of the Republic of Zimbabwe, Robert Mugabe, who is also Chancellor of the University of Zimbabwe. These meetings will be held with the entire student body with a thrust to address issues raised in this document and answering the fundamental question: *'Whither University of Zimbabwe: An autonomous credible institution of higher learning or a bureaucratic extension of the Ministry of Higher Education run by the Ministry of Home Affairs?'*

A strongly worded letter of protest will be sent to Moven Mahachi restating that Churchill Road is the boundary for the notorious emergency powers. If the above efforts are frustrated, other forms of struggle will be embarked on. There will be no compromise whatsoever. This university is the last island of democracy in this country and we will fight to the bitter end and hilt to sustain these democratic rights and extend them to the generality of the masses of Zimbabwe. You cannot push a cat into a corner. After all, we are not cats but tigers!

Defeat is not on our agenda!

A luta continua!

(Guevara, 1961) (Jackson, 1972) (Marx, 1969)

13 The struggle continues unabated

The university is eventually opened, and students are forced to sign a document which seeks to restrict their activities. The objective is to harass, intimidate and cower them, and thus turn them away from the struggle. We are finally released from detention after extensive physical and psychological torture. However, they do not break us. This speech to the UZ Students' Union General Meeting on 23 April 1990 signifies our 'no retreat, no surrender' spirit. The struggle has to continue.

Comrades, greetings and welcome to the home of student struggles. Count it a privilege not to be wasted that you are now part of this ongoing struggle. Naturally, you would want to discover and actively participate in the pursuance of the revolution. Admittedly, those who begin a revolution may not see its end results. But that must not stop or discourage you from participating positively in the struggle.

Student politics is embodied in the Students' Union Constitution as a democratic right and not a privilege that might be withdrawn. The Constitution openly states that a scientific socialist stand shall be employed in pursuance of national objectives with the students' participation in the affairs of the country.

The aims and objectives of the Constitution sanction a provision and development of social, intellectual and political activities coupled with a responsible and patriotic attitude among students.

The Students' Union recognises the existence of socio-economic classes within the country and their negative repercussions on the masses. It is the endeavour of the union to actively participate in the eradication of this obnoxious class structure in pursuit of an egalitarian society. We despise capitalism beyond expression. We support the struggle of the exploited and oppressed working class against the propertied and blood-sucking international capital and its local puppets (the comprador bourgeoisie).

While as a body politic the Students' Union does not participate in party politics, it is a fundamental and democratic right of students to participate in national politics and development. As a result of the student's worker and peasantry background, he suffers the pinch as well. At the same time, he is also a member of the aspiring intelligentsia. He is equipped with the tools of scientific analysis which enable him to explain the socio-political and economic bankruptcy characterising our nation.

Indeed, the students have been at the forefront of the struggle for a better nation. The Anti-Corruption Demonstration of 1988 and the 1989 class boycott were about social ills that were denounced in the strongest terms: national corruption, accommodation crisis, unemployment, price hikes and white elephants. These activities reveal the involvement and commitment of students to the national struggle.

It is thus imperative that students intensify their participation in national politics. This is critical in view of the movement towards the establishment of a one-party state in this country. This is being done with no respect to our fundamental human rights. The students should be the vanguard standing against this tendency. This can only be done through the maintenance of a strong and politically conscious union. That is why the struggle must continue unabated.

A luta continua!

(Marx, 1969)

14 Disruption of student participation on May Day

The solidarity and collaboration between workers and students is growing. The workers' leaders, the ZCTU, are slowly getting radicalised as the Mugabe regime starts to persecute them too. It becomes our tradition every year to attend Workers Day on 1 May in solidarity with our comrades. However, the relationship between the workers and the students is still tenuous. On May Day 1990 at Rufaro Stadium, when government functionaries decide to throw us out over our revolutionary posters, the ZCTU backs down. They do not effectively defend the students. They seek accommodation with the Mugabe regime, as students are being brutally attacked by ZANU-PF youths. Following that violent disruption of our participation in the Workers Day activities, I issue the following statement on 2 May 1990.

The Students' Union vehemently and unreservedly condemns in the strongest of terms the violation of our fundamental inalienable democratic right to show solidarity with the working class on May Day 1990. As is our tradition and practice of revolutionary, participatory democratic solidarity, two busloads of students went to Rufaro Stadium, armed with nothing except two banners and posters to join the workers. Some of the posters consisted of single words such as '*Mazimbavha*' (You thieves) and '*Hamunyari*' (Don't you have any shame). Once inside the stadium, the students were instructed to surrender their posters if they were to remain in the stadium and participate in the proceedings of the day. It was argued that President Robert Mugabe should not be exposed to posters with insulting working-class slogans.

Naturally, we principally rejected this naive mystification of an individual. We declared that we were going ahead to march in the stadium and show the President our posters. Senior police officers, government bureaucrats and members of the CIO threatened to use the violent Riot Police Squad to stop our participation. We challenged them to go ahead and manifest their fascist terror tactics before the generality of the people of Zimbabwe represented there in the stadium. We demanded to see the legal statutory instrument that they were invoking in asking us to retract our posters.

The police also demanded to know who had invited the students and also violently pulled down ZCTU anti-one-party state posters throughout the stadium. Having failed to legally throw out the students, the ZANU-PF nationalists then decided to use ZANU-PF youths. About 200 of these youths armed with knobkerries surrounded the students agitating for a violent clash. The Riot Squad and uniformed police were on the wait to join in on their side. As students, we could not find a philosophical justification or the rationale for a clash with the youth. It is an incontestable historical fact that the majority of the youth are the very victims of the system we are fighting against. They are, in fact, the unemployed and unemployable youngsters who are an integral component of the Zimbabwean socio-economic political crisis. Why fight our disillusioned, misguided and abused brothers? Logistically, we also were grossly outnumbered and the whole state machinery of violence was waiting to pounce on the students. Thus, we decided to move out peacefully from the stadium.

In the excitement that then ensued, some of the ZANU-PF youths ran amok, charging at some of our students. Resultantly, some students lost a number of clothing items such as shoes and hats. Two were brutally kicked and punched.

It is such a violation of student and worker rights that compels us to strongly condemn the ZCTU endorsement of the ZANU-PF nationalists during the recent general elections. The violation is a clear illustration that they have no agenda for the working class. There is not a single socialist in the ZANU-PF petit bourgeois party. Such a disruption only confirms, and vehemently so, our uncompromising rejection of the one-man, one-party state dictatorship that ZANU-PF intends to establish in Zimbabwe. We strongly denounce this cult of personality that now characterises the political quagmire that confronts us, a cult incapable of manifesting tolerance to dissent and rational disputation. No one is sacrosanct from criticism and mistakes.

On the one-party state, our minimum programme is very clear. There is no compromise, retreat or surrender. We are preaching an ideology of revolutionary confrontation. We say this with all humility but with authority. History will absolve us. With immediate effect, the union demands an audience with the Minister of Labour, Manpower and Social Welfare and the UZ Chancellor to seek clarification on the May Day disruption. History demands that we remain resilient and committed to a justified cause.

The struggle continues unabated.

A luta continua!

(Lenin, 1961)

15 The Students' Union rejects the one-party state

Of all the ideological and philosophical positions I have taken, the matter of the one-party state provides the best illustration of my intellectual growth and political development. I start off in high school as a fanatical proponent of a ZANU-PF one-party state as the foundational requirement for achieving a socialist socio-economic order in Zimbabwe. Now at university, having witnessed the excesses, failures, brutality and ideological bankruptcy of the ZANU-PF regime, it is time to reconsider. Even as it fought against government corruption on 29 September 1988, the Students' Union still had faith in Robert Mugabe as a leader, and ZANU-PF as an institution. That is history now. Subsequent events have changed all that. Students have been brutalised, democratic spaces have been shut down, corruption and primitive accumulation reign supreme, and Mugabe has proven to be the Looter in Chief. The union decides to formalise its rejection of the one-party state through a resolution of its supreme and ultimate platform, the General Meeting. I draft a position paper that captures the mood of the students on 15 May 1990.

The intention by ZANU-PF to press ahead with its December 1989 Party Congress, to create a one-party state in Zimbabwe by legislation, has been the subject of extensive debate and deliberation. Consequently, a number of different organisations have taken definite positions on this matter. It is in this context that the University of Zimbabwe Students' Union, obligated by historical responsibility, states its case on this pertinent issue without fear, equivocation or ambiguity.

At its General Meeting on Thursday, 3 May 1990, held in two parts, 1pm for the non-residents and 7:30pm for the residents, the motion was comprehensively debated and voted on. The General Meeting at both sessions vehemently and unanimously voted against the establishment of a one-party state in Zimbabwe. It was rejected as a phenomenon that leads to a one-person, fascist dictatorship; a brutal, tyrannical, murderous, fossilised and bureaucratised political system, characterised by an intolerant cult of personality, monopolistic politics of domination, inefficiency, corruption, looting and downright defiant petit bourgeois primitive accumulation. The union denounced all naive feudalistic arguments advanced for the one-party state by senior party propagandists as flimsy, short-sighted and unscholarly. The ZANU-PF thinking signifies unscientific, simplistic and incorrect analysis of the Zimbabwean objective reality.

The basis of the union's rejection of the one-party state concept is at two levels of analysis. The first stage is a philosophical, anthropological and ideological perception that has been expressly confirmed by the events in Eastern Europe. The second level is that ascertained by analysis of the exact Zimbabwean historical conditions and the balance of forces between the reactionary nationalists and the progressives in the loose amalgamatory mass party ZANU-PF and in neo-colonial Zimbabwe in general.

The new political thinking in Eastern Europe, characterised by restructuring, renewal, rectification and openness, is indicative of a phenomenon which is revolutionary in its essence and historical significance. This phenomenon with its drive of democratic pluralism is a manifestation that there is nothing inherently socialist about a one-party state. In fact, it is a reflection that the one-party state is necessarily incompatible with socialism.

The fight for political democracy and mass participation in these countries is a demonstrable attempt to restore the democratic and humanistic values of socialism lost during the vulgarisation and distortion of the ideology. The motivation is ridding socialist implementation of unscientific subjectivism and general ideological emasculation. There is nothing wrong with socialism as an ideology but it must be embraced in an environment of multiparty democracy. It's our submission that the first task of the working class is to win the battle for democracy. The proletariat cannot prepare for its victory over the bourgeoisie without a protracted, consistent revolutionary struggle for democracy. Thus, on the basis of these lessons from Eastern Europe, we deplore, denounce and violently reject the one-party state concept and system.

The second level of rejection is largely dictated by the events in Zimbabwe over the past 10 years and the experiences of other neo-colonial one-party and one-man states in Malawi, Zaire, Zambia, Kenya and elsewhere in the Third World. The 10 years of independence in Zimbabwe, in particular the last five years, were marked by a profound denigration and degradation of basic tenets of fundamental inalienable democratic rights of assembly, association and expression. There was a negation of working-class demands consisting of the right to work, the right to a living wage, the right to better working conditions and the right to education and social security.

There has been excessive use of the notorious repressive emergency powers (inherited from Ian Smith) against striking workers, the doctors, PTC technicians, NRZ workers and recently the nurses. The ZANU-PF government has failed to manifest tolerance to criticism, dissent and general rational disputation and this led to arrests, detentions, physical and psychological harassment of trade unionists, opposition politicians, lecturers and students under the same UDI emergency powers. This culminated in the irrational and unprecedented closure of the University of Zimbabwe on 4 October 1989.

Zimbabwe has witnessed the destruction and terrorising of free professional journalism and the stifling of democratic debate and dialogue. The separation of powers between the Executive, the Legislature and the Judiciary has been violated and threatened, as evidenced in the cases of the 1989 Kariba by-election and that of Ian Smith's salary saga.

The experiences of the recent general elections, characterised by intimidations, violence, killings and outright naked rigging, are a monumental and flourishing illustration of the inability of ZANU-PF to accommodate opposition parties and cannot pass, by any standards, for free and fair elections. There also has been a growing alliance between the nationalists and international capital and hence their attainment of comprador positions. This has led to their stunning inability to resolve revolutionary demands for land, control and management of the economy and general advancement and betterment of the material conditions of the working class and the peasantry.

On the basis of the above submissions, it is the clear position of the Students' Union that a ZANU-PF one-party state will be an intolerant and corrupt petit bourgeois one-party state against the working class, the peasantry and the generality of the intelligentsia including students. Thus, on the basis of these historical experiences in Zimbabwe, the union unreservedly rejects the one-party state in Zimbabwe with the contempt it deserves.

Therefore, the union resolves to activate and articulate a minimum programme to sustain and maintain national democratic rights by vigorously and committedly opposing a de jure one-party state. We envisage and call for the establishment of a broad-based mass democratic movement consisting of progressive organisations of workers, farmers, consumers, peasants, lecturers, teachers, students, unemployed people, churches, political parties and the rest of the professional fraternity, to openly and fearlessly campaign against the legislation of the one-party state. It is imperative, however, that it be understood in no uncertain terms that this is a bare minimum programme for the union, but also a precondition for the union's maximum programme which is to fight for the establishment of a truly egalitarian socialist Zimbabwe.

The union is very wary and conscious of the pitfalls of the debate on democracy. As long as the debate remains imprisoned in the four walls of liberalism and social democratic tendencies, then it's our submission that the debate has not yet begun. It is the union's position that in the present historical context democracy expresses an ideology of resistance and struggle of the large masses and popular classes of the people. It is the summation of the experiences of struggle by the generality of people as they thrive to improve their material conditions. Hence, in this framework we envisage and define the essence of the maximum programme, an agenda characterised by violent revolutionary confrontation as the struggle by the working class, the peasantry and the progressive intelligentsia against moribund and racial monopoly capitalism continues, as contradictions continue to radically sharpen. Yes, the ultimate objective is to seize and smash the oppressive system and replace it with an egalitarian and equitable society. This struggle continues unabated. There is no compromise, retreat or surrender!

Abasha the one-party state!

A luta continua!

(Fanon, 1963) (Lenin, 1961) (Marx, 1969) (Guevara, 1961)

16 Students' Union finances: Combating looting

While the student movement is ostensibly radical, progressive and principled, we have our share of student leaders and ordinary union members who have corrupt and consumerist tendencies. There are cases, though limited, of abuse of union resources and facilities. We try to nip such inclinations in the bud. It is in pursuance of that objective that I issue the following statement on 20 June 1990.

The Student Representative Council places prime importance on the responsible management and control of Students' Union finances. It takes cognisance of the uncompromisable need for accountability and responsibility in the execution of any financial duties. In this vein, we define the essence for members of the SRC, being the custodians of these funds, to subscribe to a non-reducible minimum bottom line of being above board. Corruption, looting and general financial abuses should be brutally and mercilessly crushed among members of the SRC. Drastic measures should be taken against anyone involved, by any means necessary.

It is in this light that the SRC takes seriously the handwritten document pinned on the halls of residence on Tuesday, 19 June 1990. The principle and spirit of criticism behind the document is quite positive and demonstrable and hence should be encouraged. It is an inalienable democratic right of every member of the union to express criticism of the SRC. The current members of the SRC will never ever try to stop members from criticising the SRC structures, members or policies. We thus appreciate the efforts of the comrade whose document is in discussion. As an SRC we find his allegations shockingly wild and highly unsubstantiated but we do not dismiss them.

We take this opportunity to invite members of the Students' Union who have witnessed any abuse of union money, property or facilities by the SRC members, SRC committees, union clubs and societies or by individual members of the union, to please give the union as much detail as possible including names of the involved culprits, amounts and facilities involved, dates, time (if possible) and scene or venue of the criminal activity. What we are looking for is information and not names of those providing it. Hence, feel free not to give us your name in the exercise. But if you feel convinced and committed enough, we will sincerely appreciate your physical participation in the giving of this information. There will be an information box in the Students' Union secretary's office. The following SRC members will be points of deposition of information: Chinyaradzo Munodawafa, Gabriel Chaibva and Edward Chagonda.

When all information is collected, investigations will be instituted by the union disciplinary machinery. A violent axe will take toll of anyone implicated. There is no compromise!

Yes, it is a historical trend that when an SRC is approaching the end of its term of office, its tendency towards the culture of consumerism and looting is escalated. Resultantly, we urge the generality of the union members to be vigilant and jealously guard union funds and facilities from any looting of any kind or level. This SRC commits itself to a tough, merciless abrogation of unprincipled looters from the SRC and elsewhere in the union with the same principled vigour that we confront and castigate corruption in the nationalist government of Harare. This SRC, unlike any other previous councils, will present its financial statement before the end of its term of office and not after, as has been the corrupt tradition. At this forum, the brunt of accountability will be grounded to the bolt. It will be a no-holds-barred General Meeting.

Comrades, as we try to resolve our internal contradictions, be they political, financial or social, let's bear one concept in mind – that these problems are non-antagonistic contradictions – and hence let us resolve them amicably within unity.

Let us be very careful and wary of certain elements instigated by external forces from central government, bent on discrediting and undermining the fundamental contributions of the union, yesterday, today and tomorrow, to the socio-geo-economic-political debates raging on in the country. They intend to compromise the credibility of the student leadership and hence undermine its ability to take and articulate radical principled class positions against the nationalist regime.

Yes, there should be vigilance to combat looting and consumerism in the SRC. However, this should be crowned by vigilance to ensure that the leadership of our clubs, societies and the SRC is not hijacked by paid agent provocateurs from central government who are bent on confusing, dividing and then fatally destroying the Students' Union and what it has principally stood for and continues to stand for.

Members of the union must make deliberate efforts to actively expose and flush out these political malcontents. This becomes very pertinent and relevant as we move towards SRC elections early next term. Surely if a student in exercising his democratic right to criticise the current SRC finds himself working out an operational strategy with *The Herald* and members of the CIO then that only serves to cloud his sincerity and inevitably seriously compromise his motive.

Comrades, we owe this Students' Union to history and posterity. It does not belong to a current SRC. Hence, let us resolve our internal contradictions amicably in the context of unity of purpose. Only then will history unequivocally absolve us!

The struggle against looting and the culture of consumerism in the union continues unabated!

A luta continua!

17 Students' Union graduate employment drive

A problem is creeping into the Zimbabwean economy – the unemployment of qualified graduates. This is in addition to the perennial unemployment problems across the different sectors at lower skills levels. Consequently, we embark on a graduate employment drive and issue the following statement in Harare on 25 July 1990.

It is with profound disgust and apprehension that the union notes the unabated rise in unemployment levels in this country. This national unemployment crisis has reached such proportions that even skilled and trained manpower is grossly underutilised. Our own graduates from this university have been no exception.

During the recent graduation ceremonies, the SRC made a deliberate effort to establish the employment levels among the 1989 graduates. The statistics were shockingly frightening. Quite a significant number has not procured employment and of these some could not even afford the traditional gown and cap. Others were seriously underemployed in the fields or trades that they were not trained in, and are mercilessly underpaid, being given meagre and mediocre temporary wages in denigrating working conditions.

Therefore, the SRC is organising a Graduate Employment Strategy Day. The prime purpose of this day is to effectively explore national job trends and study the general socio-economic-industrial trends that affect employment with a particular emphasis on graduate employment. Employer organisations will participate, exhibit and recruit students. In particular, the Employers Confederation of Zimbabwe (EMCOZ), the Confederation of Zimbabwe Industries (CZI) and the Zimbabwe National Chamber of Commerce (ZNCC) have been approached and have expressed their willingness to participate. Other employer groups yet to confirm are the Public Service Commission

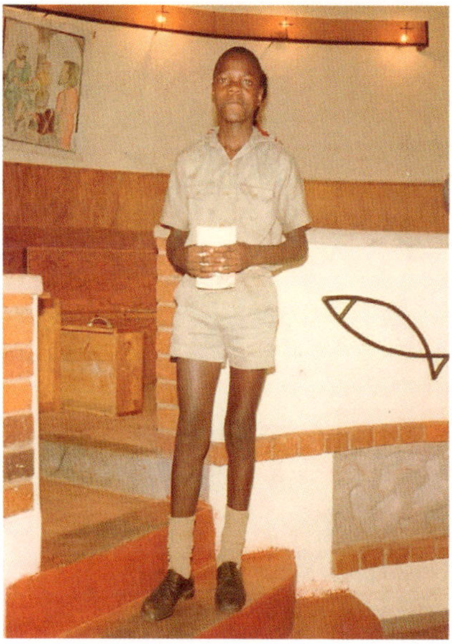

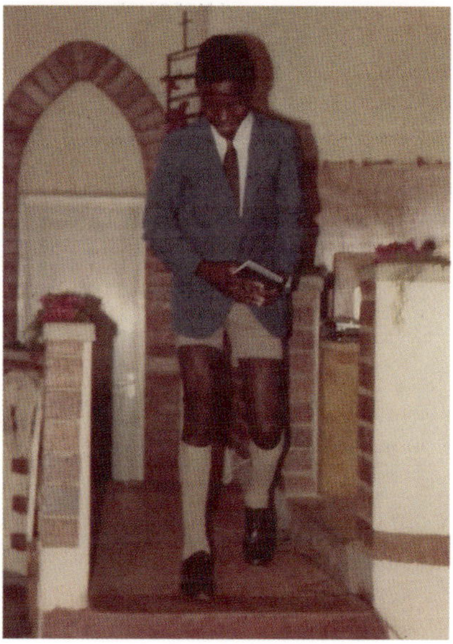

TOP LEFT: *With my siblings Audrey (back), Tsitsi and Rosemary, in Mutambara village, 1973 (Now Dr Audrey Mutambara, Prof. Tsitsi Mutambara and Dr Rosemary Mutambara)*

TOP RIGHT: *Author, aged 6, 1973*

BOTTOM LEFT: *Author winning Grade 5 Top Student Book Prize, Hartzell, 1979*

BOTTOM RIGHT: *Author winning Form 1 Top Student Book Prize, Hartzell, 1981*

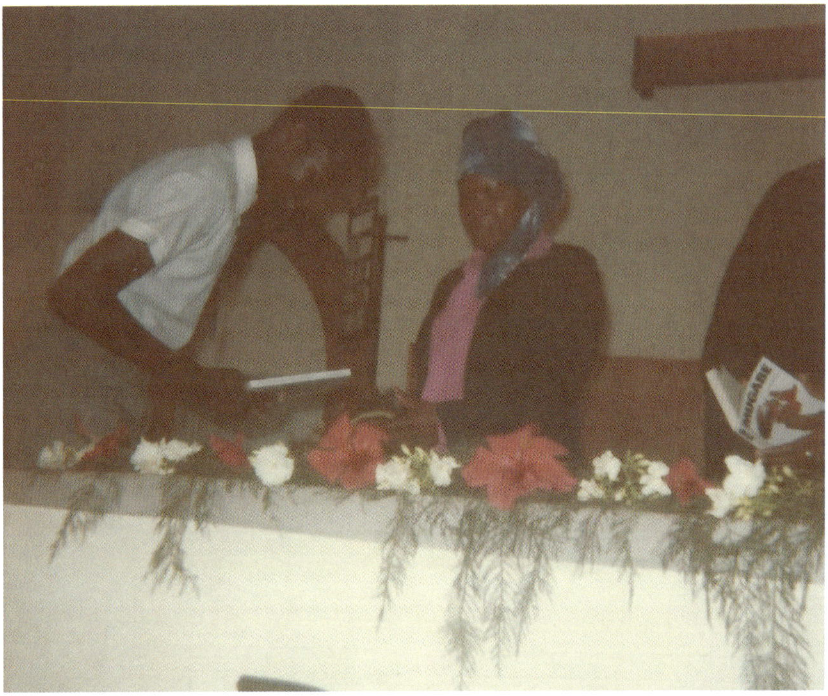

TOP: *Author (in white) winning Form 2 Top Student Book Prize, Hartzell, 1982*
BOTTOM: *Author winning Form 3 Top Student Book Prize, Hartzell, 1983*

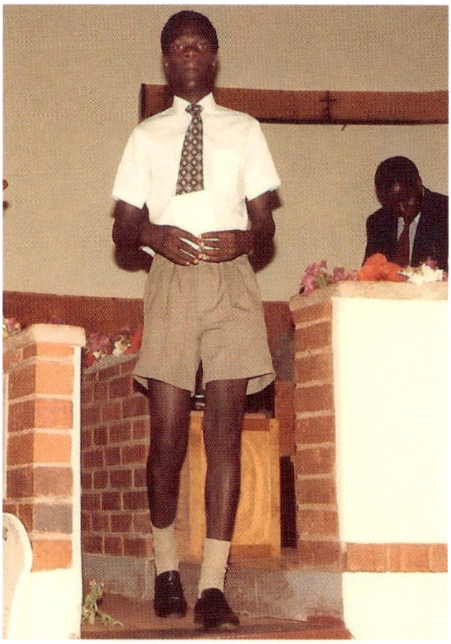

TOP LEFT: *Author winning Form 3 Top Student Book Prize, Hartzell, 1983*
TOP RIGHT: *Author winning Form 4 Top Student Book Prize, Hartzell, 1984*
BOTTOM LEFT: *Author winning Form 5 Top Student Book Prize, Hartzell, 1985*
BOTTOM RIGHT: *Author and family celebrating five Form 6 Subject Book Prizes, Hartzell, 1986*

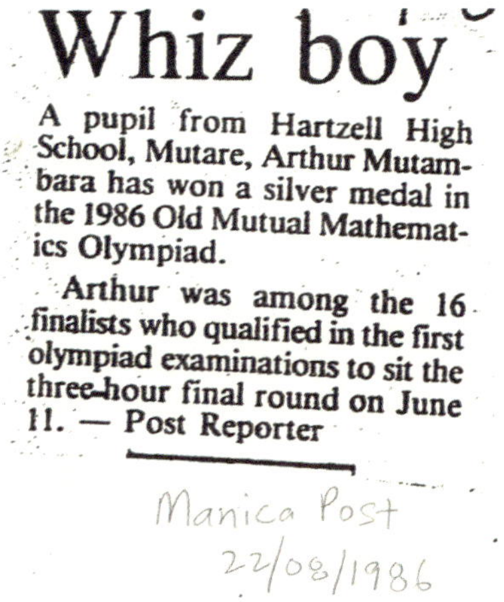

Whiz boy

A pupil from Hartzell High School, Mutare, Arthur Mutambara has won a silver medal in the 1986 Old Mutual Mathematics Olympiad.

Arthur was among the 16 finalists who qualified in the first olympiad examinations to sit the three-hour final round on June 11. — Post Reporter

Manica Post
22/08/1986

TOP: *Author receiving notice of award of the Mathematics Olympiad Silver Medal from Mathematics teacher, C. Mvere; thereafter makes a speech before the whole school, Hartzell, August 6, 1986*

BOTTOM LEFT: *Article in the* Manica Post, *Mutare, 1986*

BOTTOM RIGHT: *Winning five Form 6 Subject Book Prizes, 1986*

Author receiving the Mathematics Olympiad Silver Medal from Prof. Phineas Makhurane, 6 August 1986

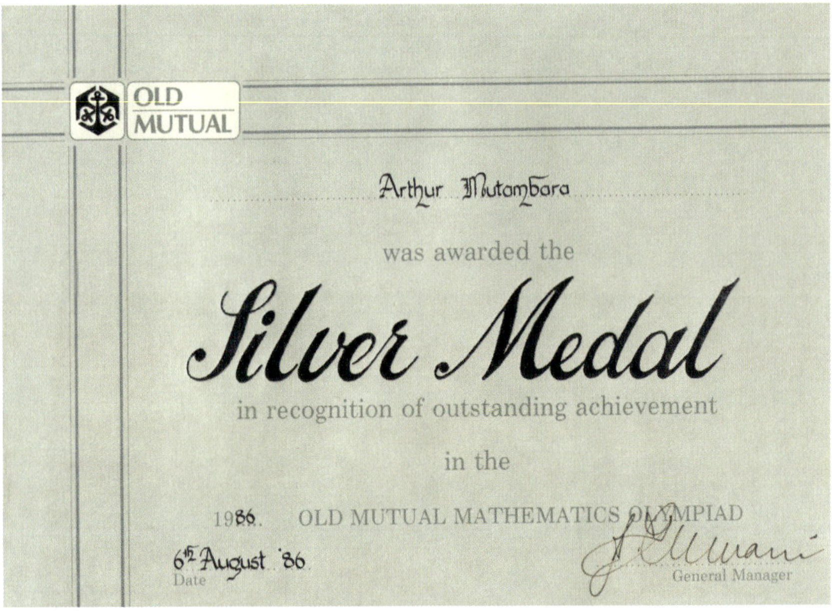

OLD MUTUAL

Arthur Mutambara

was awarded the

Silver Medal

in recognition of outstanding achievement

in the

1986. OLD MUTUAL MATHEMATICS OLYMPIAD

6th August '86
Date

General Manager

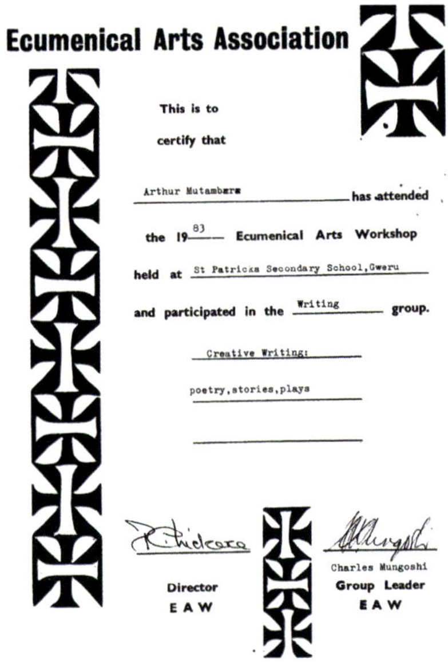

Ecumenical Arts Association

This is to

certify that

Arthur Mutambara has attended

the 1983 Ecumenical Arts Workshop

held at St Patricks Secondary School, Gweru

and participated in the Writing group.

Creative Writing:

poetry, stories, plays

Director
EAW

Charles Mungoshi
Group Leader
EAW

8 Zimbabwean students in tough essay contest

THE HERALD 4/12/86

Herald Reporter

EIGHT Zimbabwean students will compete with their counterparts in other Commonwealth countries in essay writing after emerging winners in a similar competition by the Commonwealth Parliamentary Association at national level.

The eight, who received prizes last night at a dinner in Harare hosted by the Speaker of Parliament, Cde Didymus Mutasa, beat other students from various schools throughout the country in writing an essay on one party state.

They are Enock Chikweche of Chaplin High in Gweru; Zanu Mataruka of Milton High in Bulawayo; Agmos Moyo of Gokomere High in Masvingo; Arthur Mutambara of Hartzell High in Mutare; Mark Ngano of Lord Malvern High in Harare; Smokin Siziba of Dadaya High in Zvishavane; Lovemore Zano of Allan Wilson in Harare and Onias Zivanai of Chipindure Secondary in Bindura.

Speaking at the occasion, Cde Mutasa said the purpose of the competition was to encourage students in the high schools to indulge in political thought and writing.

"This arises from our realisation of the fundamental need to give the future leadership of Zimbabwe some political aim or goal in education and orientation at an early age," he said.

"We sincerely believe that high school students should delve into the political issues of our country before they go to join institutions of tertiary education, the labour force or become drop-outs."

On the performance of the students who took part, Cde Mutasa said he had read some of the essays and had noted their high standard.

CDE MUTASA

"The students displayed a profound understanding of the issues they discussed."

He thanked teachers, headmasters and regional officers of the Ministry of Education who took part in selecting the winners and helped "us identify some of our future political leaders".

TOP: *The Mathematics Olympiad Silver Medal*

BOTTOM LEFT: *Ecumenical Arts Workshop creative writing attendance, St Patrick's, Gweru, 1983*

BOTTOM RIGHT: The Herald *newspaper article on the one-party state essay competition, 1986*

A. Moyo, L. Zano, S. Mkwawa, Author, D. Mutasa, Z. Mataruka, O. Zivanai, E. Chikweche – One-party state essay competition award ceremony, Harare, 3 December 1986

L. Zano, S. Mkwawa, Author, D. Mutasa, Z. Mataruka, O. Zivanai,
E. Chikweche – One-party state essay competition prize-giving ceremony, Harare, 3 December 1986

PROGRAMME
FOR
PRIZE GIVING DAY FOR
THE CPA ESSAY COMPETITION

AFRICAN
C
P A
REGION

WEDNESDAY, 3rd DECEMBER, 1986

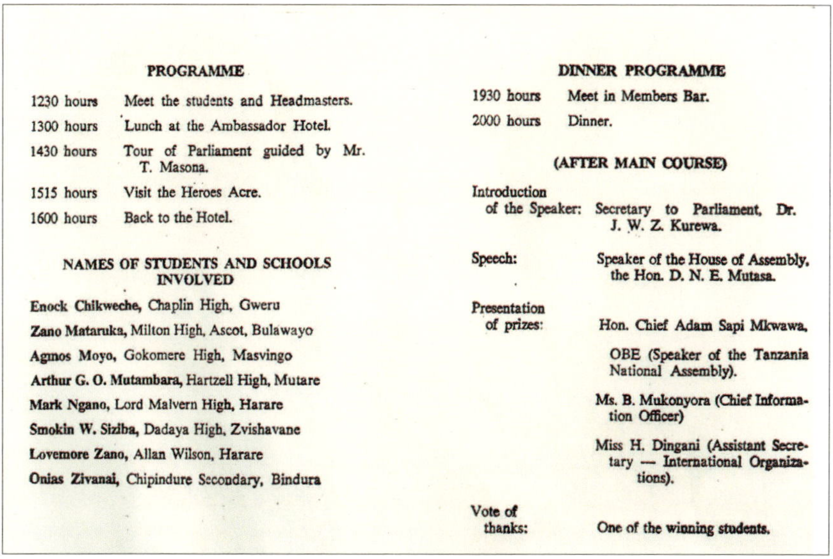

PROGRAMME

1230 hours	Meet the students and Headmasters.
1300 hours	Lunch at the Ambassador Hotel.
1430 hours	Tour of Parliament guided by Mr. T. Masona.
1515 hours	Visit the Heroes Acre.
1600 hours	Back to the Hotel.

NAMES OF STUDENTS AND SCHOOLS INVOLVED

Enock Chikweche, Chaplin High, Gweru
Zano Mataruka, Milton High, Ascot, Bulawayo
Agmos Moyo, Gokomere High, Masvingo
Arthur G. O. Mutambara, Hartzell High, Mutare
Mark Ngano, Lord Malvern High, Harare
Smokin W. Siziba, Dadaya High, Zvishavane
Lovemore Zano, Allan Wilson, Harare
Onias Zivanai, Chipindure Secondary, Bindura

DINNER PROGRAMME

1930 hours	Meet in Members Bar.
2000 hours	Dinner.

(AFTER MAIN COURSE)

Introduction of the Speaker:	Secretary to Parliament, Dr. J. W. Z. Kurewa.
Speech:	Speaker of the House of Assembly, the Hon. D. N. E. Mutasa.
Presentation of prizes:	Hon. Chief Adam Sapi Mkwawa, OBE (Speaker of the Tanzania National Assembly).
	Ms. B. Mukonyora (Chief Information Officer)
	Miss H. Dingani (Assistant Secretary — International Organizations).
Vote of thanks:	One of the winning students.

TOP: *One-party state essay competition prize-giving day programme, Harare, 1986*
BOTTOM: *One-party state essay competition prize-giving day programme, the details, Harare, 1986*

TOP LEFT: *Author, Form 4, Hartzell, 1984*
TOP RIGHT: *Author, Form 6, Hartzell, 1986*
BOTTOM LEFT: *Author, UZ, 1987*
BOTTOM RIGHT: *Author, UZ, 1988*

Author, Mrs Katsande (Anglo), H. Mukori, S. Ndiyamba, A. Mutiti, B. Magara, K. Dube, G. Dzinomwa – Anglo American (WCC) scholarship winners, Harare, 1987

TOP: *Flight to WCC for the Anglo American scholarship interviews, April 1987 (first time on a plane!)*
BOTTOM: *The graduation of Tsitsi Mutambara (Author's sister), Author, T. Mutambara, S. Nyatsanza, R. Mutambara (author's sister) - UZ, July 1987*

UZ SRC 1988–89; Seated: *O. Ntabeni, F. Mutyavaviri, E. Mbwembwe, Author, T. Kufa;* Standing: *T. Shava, B. Miti, R. Muchirahondo, S. Mkandla, D. Chibaiwa, P. Chidhakwa, I. Murambatsvina; Absent F. Charumbira, H. McConville, P. Chimonyo; UZ, 1988*

UZ SRC 1988–89 'Football Team'

TOP: *Attending the graduation ceremony as SRC officials, E. Mbwembwe, Author, F. Charumbira, UZ, 1989*

BOTTOM LEFT: *At the magistrate court, after acquittal, S. Dube, Author, S. Mkandla, R. Muchirahondo, Harare, 1988*

BOTTOM RIGHT: *Author speaking at a conference, UZ, 1988*

TOP: *Celebrating victory as new SRC President, T. Govere and Author, UZ, 1989*

BOTTOM LEFT: *Author's office, showing the sources of inspiration (Malcolm X, Che Guevara, Marx, Sankara)*

BOTTOM RIGHT: *Author's office, showing the sources of inspiration (Mandela, Lenin, PLO)*

TOP LEFT: ***Author's office, showing the sources of inspiration (Che Guevara, Marx, Lenin, Engels)***

TOP RIGHT: ***Author's office, showing the sources of inspiration (Lenin)***

BOTTOM: ***Author in front of UZ Students' Union, UZ, 1990***

UZ SRC 1989–90; T. Bingudza, I. Mukeredzi, E. Munodawafa, D. Chademana, M. Ncube, Author, C. Takafakare, G. Chaibva, E. Chikweche, T. Gowera; Absent; T. Ndebele, Z. Masiye, M. Karima, E. Chagonda, F. Moyo

UZ SRC 1989–90; D. Chademana, T. Bingudza, C. Takafakare, T. Gowera, E. Chikweche, Author, E. Munodawafa, F. Moyo, M. Ncube, I. Mukeredzi, G. Chaibva; Absent; T. Ndebele, Z. Masiye, M. Karima, E. Chagonda

TOP: *UZ SRC 1989-90: M. Ncube, C.Takafakare, I. Mukeredzi, T. Bingudza, T. Gowera. F. Moyo, D. Chademana, E. Munodawafa, E. Chikweche, Author, G. Chaibva; Absent; T. Ndebele, Z. Masiye, M. Karima, E. Chagonda*

BOTTOM LEFT: *Author addressing students during Orientation Week, with Vice Chancellor W. Kamba, UZ, 27 April 1990*

BOTTOM RIGHT: *Author addressing students during Orientation Week, UZ, 27 April 1990*

Author addressing students during Orientation Week, with Vice Chancellor W. Kamba, and Pro Vice Chancellors P. Makhurane and E. Ngara, UZ, 27 April 1990

TOP: *After addressing students during Orientation Week, sharing a joke with Vice Chancellor W. Kamba, Pro Vice Chancellor P. Makhurane looks on, UZ, 27 April 1990*
BOTTOM: *Author leading the graduation procession with D. Chademana; S. Nzombe and D. Vuma walking behind them, UZ, 13 July 1990*

Author confronts R. Mugabe about the one-party state, Prof. W. Kamba tries to mediate, College Green, UZ, 13 July 1990

Reception for student affairs consultant J. De Gidio (middle), W. Kamba (left), Author (right)

PRESENTED

by the University Senate of the

UNIVERSITY OF ZIMBABWE

to

ARTHUR G O MUTAMBARA

as a prize for

University Book Prize for being one of the best student in the BSc Eng Hons Part II (Electrical) Course and Examinations

Academic Registrar

Author's UZ Book Prize for Electrical Engineering Part II Results, 1988

UNIVERSITY OF ZIMBABWE : FACULTY OF ENGINEERING

B SC(ENG) HONS PART II

ELECTRICAL ENGINEERING

COURSE / NAME	MATHEMATICS MT 204/205	ADVANCED ELECTRICAL PRINCIPLES EE 203	ELECTRICAL MEASUREMENTS AND INSTRUMENTATION EE 204	ELECTRICAL MACHINES EE 202	ELECTRONIC CIRCUIT DESIGN EE 201	DIGITAL ELECTRONICS EE 206	APPLIED MECHANICS ME 201	THERMO FLUIDS ME 204	AGGREGATE	COMMENTS
27. Mpofu G T	III	F	II_2	III	III	III	III	III		Supplementary in Advanced Principles
28. Murwira M D	II_2	I	II_1	II_1	I	II_2	III	III	II_2	Pass
29. Mtetwa W K	II_1	F	II_2	III	II_1	III	III	III		Supplementary in Advanced Principles
30. Mudonhi M E	II_2	II_2	II_1	II_2	III	III	II_2	III	II_2	Pass
31. Munwiro K T	F	III	II_2	III	III	F	III	F	F	Supplementary in Math + Digital
32. Munyaradzi I	II_2 *	F	II_2 *	F	F	F	F	F	F	Discontinue
33. Mushosho R	III	F	II_1	III	II_1	III	II_2	II_2	II_2	Proceed
34. Mutambara A G O	II_1	II_2	I	I	I	II_1	II_2	II_1	I	Pass (U Z Prize)
35. Muwanigwa K D	III	II_2	II_2	F	II_1	III	III	F	III	Supplementary in Electrical Machines
36. Muzhuzha N	II_2	II_2	II_2	III	II_2	II_2	III	F	III	Proceed
37. Nyakutambwa T T	II_2	II_2	I	II_2	I	II_2	II_2	II_1	II_1	Pass
38. Nyamapfene A Z	III	III	II_1	III	II_2	II_2	III	III	III	Pass
39. Nyamupingidza R G	II_2	II_2	II_2	I	I	II_1	F	III	II_2	Proceed

DATE: 12/12/88

R. Z[illegible] DEPUTY REGISTRAR (ACADEMIC)

THE SMITH PREDICTOR CONTROLLER

ARTHUR G O MUTAMBARA

Project Advisor: Professor R K APPIAH

THIRD YEAR PROJECT

This project was submitted in partial fulfilment of the Third year Electrical Engineering course.

Department of Electrical Engineering

Faculty of Engineering

University of Zimbabwe

1989

UNIVERSITY OF ZIMBABWE

Department of Electrical Engineering

Final (Fourth) Year Project

A SWITCHED MODE POWER SUPPLY

By ARTHUR G.O. MUTAMBARA

Supervisor Mr. E.T. Kapuya

Year: 1990

TOP: *Author gets a First Class aggregate and wins the UZ Book Prize for BSc (Hons) Part II Examination Results, 1988*

BOTTOM LEFT: *Author's BSc (Hons) Third Year Project Report, UZ, December 1989*

BOTTOM RIGHT: *Author's BSc (Hons) Final (Fourth) Year Project Report which is awarded a First Class Pass, UZ, December 1990*

UZ Electrical Engineering graduation class of 1991, Harare, 1990

LEFT: *Author, BSc (Hons), Electrical Engineering, UZ graduation, 12 July 1991*
RIGHT: *Author, BSc (Hons), Electrical Engineering, UZ graduation day, 12 July 1991*

Author and R. Mugabe, UZ graduation day, 12 July 1991. After an attempt to refuse to kneel down!

TOP LEFT: *Author, BSc (Hons), Electrical Engineering, UZ graduation day, 12 July 1991*

TOP RIGHT: *Author, Merton College Freshman, Oxford, October 1991*

BOTTOM: *Author attending the Rhodes Ball, with Charlotte and Mulenga (the Author does not touch the alcohol!), Rhodes House, Oxford, 1992*

Merton College Freshmen (and Freshwomen), Oxford, October 1991

Incoming Rhodes Scholars, Rhodes House, Oxford, October 1991

(PSC), building societies and banks, parastatals, the Chamber of Mines, army, air force and police. As there will be a raging and comprehensive debate to come up with a socio-economic panacea to resolve the unemployment and underemployment crisis, the Zimbabwe Congress of Trade Unions (ZCTU) and the Zimbabwe Institute of Development Studies (ZIDS) will be invited to effectively participate.

The Graduate Employment Day will be for a whole day in the UZ Great Hall.

Each of the participating organisations will run an exhibition stand, address students and answer questions from students, hold preliminary interviews for students interested in joining their organisations, and hence actually recruit students for employment. Details such as date, timetable and programme layout will be released soon, as they are being finalised with employer organisations.

It is imperative that the entire union gives the SRC strong backing in this endeavour, in particular the final year students who will soon be joining the already flooded job market. Let us all support this cause and hence boldly ascertain and guarantee the right to work for all graduates of this great university!

18 Increase in payout! Victory for a fighting union!

In addition to taking up and tackling national issues, we also address both the sectional interests and primary needs of the students: accommodation, food, teaching resources and financial allowances – the highly sought-after payout. For some time, we have been pushing for an increase in the student payout. I release the following statement on 30 July 1990, after victorious negotiations.

The Ministry of Finance, Economic Planning and Development, which is the National Treasury, has granted an increment to the grant and loan facility for UZ students. This increase is to be backdated to the beginning of this academic year and consists of a non-reducible minimum bracket of 15 per cent to 20 per cent. This percentage range is definitely likely to go up as the SRC goes into another fierce and comprehensive battle with the administration this week, to counter any attempts to institute destabilising increases in accommodation and academic fees.

Further, the SRC has managed to bring forward this term's payout dates. The planned administration dates were 6 and 7 August 1990, but bearing in mind in particular the plight of the non-resident students, the SRC felt that this was thoroughly irresponsible and insensitive, hence demanded redress. Resultantly, payout dates (the old rates) are now on Thursday, 2 August 1990, and Friday, 3 August 1990. A permanent strategy has also been forwarded to the UZ administration to ensure that from now onwards payout will always be on the first day of the term after all the paperwork has been done during the vacation. This has been agreed to in principle and will be functional from next term. On the payout increase balance, the SRC has a commitment from the university registrar that all the logistical operational modalities will be speedily and expediently cleared and the payout will be paid out to students within the next 10 days, backdated to the beginning of the year.

A proposal has also been advanced to the administration to incorporate a permanent in-built mathematical self-adjusting mechanism to ensure that payout is adjusted annually in direct relationship to the rise in the cost of living and inflation levels. Thus, and effectively, we expect the payout to go up again at the beginning of 1991. This is a matter of principle and there will be no compromising whatsoever!

Comrades, the background to the above revolutionary breakthrough is characterised by active protracted student struggles as nothing was given on a silver platter. On 7 May 1990, the SRC sent a memo to the Vice Chancellor demanding two meetings – one with the Minister of Higher Education and the other with the UZ Chancellor, the national President – to discuss the payout issue and another eight items on a proposed agenda. None of these meetings have been facilitated and no official response has been received from the Vice Chancellor up to now. On 21 June 1990, before the end of last term, a union General Meeting took a definite position on this issue. It demanded that the student support rates, that is, payout, should be increased at the beginning of this term by any means necessary – including violent revolutionary confrontation. This decision was made unambiguously clear, in no uncertain terms, to the Dean of Students, the Registrar, the Vice Chancellor and the Ministry of Higher Education. In the same vein a positive response was demanded before the end of the vacation.

Yes, admittedly the UZ administration responded actively, but still the general bureaucratic and reactionary attitudes were manifested. This was aggravated by deliberate dragging of cold feet by the technocrats at the National Treasury, all this culminating in a designed conspiracy to frustrate students.

Consequently, on the first day of this term, 23 July 1990, the SRC decided to send an ultimatum to the university administration categorically stating that if a definite and unequivocally concrete position on the matter is not received by 12pm (noon) on Friday, 27 July 1990, an emergency union General Meeting will be convened granting students an opportunity to decide on which mode of physical struggle to embark on. This ultimatum was met. The administration buckled under revolutionary pressure.

This is the build-up, comrades, and hence this victory is a product of comprehensive unabated struggle characterised by revolutionary confrontation and not liberal diplomatic strategies. In fact, other union demands remain unresolved. The union demands that the issue of salaries and wages for lecturers and the entirety of the university working class be granted immediate attention by the National Treasury and the Chancellor. The union further demands that if the Vice Chancellor is to be credible, he must facilitate the long-overdue meetings between the Students' Union and the Minister of Higher Education and the Chancellor of the university.

These remain demands on our agenda. There will be no compromise, retreat, or surrender. Defeat is definitely not part of our agenda!

A luta continua.

19 Payout increment: The state of the struggle

We are still pursuing the payout mandate for members of our union. The following statement outlines details of the government grants and loans payout negotiations, as of 14 August 1990.

Comrades, members of the union, I am sure by now you have seen or are in possession of the two-page financial data document that we are circulating. If not, go to the nearest notice board. The first page contains the administration's proposals on the revision of university fees and the second page contains the SRC proposals. Please comrades, study these documents carefully.

As is clearly stated in the document, the government has already approved and granted the gazetted increases in the loan/grant facility and the only stumbling obstacle is the University of Zimbabwe administration which has decided to introduce grotesque and drastic fee increases as is manifested in their proposals – for example, academic fees by 16 per cent, caution fee by 33 per cent, laboratory deposit by 50 per cent, and accommodation fees an across-the-board increase of $315 (12–14 per cent). In its proposals, the SRC recommends the removal of any increase of caution fees, lab deposit, CIMAS and registration fees. It also cuts down the academic fees increment to 10 per cent and accommodation fees to a fixed 8 per cent.

Summary: Net increase in payout for one year

k. Administration proposal (Zimbabwe $)

	Arts	Science	Medicine	Vet Science
Shared (1)	140	165	170	200
Shared (2)	140	165	170	200
Single (NH)	140	165	170	200
Single (Med Res)	-	-	170	-
Non-Resident	455	480	485	515

l. SRC proposals (Zimbabwe $)

	Arts	Science	Medicine	Vet Science
Shared (1)	345	421	424	454
Shared (2)	328	404	407	437
Single (NH)	320	396	399	429
Single (Med Res)	-	-	386	-
Non-Resident	530	606	609	639

The administration has agreed in principle to adjust their position to take cognisance of the interests of the students. A definite position in terms of the time framework for processing all the details from the administration will be coming from the administration in writing. For those students sponsored by other organisations and ministries, once the details are finalised, an official administration statement will be sent to them so that they can adjust accordingly. It is imperative that the union strongly reminds the administration that the government increments were only granted after students had strongly pressed for them and that the reason was to increase the realisable payout and not increase fees.

Logic and rationality must prevail. The struggle continues.

A luta continua.

NB: The administration data document is written 'not for publication' but we have decided to publish it to students because we do not believe anything should be secret about the planning and management of student finances, more so when the UZ administration technocrats do not seem to be sensitive to the socio-economic interests of the students.

20 Graduate employment strategy day

Having identified the challenge of graduate unemployment, we work with the university authorities, industry, government and civic society to develop solutions. The statement outlining our collective efforts to solve the issue is released on 20 August 1990.

The plans to institute an effective Graduate Employment Drive have reached an advanced stage. The occasion has been set for the whole of Tuesday, 25 September 1990 in the Great Hall. This will be the Graduate Employment Strategy Day. After thorough consultations with different employer organisations and the university authorities, a planning committee is established. It comprises the following:

1. Cde (Dr) D. Chanaiwa, EMCOZ
2. Cde M. Gate, CZI
3. Cde Milliker, CZI
4. Cde A.G. Dry, ZNCC
5. Cde T.I. Kona, Assistant Registrar, Information
6. Cde F. Bvindi, Assistant Registrar, Student Records and Registration
7. Cde T.N. Mkwananzi, Deputy Dean of Students
8. Cde S. Sibanda, Assistant Registrar, Admissions Office
9. Cde G. Chaibva, External Affairs, SRC
10. Cde A.G.O. Mutambara, President, SRC

This committee has already met to discuss general planning of the occasion, the day's form and substance, targeting of the programme, funding, advertisement and publicity to companies and employer organisations. The day will be effectively publicised through a wide spectrum of media channels such as radio, television, magazines, local newspapers and business magazines/papers. In particular, the committee has managed to secure a special supplement (16-page tabloid) in *The Business Herald* on 20

September 1990. It is imperative that the role of the university in the process of manpower development is realised by the commercial and industrial sectors, and thus some basis for possible graduate recruitment is laid.

It is the unequivocal intention of the committee to make the Graduate Employment Strategy Day an annual day on the calendar of the university, while simultaneously ensuring that career guidance, discussion of job trends, and analysis of socio-economic-political trends affecting material interests of graduates become a continuous uncompromisable process at the university. Furthermore, the participation of commerce and industry in the designing and structuring of academic curricula should be ascertained.

Comrades, the union has an obligation to guarantee the fulfilment of the socio-economic material interests of graduates from this university.

The right to work is an uncompromisable, inalienable and fundamental democratic demand. This is a demand that should be met by any means necessary.

A luta continua.

21 In response to a mischievous and bankrupt appraisal

After completing the BSc engineering programme, we must go through an industrial engineering pupillage programme in order to qualify as professional or chartered engineers. I am doing my training at Wankie Colliery Company (WCC), which is evolving out of the ambit of Anglo American, as the management agreement between the two ends. Since at UZ I was on an Anglo American Scholarship, awarded through WCC, I am bonded to work for WCC. However, after I get the Rhodes Scholarship, WCC agrees in principle to release me, when the Oxford academic year starts in September 1991. As I settle into the training programme, new challenges arise at WCC. There are unqualified and incompetent white engineers who are working as professional engineers. Being unqualified and white, they are racist and insecure towards young freshly qualified black engineers. They try to undermine and frustrate them. I decide to challenge this debilitating situation. One such incompetent engineer decides to humiliate me by abusing his role as my supervisor. On 6 May 1991, I craft a robust rebuttal to a subjective industrial performance appraisal of me that he has submitted.

Appraisal as an organisational tool demands concrete objectivity, rationality, clarity of trade objectives and sharpness of exposure to the activities of the appraised. It indisputably demands professionalism and confidence on the part of the appraiser. As a process, an appraisal is a summation of both the negative and positive attributes of the shop floor experience of an employee with the view of ascertaining the viability and value of his social labour productivity. It is within this theoretical framework, and guided by the above conceptualisation, that a candidly critical analysis of the 'Reynolds Appraisal' is carried out.

1. As a supervisor, Reynolds has blatantly glaring limitations. In a nutshell, he is intellectually limited, professionally bankrupt, a victim of preconceived ideas and thoroughly crippled by an inferiority complex. The point of departure is his professional training – an electrical linesman. He is not a graduate of any university. He has never been a graduate pupil learner. He is not a member of any level of the Zimbabwe Institute of Engineers (ZIE) and he is not a member of any professional electrical engineering bodies, such as IEE and IEEE, for that matter. Given this professional background, it is common cause that there is no objective basis for him to supervise, let alone appraise, a graduate pupil learner. It is very clear from the regulations of professional bodies, in particular the ZIE, that for any graduate training to be recognised, one must train under a qualified professional accredited engineer. It is a pity that such an academically limited supervisor is not enterprising enough to join these bodies to compensate for his glaring limitations. In fact, this chap is not an engineer and has been promoted beyond his humble capabilities. It is a strong recommendation that his appointment be reviewed and the necessary adjustment effected. It is a matter of principle.
2. The above supervisor being one of mediocre intellectual acumen, compounded by academic deficiency, has an inordinate fear of university graduates. Hence, he tries to overcompensate by castigating them under the guise of practical experience, thus boosting his ego and self-image. We cannot allow anyone to fall victim to these personal inadequacies. In fact, he has a history of frustrating black graduates. Granted, there is no bridge, nor substitute, for practical experience. I definitely need it and I am getting it from the WCC. But I do not need anyone to frustrate and demotivate me in the process. In any case, cognisance should be taken of the fact that engineering is a professional academic field. There is a basic non-reducible minimum amount of academic training and a pre-requisite minimum amount of intellectual aptitude that is required for one to be a proficient, confident engineer. With all due respect, the above supervisor has neither of these qualities. An organisation does not need an engineer who feels inadequate and out of place in the midst of qualified graduate engineers. This supervisor belongs to this category of insecure pseudo-engineers.
3. On exposure to my activities and the commensurate supervision granted, disorganisation and outright irresponsibility are manifest. The supervisor did not at any point work with me, nor did he seem to have time to inspect my work. Thus, it is my submission that he was never exposed to the work I was doing and hence his knowledge of my capabilities and weaknesses is downright nebulous and dubious. Hence there is no objective basis for his mischievous comments.
4. According to the WCC Electrical Engineering training programme, I am supposed to spend three to four months in Transmission and Distribution (T&D). During this period, a project is supposed to be executed if any

is available. After three months, I brought up the departmental transfer issue and it was at this point that he brought up vague disjointed ideas about a project coming in a month's time. It was a four- to five-month project which would mean an effective eight months in one department. What a grossly incompetent supervisor! Of course, I could not accept this zoo of mismanagement and the training centre transferred me to the Opencast Mine.

5. There is one subtle subjective factor that clouds the judgement of this supervisor. He strongly objects to my anti-racist attitude. I believe in a merciless elimination of racism by any means necessary. T&D has a history of both overt and covert racism. I have openly and unequivocally denounced this on the shop floor. I hope this supervisor is not, in fact, a white racist.
6. A very strong source of subjectivism in this appraisal is a pervasive guilty conscience of the rampant corruption that characterises T&D which this supervisor is perpetrating. This ranges from abuse of colliery equipment/facilities and outright theft of colliery equipment. I have openly condemned these actions to the supervisor and his cronies and all I get in return is its reflection in the appraisal. Corrupt activities have become a way of life at the colliery. It is very interesting that a strategic, defensive initiative is being structured through victimisation. This is a very critical issue and details will be tabulated at an appropriate forum. There will be no holds barred.
7. Pre-conceived ideas are an intense contributory factor to the confusion manifested in the appraisal. When he says 'argues a lot', he is simply alluding to my political history. I challenge him to prove a single incident in which this occurred at work. He is simply pre-judging me. In fact, I had excellent working relations with all shop-floor workers at T&D – artisans and assistants. There is not a single one I worked with and had any problem with. The same applied to taking orders and ideas from the charge-hand and foreman. All the workers at T&D will bear testimony to this and I learnt a lot from these workers. To me learning is an art; it never ends and can come from anyone at any time. Hence I learnt a lot from the assistants and B4s. This supervisor is simply downright malicious.
8. In fact, there is also a clash of styles of operation. Reynolds, as a narrow-minded supervisor, believes in reactionary officialdom (chiefdom) – of keeping your distance from your subordinates, for fear of ignorance and bankruptcy being exposed. He believes that, for you to control, you must keep your distance. I belong to a different school of thought. I believe in social interaction, granting respect to workers, motivating them and allowing them the opportunity to take initiatives. I believe in being friendly but firm. I have the confidence to explain my position or ideas to anybody anytime, so I do not need to hide. Moreover, I am not despotic and corrupt and hence I will account for all my activities

anytime. I do not need officialdom. Thus, the allegation that I am too friendly is naive and simplistic. What a shame!

9. On the basis of the above submissions, the categorical imperative is very clear. The granted appraisal is a product of glaring subjectivism and was made by a supervisor not competent to make it. This effectively renders the appraisal void, meaningless and hence inadmissible. It must be rejected with the contempt it deserves. It is an insult to organisational competence. In a big company such as WCC, such bankrupt, vindictive, narrow-minded officials destroy the reputation of the company, thus denigrating organisational efficiency. It is a strong recommendation that the company revamps its system of worker appraisal reducing subjectivity and reinforcing objectivity. Appointment structures should be reviewed in order to promote adequately equipped supervisors and demoting those that have been promoted above their limited abilities.

This comprehensive response has been detailed with a view of defeating the desired effect of this appraisal – frustration and demotivation of a trainee. Many have been frustrated before, others are being frustrated now and more will be frustrated in future. This is only a candid case study – a microcosmos of the larger macrocosmos. The question is, how many cases do we have like this at the colliery? What are we doing about it? Out of frustration, people become disillusioned, disenchanted and disgruntled. In the past, some resorted to flight and surrender. But I am saying 'no' to deliberate and conscious frustration. This has gone on for too long at the colliery unchallenged, and in some cases perpetrated by illiterate racists. No! The honeymoon is over. It is time to stay put and do some fighting.

The lines of battle have been drawn.

Abasha demotivation.

Abasha frustration.

The struggle continues unabated!

22 WCC Opencast Department: Perception of the snags and hitches

In addition to the challenges of unqualified white racists undermining black professionals at WCC, there is also the matter of endemic corruption and abuse of company assets by the same whites. To protect themselves, they involve senior black WCC managers in their corrupt activities. They take the bulk of the loot, and give the senior black managers crumbs. That is enough to compromise senior black officials into inaction. While working in the WCC Opencast Department, things get heated as I decide to take a principled stance. Again, the corrupt white managers try to use the same technique of abusing the trainee appraisal process. On 26 July 1991, I pen a document meant to expose industrial corruption and abuse of authority within WCC.

To establish an objective interpretation of any appraisal, the concrete conditions in which the appraised operated should be taken cognisance of. This perception does not seek to undermine or invalidate the contents of the appraisal form but rather to guarantee that the empirical socio-industrial-administrative context in which it was structured is clearly ascertained.

1. The supervisor (appraiser), Chris Hawksley, unlike other qualified graduate engineers, did not go through the prerequisite engineering pupillage training programme. There is no bridge or short circuit to this hands-on training scheme. As a result, he does not have the slightest clue of what the programme entails. He has no physical technical appreciation of Opencast engineering operations and, as such, he has no evident technical contribution in Opencast. Electrically, he is just completely illiterate. This lack of training leads to confusion and

disorganisation when it comes to training learners. This in turn leaves him prone to manipulation, destroys his independence of mind and thus compromises his ability to train and appraise. This incompetence can be clearly demonstrated by the following:

a. Failure to draw up a comprehensive training programme.
b. Inability to understand regulations and procedures of training as drawn up by the training centre.
c. Failure to physically inspect the learner workplace and activities.
d. Inability to organise progress meetings and biweekly reports as requested by the Training Centre.
e. Failure to meet scheduled appointments with the learner. At one point, he postponed a scheduled appointment for five consecutive days.
f. Downright laziness, coupled with phenomenal lack of interest can be the only rationale for his inability to read through a project write-up over a period of five days.
g. As a result, no discussions were carried out with the learner about a very critical project.
h. Inability to understand the process of learner appraisal and resultantly failure to comply with procedures of appraising. The form was brought to him four weeks before the departure of the learner but was only completed four weeks after the departure. As if this is not enough, at this stage, the learner was not shown the appraisal and it was sent straight to the chief engineer.
i. The absence of any physical technical involvement in the solving of engineering problems in Opencast.
j. Given these glaring inadequacies, it is common cause that Hawksley should immediately embark on a two-year uninterrupted pupillage training programme like every other graduate. This is mandatory.

2. Top management in Opencast is too centralised in one pair of hands – those of Murdoch-Eaton. This manager has created oligarchical indispensability around himself to such an extent that Opencast becomes synonymous with Murdoch-Eaton. This one-man bureaucratic administrative command leads to outright abuse of authority, organisational insensitivity, corruption, general looting and pilfering, blackmail of top Wankie Colliery management, application of undue pressure on junior supervisors, low shop-floor morale, demotivation, victimisation and resultantly a drop in production rates. This organisation, WCC, should be in a position to dispense with the services of anybody and this includes the Opencast Department manager. In fact, one wonders whether those with the positional power to supervise him have the confidence to monitor his activities. It is a categorical imperative that this authority be decentralised and that an assistant manager be appointed immediately as provided for in the company organisational structure. As for corruption and looting, anyone sincerely concerned with addressing this scourge

should think in terms of revamping the entire colliery. This should be done through an external tribunal, for inside the colliery the question is: Who is clean enough to punish whom? It seems very fashionable to crush corrupt junior officers but the question is: Who is going to deal with corrupt senior managers such as HODs? A permanent, equitable and just solution should be found to this socio-economic cancer.

3. Of particular interest at the Opencast mine is the case of a belts man who was recently appointed diesel plant fitters' foreman. This chap has no professional or academic training as a diesel plant fitter. Neither does he have any experience of working as a diesel plant fitter in any capacity, be it semi-skilled or unskilled. He has worked as an unskilled mechanical fitter (but never as a diesel plant fitter) and was, for more than a year, illegally and unofficially appointed assistant section engineer by Opencast Department management. What beats any logic is the fact that the diesel fitter foreman's job was widely advertised in the national press by the human resources department. Did this department endorse the appointment, and if it did, what is its rationale? If it did not endorse it, then who did and what is their objective justification? In the Opencast diesel plant fitters' section, there are able, professionally and academically qualified diesel plant fitters, some of whom have eight to nine years' relevant experience. Well yes, they do have their own limitations, just like anybody else, but the issue is: What gives the belts man an edge over them? In any case, what is a foreman? Is that appointment professional, technical and ethical? What is the personal reputation of this individual with respect to evidently established looting in Opencast? Who benefits from his appointment as foreman?
4. Opencast remains the most backward working environment in the colliery. It is characterised by autocratic repression, shop-floor disrespect, class segregation and a deafening culture of silence. There is no respect of the worker even at social functions. It is the only place in the colliery where, when you have a shop-floor party or reception, there is clear class distinction – two drink outlets, two parties in one and no mixing across the class barrier. This is the case no matter how small the group is. What an emphasis on labour aristocracy?
5. Confronted by such a quagmire of problems, the graduate learner tried, in his limited capacity, to combat and redress them. It was during such efforts that he came into conflict with the Opencast Department manager and the then assistant section engineer, who later became foreman of diesel plant fitters. It is a very strong view that these two colliery employees took advantage of the naivety, lack of confidence, lack of industrial training and the general inexperience of Hawksley to unduly influence him to make most of those subjectively negative remarks about the graduate learner. As he is, Hawksley is not aggressively negative. It is unfortunate he allowed himself to be used.
6. When all is said and done, this response is not meant to absolve the

graduate learner but rather to expose a detailed account of his situation at the Opencast mine. The prime motivation being to ensure that top Wankie Colliery management takes cognisance of these problems. We owe this organisation (WCC) to Zimbabwean posterity. It is the duty and obligation of every colliery employee (the WCC Managing Director, Mr Kudzanayi Bwerinofa, included) to confront and not avoid problems, to solve and not work around problems. Professionalism knows no cowardice. It knows no compromise but bold effectiveness.
The struggle continues unabated.

1. Section Engineer, Chris Hawksley
2. Chief Engineer, John Dudman
3. All those officially involved in the appraisal process
4. Any such person or persons who have seen Hawksley's appraisal

(The people listed above received copies of this communication.)

SECTION THREE

Out into the Big Wide World

1991–2002

The context, circumstances and issues

I have served my political apprenticeship and acquired some powerful oratorical, analytical and writing tools – which make me stand out among the infant Zimbabwean opposition forces. I am in the ideal position to build on those intellectual foundations when I spread my physical and metaphorical wings and head abroad for further study and employment opportunities in the United Kingdom and the United States. The platform has been built and I need only to improve and expand on it.

The unfolding political instinct in me does not neglect my student constituency and I take up their issues with vigour and consistency. In fact, at this stage, I understand and embrace the importance of both academic excellence and social responsibility. Revolutionary and radical political activism must be buttressed by a distinguished academic career. I am always aware that I can go further in education, as well as socially and politically, if I spread my wings and look abroad for further education.

My winning application essay, for both the Rhodes Scholarship to the University of Oxford and the Fulbright Scholarship to the United States, shows clearly, though, that my commitment is to improving myself first so that I can return and make a better and amplified contribution to my country. Primarily because of distinguished academic excellence and outstanding leadership roles at UZ, I am awarded both scholarships. I choose the Rhodes Scholarship and head to Merton College at the University of Oxford, where I enrol for an MSc in Computer Engineering in September 1991. In October the following year, I register for a PhD in Robotics and Mechatronics.

At the University of Oxford, I am elected President of the Merton College Middle Common Room (Graduate Union) and President of the Oxford University Africa Society (OUAS). In my role as an elected student representative, like before, I do not shy away from speaking out on some of the entrenched and uncomfortable realities of college life. Some of these thoughts and issues I express on 14 June 1993, in my end-of-year address as MCR President. I also present a paper on understanding the motivation, content and impact of the UK Department for Education (DFE) reform of UK students' unions. I also tackle the Oxford experience from an overseas student's perspective, and challenges faced by black and African students in Oxford. I am also a regular in the Oxford Union debating chamber, the oldest one in the world. On a couple of occasions, I win the best speaker award. This is the case, on 11 November 1992, when I clinch the most outstanding speech prize during the debate on Western governments' commitment to the environment. As President of the OUAS, my colleagues and I host debates and distinguished speakers. On a number of occasions, I am the keynote speaker, and preach the Pan-Africanist gospel, economic independence and empowerment, social justice and the primacy of democratic governance.

Further ideas I explore and articulate during my time at Oxford include the implications of the collapse of communism in Eastern Europe, the new impetus for Pan-Africanism, and the Japanese economic success story. The world is changing, with the fall of the Soviet Union and its allies, which causes me to think broadly and philosophically about the future of the politics of the Left. I am clear that just because the West seems to have 'won' the Cold War does not mean its systems and ideology are just. The article I share on the Zimbabwe Network (Zimnet) platform on 6 January 1994 provides my perspective on socialism after the changes in Eastern Europe. I also speak and write about the challenges of post-colonialism – but particularly on the minds of young Africans, who have been the victims of decades and even centuries of cultural imperialism. My speech at the SCUSA 2nd Colloquium on post-colonialism at the University of Manchester, on 14 May 1994, lays and delves into these matters.

In September 1994, I attend a 21st Century Trust conference at the Klingenthal Castle in Alsace, France. The Trust brings together the rising generation of leaders worldwide, aged under 40, from government, business, NGOs, academia, media and other sectors. Its conferences provide a forum where these exceptional individuals, who otherwise would not have a chance to meet, identify the major challenges and opportunities facing them and the world in the decades ahead. The theme of my conference is: '*What is a nation? The limits of self-determination*'. The discussions are led by Mr Edward Mortimer, a columnist and leader writer of the London-based Financial Times. As globalisation transforms how we relate to one another across national and professional boundaries, it is essential that future decision takers and opinion leaders from all walks of life have the opportunity to learn from one another and to test their ideas in an international and inter-disciplinary context. This is the rationale behind the activities of the 21st Century Trust.

While at Oxford, Zimbabwe is never far away from my mind. This is clearly demonstrated in the response I write, on 13 November 1993, to a letter that I receive from Professor Masipula Sithole.

Oxford intrinsically attracts, from around the globe, extremely bright students for both its undergraduate and graduate programmes. Every year, over 100 new Rhodes Scholars come into Oxford from all over the world: Africa, Australia, Canada, New Zealand, Europe and the United States. In fact, the United States provides the lion's share of Rhodes Scholars, with the US Ivy League schools dominating. Many other competitive awards such as the Marshall, Beit and Commonwealth Scholarships, also bring academic superstars to Oxford. Thus, the university becomes the 'who's who' in the world, in terms of academic and research excellence, student leadership, and future success promise. Furthermore, the university is well resourced in terms of professors, researchers, academic resources and social amenities. Of particular interest is the prestigious Oxford tutorial system, where undergraduates are taught, one-on-one or, at the most, two students per tutor. The colleges, departments and research groups are thoroughly well endowed. As a graduate student, the type of subject you can study is not limited by your college. All teaching of graduates is carried out in the departments. As a result, you can invariably read for any course you want. While the university is obviously very strong in the traditional Liberal Arts subjects, such as History, English Literature, Law, Politics, Philosophy and Economics, it is also internationally recognised in advanced science and technology areas, such as Neurosurgery, Astrophysics, Chemical Engineering, VLSI design, Artificial Intelligence, Robotics and Mechatronics. When all is said and done, Oxford University is a world-class, dynamic and competitive academic institution in the business of ideas, thought leadership, teaching, research, intellectual innovation and self-development, arguably, ahead of such places as Harvard, Yale, MIT, Stanford and Cambridge.

In terms of personal academic success, the university is intensely competitive, to get in, stay in and to graduate from. Both undergraduate and graduate academic programmes are quite tough and exacting, and students are subjected to a rigorous and taxing examination system. The university and college authorities do not hesitate to fail and dismiss students who do not measure up. In fact, in some departments, failure of students is celebrated as an indicator of the prestige of an academic programme. Because of academic pressure, cases of suicide do occur. This mainly happens among the undergraduates. You get a 17-year-old, 4 A grades at Advanced Level, who has never been number two, then comes into Oxford, and becomes number 25 out of a class of 30, for the first time. Some ambitious young people cannot handle that. Many extremely bright students came to Oxford and left without degrees. The clearly very intelligent President Bill Clinton, a US Rhodes Scholar, is a classic example.

Despite my hectic political activism at Oxford, I thrive and excel academically. I deploy the principle of combining academic excellence and social responsibility. The MSc programme consists of a taught course with rigorous exams, and a research project leading to an MSc dissertation. The written examinations are the hardest ones I have ever taken. However, I crack them. Taking written exams in Oxford is a formal exercise where you dress up in sub fusc – a white shirt, a dark suit and a white bow tie – and put on the gown and mortar board of your previous degree. Undergraduates put on a commoner's gown and mortar board. After passing the written exams, I successfully submit my MSc dissertation titled '*A Formally Verified Modular Decentralized Control System*'. The research is inspired by the work of the world-renowned Computer Scientist and Head of the Oxford Programming Research Group, Prof. Tony Hoare. My supervisor is Prof. Jeff Sanders, who belongs to the same research group, in the Oxford University Computing Laboratory. Thus, after a year of distinguished academic work, I graduate with an MSc in Computation (Computer Engineering) on 28 November 1992.

After finishing the MSc, I proceed to tackle PhD studies in Mobile Robotics and Mechatronics. After a short two years and two months, on 22 December 1994, I am done with my doctoral research and submit my thesis for examination. That is a record completion time. The title of my thesis is '*Decentralized Estimation and Control with Applications to a Modular Robot*'. My PhD supervisor is Prof. Hugh Durrant-Whyte, a leading authority in the fields of Mobile Robotics and Mechatronics. I receive further guidance and insights from Prof. Michael Brady, Head of the Oxford Robotics Research Laboratory, Prof. Rodney Brooks, the Director of the MIT Artificial Intelligence Laboratory, and Prof. Edward Crawley, Head of the MIT Aeronautics and Astronautics Department.

The activity of orally defending a doctorate thesis, the viva voce, at Oxford is very formal. You dress up in sub fusc and put on the gown and mortar board of your Master's degree, and then face two leading experts in your field, one from Oxford and the other from an external institution. In my case, it is Professors Ron Daniel and Peter Fleming, from Oxford and Sheffield universities, respectively. On 21 February 1995, as I enter the PhD viva voce room, dressed up and all, I am a bit nervous but solidly prepared. The two Professors have copies of my thesis, opened. It looks like they have extensively read it and they have made copious notes. I have my copy of the thesis, but as I sit down, I do not open it. I just put it on the table and face them. I do not have notes or any other materials.

After a brief exchange of pleasantries, the examiners launch the traditional first set of related questions that any PhD candidate must prepare for: 'So, *Mr* Arthur Mutambara (there is an emphasis on the title *Mr*, because a doctoral candidate aspires to have the designation *Dr*, and the viva voce determines whether that transformation takes place), what are you saying in this thesis which has never been said before? What are your new contributions to your chosen field of study? How are you extending the frontiers of knowledge?' Now, these are loaded questions coming from world experts in my area of study, each with more than 25 years of teaching, research and publications. I have to know my story. However, I am ready for them. In fact, I am over-prepared. Without opening my copy of the thesis, I start to clearly and confidently articulate in detail – the new ideas, mathematical proofs thereof, novel applications, literature review, references, thesis chapters and pages – my five unequivocal contributions to mobile robotics. When I get to contribution number four, without opening my thesis, one of the examiners stops me and exclaims: 'All that detail, off the cuff like that!' At that moment, three minutes into my viva voce, I know that I have got my doctorate. I continue, with my extempore and unaided, but flawless, narration. The viva voce proceeds with further interrogation and discussions. However, it is now just a formality. The whole exercise takes just over 45 minutes. I pass my doctorate defence without any requirement for changes. There is not even one typographical error to be corrected! This is splendid.

When I inform the Dean of Graduate Students in Merton College of my good fortune, he refuses to believe me. He has to verify with my supervisor and university department. Well, I do not exactly blame him. Getting a doctorate from the University of Oxford is fraught with challenges. Some students drop out of the doctoral programmes, while others take up to six years to finish. A viva voce can take up to three hours, and the aftermath can be one of several outcomes, such as complete failure, a two-month thesis rewrite and resubmission, changes requiring six months of remedial effort, or an additional year of work before resubmission of doctoral thesis. Rarely do you get candidates passing first time with minimum changes. This African has just cracked the doctorate in two years and two months, and passed without any changes! The traditional Oxford establishment, while pleased with my achievements, looks a bit perturbed. I guess the African has outperformed the master, in his own territory! What an example of effective counter penetration!

The graduation ceremony is quite an elaborate, celebrated and prestigious affair at Oxford. However, it is conducted in Latin. All I hear is my name and that of my degree programme. I go through that process twice, for my MSc, on Saturday, 28 November 1992, and for the PhD, on Saturday, 4 March 1995. On both occasions I start the ceremony in the Sheldonian Theatre, wearing sub fusc and my previous degree's gown, hood and mortar board. Hence for the MSc ceremony I wear my UZ BSc Electrical Engineering graduation attire, and for the doctorate, I put on my Oxford MSc graduation regalia. Each Oxford College Dean leads his or her graduands into the Sheldonian Theatre, and presents them to the Oxford University Vice Chancellor. The graduating students then go outside the theatre where the College Deans and their staff help them change into their new degree gowns, hoods and mortar boards. The graduands then re-enter the Sheldonian Theatre donning the full graduation regalia of the new degrees they have just taken. All these processes and procedures which culminate in this literal de-gowning and re-gowning are conducted in Latin. For the PhD, there is a further process, where graduands are formally admitted into the Ancient House of Congregation of Doctors and Regent

Masters of the University of Oxford. As part of the graduation ceremony, dressed up in my new doctoral regalia, I sit in the special section of the Sheldonian Theatre with the high priests and gods of academia.

The Oxford obsession with formal dress extends to social functions. The elite, expensive, and uniquely Oxonian *balls* are black tie dinner events, requiring a tuxedo, a black bow tie, a cummerbund and a special white shirt. I attend the Rhodes Ball two years in a row, and grace the Merton Ball three times. At Merton College, every evening there is *formal hall* supper where a jacket, a necktie and an academic gown are required. Every night! I gleefully go through all these rituals. After partaking in such Oxonian bourgeois decadence, in addition to other extracurricular activities, and with my academic agenda accomplished, I guess I can now say I have had the full experience of Oxford – the City of Dreaming Spires, the citadel of knowledge. It is time to move on.

At the prime age of 28, armed with an MSc in Computer Engineering, and a PhD in Robotics, I head right into the belly of the beast – the United States – from 1995 to 2002, where I am a Research Scientist at NASA, Professor at MIT and Management Consultant at McKinsey & Company, among other interesting assignments. Thought leadership engagements during this sojourn include African-American struggles, general US politics, and the African-American versus African dynamic. I have a strong bond and camaraderie with a fellow Rhodes Scholar from Zimbabwe, Cyril Ruwende, and two US Rhodes Scholars, Andre Namphy and Trina Williams. The three, who were my juniors at Oxford, are still there, while I am now in the United States. From 1995 to 1998, through electronic mail, I share with these three, and a few other colleagues, my detailed and extensive reflections on US society, politics, economics and culture. We also share thoughts on personal matters.

As I embrace black consciousness, African-American history, the variegated black struggles, and the perennial challenges of the US working class, I engross myself in the literature of my favourite black revolutionaries such as Malcolm X, the Black Panthers (Huey P. Newton, George Jackson, Fred Hampton and Eldridge Cleaver, Kathleen Cleaver, Bobby Seale), George Padmore, Frederick Douglass and W.E.B. Du Bois. I also tackle contemporary issues in the black community. I study and delve into hip hop culture. In fact, I know more about hip hop than my young US students, both black and white. They cannot believe this, neither can I. The upshot of it is that because I am thoroughly immersed in their youth culture, they respect my views on politics, society and the economy. Hence, I am very effective in my thought leadership mission with them. 'The Professor drops knowledge,' they often opine in hip hop lingo.

I go around the US giving public lectures at Ivy League Colleges and Historically Black Colleges. Some of the schools I speak at are Harvard, MIT, Stanford, Florida A&M University – Florida State University (FAMU-FSU), the University of Virginia, Tennessee State and North Western. Some of the topics I develop and cover include the following: 'Rap and revolution, the political implications of the hip hop nation'; 'The US black history that the US government does not want you to know'; 'The FBI's war on black people'; and 'The case for a primer in intellectual self-defence'.

All these presentations are evidence-based and data-driven. I meticulously lay out the research and documentary evidence for every position that I advance. I use audio and visual tools, such as documentaries, TV interviews, news clips, declassified US government reports, audio tapes, pictures, infographics and PowerPoint slides. My favourite documentaries are from the 1960s and 1970s, such as the *Eyes on the Prize* series. With all these presentation innovations my public lectures are quite a hit on US campuses. One specific public lecture I give is at Vanderbilt University, on 25 January 1999. It is titled: 'The FBI's war against Martin Luther King, Malcolm X and the Black Panthers.' It is oversubscribed and is thoroughly well received. However, there are a few complaints from some conservative professors at this predominantly white university. They are overly defensive of the FBI, the US government and the white power structure. The lecture is a topical subject within the university for weeks thereafter.

I also address among my hosts the sensitive subject of 'The African-American and African relationship: what it is, and what it should be'. This is a very crucial subject because there is a lot of unnecessary misunderstanding and resultant acrimony between these two communities. This is further complicated by white people who try to play one group against the other, and the general lack of knowledge about Africans and the African continent within most of the African-American communities.

Most of these addresses to the African-American communities and US campuses are not presented in full in this book, since the focus is on the Zimbabwean and African aspects of the thought leadership journey. I also revisit my favourite theme from UZ and develop it into a presentation that I give to African-American and African students at a number of US universities, 'The case for both academic excellence and social responsibility'. On 9 February 2000, I speak on this topic to the MIT Black Graduate Union. I emphasise that you do not impress me if you come top of your class, if books are all that you do. A bookworm or nerd who gets the top grades is to be shunned. Similarly, a perennial and radical activist who fails in their studies, never graduates, or is at the bottom of the class, should not be respected or celebrated. That is how I push for academic excellence coupled with social responsibility.

Not only that, I walk the talk. From 1995 to 2002 in the United States, as I pursue the revolutionary path of political activism, thought leadership and societal change, my professional work involves Robotics and Mechatronics teaching and research at various institutions which include FAMU-FSU College of Engineering, NASA Lewis Research Center (now John Glenn Research Center) in Cleveland, Ohio, the John F. Kennedy Space Center (KSC) in Florida, the NASA Jet Propulsion Laboratory (JPL) and California

Institute of Technology (Caltech), both in Pasadena, California. At MIT, I work with the Artificial Intelligence Laboratory (MIT AI Lab) and the Controls Research Group in the Aeronautics and Astronautics Department. I also teach classes in this department, what is called Course 16 at MIT. My subjects are Advanced Control Systems and Introduction to Computer Architecture. At FAMU-FSU College of Engineering, I teach Dynamic Systems II, Control Systems, Advanced Robotics, Introduction to Robotics and Mechatronics, and Advanced Robotics and Mechatronics. I establish Mobile Robotics and Mechatronics research laboratories both at MIT and FAMU-FSU College of Engineering.

All these academic endeavours are not without amusing and invidious incidents with political undertones. In February 2000, at MIT, during my first Advanced Control Systems lecture, two white Professors in the department decide to attend my class. They explain their presence by saying they want to see how I present the subject matter in order to efficaciously link my material to theirs, as our subjects are related. I am not convinced. I suspect they are just checking to see whether the African can effectively teach at MIT – the top Engineering school in the world! Well, I have to deliver. When I am done, the entire class of 26 students stands up in a rousing standing ovation. This is not even a seminar. It is a class lecture. The two observing colleagues sheepishly leave the room and go straight to the Department Head, Prof. Edward Crawley, who later shares with me the content of their discussions. 'I have been teaching here at MIT for 15 years. I have never seen such a rousing standing ovation given for a class lecture. This guy is good,' one of the wowed colleagues says to Prof. Crawley. I quietly say to myself: 'How patronising. Even with your 15 years at MIT, what makes you think that you are, or you understand, the benchmark or reference point for teaching ability or skill? Surely, an African or a black person can have capacity and ability, beyond and unexperienced by the best of white achievement. Black success or ability does not need to be referenced to, benchmarked by, or constrained by white standards. There is no need for such validation.'

Another amusing altercation occurs at the NASA Lewis Research Center in July 1997, during discussions about applications of my mobile robotics research results to US Unmanned Military Vehicles (UMVs) and the NASA Mars Sojourner Rover. In attendance are top officials from NASA, the US Army and MIT. This is a high-level, top-secret meeting whose contents and outcomes the US researchers and scientists would not want to get to their competitors, in particular the Russians and the Chinese. The US Army Chief Research Scientist – who is also a retired Four Star General – chairing the meeting, sternly looks at me and says: 'Where are you from?' I say, 'Zimbabwe'. 'Well, we are not about to be attacked by that small country. You can stay in the meeting.' 'How rich?' I quietly ponder to myself. 'As if you have a choice! These are my ideas we seek to apply to UMVs and the Mars Rover. Without me, there would be no meeting. In any case, how do you know that my loyalty does not lie with the Chinese or the Russians?' Well, well, that is how it is. White supremacy always wants you to feel that it is doing you a favour, even when you are the one holding all the chips.

I attend and present papers at academic and research conferences all over the world. In keeping with my personal commitment to academic excellence, I publish over 45 refereed journal articles in the field of Robotics and Mechatronics, and two Electrical Engineering books that are widely used for teaching and research in Graduate Schools in the US, Europe, China, Japan and Africa: *Decentralized Estimation and Control for Multisensor Systems (1998),* and *Design and Analysis of Control Systems (1999).*

In the future, in the years 2015 to 2017, there is a big global debate, mainly in South Africa and at the University of Oxford, about the legacy of Cecil John Rhodes. The battle cry is: *Rhodes Must Fall!* I chuckle. This is because in 1998, I address this issue in my first book. This is what I write, among other remarks, in the book's acknowledgements section:

> *'I attended Oxford University as a Rhodes Scholar and visited robotics research laboratories (in both academia and industry) in the United States of America, Japan, Germany and the United Kingdom while presenting papers at international conferences, courtesy of funds provided by the Rhodes Trust. Consequently, financial acknowledgment goes to the generality of the struggling people of Southern Africa who are the living victims of the imperialist Cecil John Rhodes's plundering and looting activities. Every Rhodes Scholar should feel a sense of obligation and duty to the struggle of the victims of slavery, colonialism and imperialism throughout the world.'*

The dedication for the same book is as follows:

> *'This book is dedicated to oppressed people throughout the world and their struggle for social justice and egalitarianism. Defeat is not on the agenda.'*

After a big and vicious fight with my publisher who does not want these statements in the book at all, I compromise and take out the *'plundering and looting activities'* bit. The rest of the remarks remain in the book: *Decentralized Estimation and Control for Multisensor Systems!* Therefore, my response to the great excitement of the Rhodes Must Fall Movement of 2015 to 2017 comes from 1998. It is pleasing to see that the world is catching up with me. I am not too sure whether they know how best to do that.

A number of African student associations throughout the United States also get my special attention. I address them mainly on issues related to Africa. For example, on 26 April 1999, I give a keynote address during the Stanford University African Students' Week, concentrating on the state of the African continent. As I settle in the United States, I also start to consciously guard against subtle forms of racist thinking and become more Africanist and Afrocentric in disposition. I come to strongly embrace the concept of the power to define. In views I express on the Zimnet discussion platform, on 22 June 1996, I explain why we object to the use of the term 'tribalism'. In further discussions, I also make it clear that I believe that, as black people or Africans, we are our own liberators. None but black Africans can truly free black Africans. In fact, I address the controversial and contentious problem of involving white liberals in predominantly African struggles. Then comes the emergence of my 'unity is strength' thinking when I urge African cooperation and support for institutions like the Southern African Development Community (SADC) and the Organisation of African Unity (OAU). (The OAU is later transformed into the African Union (AU) in 2002.) I also start championing technology as the key equaliser for Africa to make that giant 'leapfrog' from poverty to prosperity, thus improving the quality of African lives. I give a speech to launch a science and technology advocacy entity at MIT on 15 March 2000. It is an African technology and science strategy rooted in innovative paradigms and solutions for the continent.

In all this intellectual and activist type involvement, I never lose sight of the Zimbabwean agenda. I keep in touch with Zimbabweans in the United States, and throughout the world through the Zimnet platform. I am constantly in touch with the comrades on the ground in Zimbabwe. As I start dipping my toes into the politics of my home country, I am fearless in my criticism of both ZANU-PF and the inept opposition, but shun grandstanding in favour of real, concrete suggestions for political, social and economic progress. As I directly re-enter the big debates of Zimbabwean politics, I make it clear that any solution to the crisis facing the country should not be left only in the hands of the politicians, but should involve civil society, entrepreneurs, academics and industrialists. Any change which comes, I say, should be built on solid ideas and programmes, and not merely on opposition to ZANU-PF. At the same time, I demonstrate my political even-handedness by pointing out that the liberation legacy that ZANU-PF immorally appropriates cannot, and should not, be ditched in the name of political expediency. That legacy belongs to all Zimbabweans, including the opposition parties. My own ideas are now starting to be expressed in detail, particularly when it comes to issues like land revolution, technology innovation, industrialisation, economic empowerment and regional integration. On 6 March 1999, while on a visit to Zimbabwe from MIT, I give a public lecture organised by the Southern African Political Economy Series (SAPES) Trust. The presentation focuses on the crisis in Zimbabwe. I advocate for an imperative and exhaustive agenda covering constitutional matters, political governance issues, electoral concerns and politics of the stomach – the economy. On 27 March 2000, I am back in Harare and give another public lecture urging Zimbabweans to clearly understand the nature of their challenges, and systematically shape the way forward.

The years 2001 and 2002 are my last years in the United States. Towards the end of 2000, while at MIT, where I am teaching and doing research in the Aeronautics and Astronautics Department, I decide that I must broaden my exposure and experience beyond technology, engineering and rocket science. In addition to understanding and mastering world politics, black struggles and the African agenda, I need a primer in business leadership in order to comprehend and navigate the interconnected and globalized world of commerce. I must understand business, management, entrepreneurship and finance. In particular, I want to master corporate strategy, project execution, corporate finance, operations management and branding. McKinsey & Company – the world's number one global management consulting firm – is the answer. They hire MBAs from top business schools like Harvard, Wharton and INSEAD, but also recruit non-MBAs with STEM (Science, Technology, Engineering, and Mathematics) PhDs from top schools like MIT, Oxford, Stanford, Imperial College, and Cambridge, and then give them MBA-type training on the job. They call it the McKinsey Mini-MBA route. This is the trajectory I should pursue.

However, because of its unparalleled prestige and oversubscription by exceptionally qualified applicants, McKinsey is highly selective and brutal in its hiring process. The case study based interview process consists of four daunting, excruciating and torturous rounds. It is the toughest recruitment exercise that I have ever undergone. Nonetheless, I triumph! I join the McKinsey Chicago Office in the State of Illinois, from 8 January 2001. It is a tremendously great experience. For the next two years, I provide strategic advice to senior executives, directors and business leaders of top US companies, mainly those in the Fortune 100 category. In terms of industry sectors, I cover ICTs, telecommunications, automotive assembly, electrical power, natural gas, manufacturing, financial institutions, pharmaceutical companies and medical products. With respect to functional expertise, I am involved in technology management, corporate strategy, global strategy, corporate finance, post-merger management, business building, entrepreneurship, operations strategy, branding, marketing and implementation management.

As I approach the middle of 2002, my US tour of duty is coming to an end. It has been just over seven years in the belly of the beast – the United States. What a ride! Now, Africa is beckoning. Zimbabwe is beckoning. It is time to respond to the needs of the motherland. With my frequent visits to the continent and the public lectures I give, it seems I am becoming part of the breath of fresh air that Zimbabwean politics – and indeed, the politics of the rest of the African continent – so desperately needs. It will not be long before I heed my African people's clarion call. Soon it will be time to take the plunge!

(Nkrumah, 1965) (Fanon, 1963) (Anholt, 2007) (Mutambara, *Decentralized Estimation and Control for Multisensor Systems*, 1998)

23 My educational objectives

As I come to the end of my fourth and final year of the electrical engineering degree programme, I am anxious to attend graduate school outside Zimbabwe. In particular, I am interested in the United States and the UK. The two key sources of funding that I pursue are the Rhodes (University of Oxford) and Fulbright (US universities) Scholarships. They both require an application essay; that is, a statement of educational objectives. I submit the following essay on 5 September 1990. I later go for interviews and I am awarded both scholarships. I choose the Rhodes Scholarship.

My perception of education is that it is that part of the superstructure which envisages a profound and complete socio-political-economic development of individuals, thus making them more viably participative and hence a vibrant, integral component in the development of a country. It is in this context that I conceptualise my educational objectives.

By January 1991, I will be a qualified holder of a Bachelor of Science Degree with Honours in Electrical and Electronic Engineering. This will be at least at the level of an upper second class. I am aiming consistently and committedly at a first-class degree. I feel propelled and obliged to further my academic work to the Master of Science (MSc) level and further to Doctor of Philosophy (PhD) status. Engineering is a rapidly changing profession with technological advancement. Hence, for me to effectively contribute to my country, a Third World country, I need to further my academic training.

Having attained a PhD in a specialised area of Engineering (Major Area – communications, computer and systems, Specific Area – digital communication systems), I envisage a situation whereby I will effectively contribute to my country's progress and advancement by becoming a conversant design or consultant engineer in a big company like Wankie Colliery Company or the Posts and Telecommunications Corporation

(PTC). Most importantly, I will be very effective in the professional field of lectureship in the Faculty of Engineering at the University of Zimbabwe. This field is very important as the government plans to establish a technologically biased university in Bulawayo and the plans are already under way.

Engineering is a professional field and this demands thorough industrial practical exposure. Despite the fact that I am just completing my degree, I have had comprehensive exposure to industry. Since my first year in 1987, I have had three sets – each set consisting of four months – of industrial training under qualified engineers with Wankie Colliery Company Limited, this culminating in 12 solid months of profound industrial training. For the past three years, I have been an electrical laboratory practical demonstrator for first, second and third year students.

From 1988 to 1989 I was Secretary General of the University of Zimbabwe Students' Union. In 1989, I was elected President of the same Students' Union and also Chairman of the Student Representative Council (SRC). I am currently holding these two posts until September 1990. The Students' Union leadership spells have given me the experience of managing the socio-political-economic interests of 10 000 students and run a union budget of $360 000. Admittedly, all this exposure can never substitute the effective experience one gains by working in the industry as a qualified engineer, but it does bear testimony to some degree of workplace responsibility I have handled. It thus offers substantiation to my application for further academic training.

In conclusion, it is my humble intention to maximally utilise my academic capabilities, not only for self-actualisation, but for the betterment and advancement of my country technologically. I hope this aspiration will be ascertained and demonstrably fulfilled.

24 Western governments have yet to prove their commitment to the environment

On 11 November 1992, I participate in the great Debate on the Environment at the Oxford Union, the world's oldest debating society. The topic is: 'This house believes that Western governments have yet to prove their commitment to the environment.' The other distinguished participants are Peter Chapman, David Blair, Sara Parkin, Jonathan Porritt, Malcolm Grimstone, Paula-Tarsa De Lima and Russell Lewis. I speak in support of the topic and win the best speaker award. I am given a bottle of champagne which, of course, I find no use for. These are my talking points for that debate.

1. Western economies
- Emphasis on markets, economic growth, and exports
- Uneven consumerism and consumption: 20% of the world (the rich Western countries) consume 80% of the world's natural resources
- Environmental degradation
- Social degradation
- Economic exploitation

2. Policy direction
- Bio-diversity (required resources, Global Environmental Fund)
- Climate change convention (global warming)
- Role of the World Bank and IMF
- Roles of transnational and multinational corporations

3. Double standards
- Environmental or green agenda is not neutral

- Context of agenda is not new
- Role of market forces and social justice
- Notion of a bigot, feeling good by talking green
- The Oxford Union and Mitsubishi
- Is there a common destiny for a super-rich tycoon, a Somali refugee, a liberal activist, and a drought-stricken peasant?
- Innovators (sponsors of debate) understand the profit imperative

4. The way forward

   a. Social justice

- Land redistribution and land rights
- Redistribution opportunities
- Resources required for redistribution
- Lobby or force governments, urban elites and transnational corporations
- The rationale for redistribution – history of slavery (400 years), colonialism (100 years), and neo-colonialism which is current
- Embrace the right to a job as a human right
- Free and fair trade with so-called Third World
- $50 billion reversal
- Promote technology transfer to the so-called Third World

   b. Other strategies

- Decentralise consumption and production
- Push for self-sufficiency and self-sustenance
- Adopt self-organising principles
- Revisit our misplaced values, such as, having a mahogany toilet seat, the importance of a tuxedo, unrestrained consumerism, and the right to waste
- Institutional changes
- Structural changes
- Increase solar power, and reduce fossil fuel dependence
- Plant more trees, promote recycling, cycle more, and drive less

25 MCR presidential campaign: A proactive socio-academic agenda

Merton College is one of the top colleges at the University of Oxford, always coming first in the unofficial rankings called the Norrington Tables. Graduate students come from all over the world, but the student population is predominantly white. Among my 1991 Freshers' group (the new undergraduate and graduate students), there are only two black students, myself and one other. After a year at Merton College, I decide to run for the Merton College Middle Common Room (MCR) President. The MCR is equivalent to a graduate students' union. It addresses the concerns and welfare of graduate students, and represents them on university committees. Why run for President? I reckon they came to Africa and colonised us, now it is time for counter penetration. The African must rule them, even if it is for a moment! The following is my presidential campaign manifesto that I release on 14 November 1992.

The central organising principle behind my candidacy is to make life pleasant to as many Merton College Middle Common Room (MCR) members as possible. I envisage an MCR at ease with itself, characterised by unbounded friendliness, a sense of belonging and, consequently, responsibility. In this vein, it is imperative that all remnants of alienation be destroyed. Given the diversity of its functions, the MCR should be a social centre where all members should feel comfortable. To achieve this, it is important to take cognisance of the non-monolithic nature of the MCR membership, identify any causative factors for apathy, broaden the spectrum of activities and resources and thus galvanise interest.

At all times, the operational strategy should be seizing the initiative and thus improving socio-academic conditions before they become problems. This is of particular significance to the issue of accommodation. The process of renovating old graduate houses must continue vigorously while minimising the disruption caused to occupants. A more assertive approach is required to get plans for the new Graduate Quad on Holywell Street off the ground. It is imperative to carry out an appraisal of the breakdown of graduate fees with a prime emphasis on college fees. While the MCR must exercise strict financial control, college subsidisation of MCR functions must increase. Consultations with college and university authorities must be unequivocal and effective. Cooperation with the local Junior Common Room (JCR) must be optimised and where possible common strategies adopted. Inter-collegiate solidarity must be reinforced through Oxford University Graduate Union (OUGU) events and joint MCR functions. Resources and facilities such as access funds and university accommodation, available through OUGU, must be maximally utilised by Merton MCR members.

This, in a nutshell, is the essence of my case.

26 On the UK students' union reforms

I win the MCR presidential elections and have a competent team to help me discharge my duties. In 1993 there is an effort by the UK Department for Education to reform UK students' unions. In response, students are cautious, cynical and in some cases hostile to the proposals. This is because there has been history of the UK government trying to break or weaken the students' unions. On 4 June 1993, I release some remarks on these reforms in my capacity as Merton MCR President.

While in principle I find the university's interim response agreeable, it strikes me as naive and apologetic. I have already sent some preliminary views on the reforms to the Oxford University Student Union (OUSU). Consequently a few remarks are made here.

Motivation behind reforms

It is pertinent to establish the central motivating principle behind these reforms. I refuse to accept the illusion that the government is a neutral arbitrator trying to improve the generality of student unions by incorporating choice, democracy and accountability. It is outright naivety for the university to assume this.

These proposals are by a Conservative Party government with vested political interests. It is common cause that student unionism, just like trade unionism, is an antithesis and a frustrating negation to conservatism. Consequently, it is no coincidence that some of the positions that student unions have taken in the past have been against Conservative government policies, and that most of the unions are run by officers on the political left. It is my strong submission that these reforms are meant to destroy and incapacitate student unions because, by and large, they have been politically unhelpful to the Conservative Party. Reforms must be made for posterity and not to serve sectional political interests. It is extremely critical that the university understands and states this observation in its response to the reforms. This will help inform the negotiation process by putting the Department for Education (DFE) proposals into perspective.

The reforms

Ill-conceived, redundant and nebulous choices characterised by opt-in provisions, voluntary-based inclusion and superfluous referenda will render unions dysfunctional and ineffectual. The reforms will require the imposition of changes to the constitutions of unions. This is because in their present form they will be violently rejected by the generality of members of unions throughout the country. The definition of the National Union of Students (NUS) as an external body defies logic. NUS is an essential extension of student representation to the national level. Defining core and non-core activities derives from the myth that unions can be made apolitical by cutting socio-political activities. It is my unambiguous contention that these activities are inextricably linked to the welfare and academic issues. In any case, establishing a set of core activities is subjective and non-exhaustive. There will always be political bias in any functioning institution, the current Conservative government being no exception. What is imperative is to ensure that the bias is democratically established after thorough consultation. It is intrinsically nonsensical to expect unions to always make politically neutral decisions. The provision of an appeal body external to unions is both redundant and unimaginative.

It would be greatly appreciated if the Merton College position on the reforms reflects these remarks, and the MCR be consulted before the position is submitted.

27 The Merton MCR: A reflective perspective

Our Middle Common Room (MCR) committee has had a successful term of office. The difference between the UZ Students' Union experience and this new exposition is the extent of structure and organisation at Oxford. We plan all the upcoming term programmes and activities in advance. Thereafter, the schedule is strictly followed. Furthermore, there is razor-sharp accountability demanded by the electorate on all matters. Delivery is tracked and measured. However, unlike UZ, here we hardly influence national politics. There is a functioning national democracy. At the end of my tenure, on 14 June 1993 I present an end-of-year address as outgoing Merton MCR President.

The arrival of an extremely enthusiastic bunch of new students graced the Merton College Middle Common Room (MCR) (the Merton Graduate Union) at the beginning of Michaelmas 1992. They found a very comprehensive orientation programme in place, organised by the 1992 committee. The term card events for Michaelmas were quite exciting, culminating in the great Christmas play. The election of a new committee at the end of the year marked the dawn of a new dispensation in the MCR. The central organising principle was envisaged as a proactive socio-academic agenda based on a sense of community, diversity, democratic disputation and dynamism.

Hilary term saw unprecedented levels of interest and diversity in MCR activities. The spectrum of events was broadened and maximum publicity executed. This empirically galvanised interest. The highlights were the MCR Talent Show, MCR Mad Hatter Party, MCR Dinner and the historic BOP of the Decade. In addition to the MCR/SCR talks, which continued to be inspiring, a speaker series was instituted. Professor R. Dworkin was a guest speaker in Hilary and Professor Norman Stone in Trinity. Professor Terry Eagleton is a candidate for Michaelmas 1993.

The politics of the fridge received unmitigated attention as the quality, diversity and quantity of food and drink increased spectacularly. A new user-friendly Battels sheet was designed to take cognisance of these changes and facilitate tracking of Battels records throughout the term. Trinity term was equally socially hectic, marked by the May Day Breakfast, MCR Dinner with a difference (held at a restaurant) and the MCR versus college staff softball. Inter-collegiate dinners were organised with Lincoln and St Johns. With the JCR, organic linkages were fused and some common events executed. Joint strategies and maximum cooperation characterised joint MCR and JCR dealings with college officers.

Within the MCR, all has not always been rosy. A motion to create a Women's Officer on the MCR committee, to be elected by a women-only vote, generated strong views for and against within the MCR body politic. In the end, the motion failed to receive the necessary two-thirds majority. This brought further aggravation. It is hoped that rather than be a source of division, this episode should be educational to every member of the MCR. It is extremely pleasing to note that interest in events and meetings has remained high. It is our duty and obligation to sustain a vibrant and dynamic common room. We owe this MCR to posterity!

Accommodation is one area where a demonstrably proactive strategy was adopted. In Michaelmas, some of the new students, in particular those at 19 Holywell Street, arrived to squalid accommodation conditions. A project of vigorously pursuing renovations while minimising disruption to occupants was put in place. It was agreed with college authorities that all new students' accommodation will be physically inspected over the summer. It was also proposed and adopted that, with any renovations and new accommodation, basic facilities such as telephones and computer terminals will be made available in rooms. This is to be the case for the new student accommodation quad.

The Room Ballot process was well structured and organised. It was also granted comprehensive publicity and hence it was implemented without any problems. Unfortunately, for this year the number of rooms on the MCR ballot has decreased due to renovations at 19 Holywell Street. With a waiting list of at least seven, this situation is grave for the MCR. Consequently, a proposal has been sent to the college to procure a house to rent out to these students. Battels negotiations between the MCR/JCR joint team and the college, to discuss increases in food and accommodation charges for next year, are in progress. The bottom line, however, is unambiguous. Any increase must be reflective of student ability to pay, in line with inflation and substantially cushioned by college subsidisation.

Which way forward, Merton College MCR? The MCR and the JCR need institutional recognition by the college and its functionaries. At the moment, there is no official representation of students on any college committee or board. Pseudo-representation is effected through informal lobbying of college officials by elected student leaders. Yes, it does produce limited results, but it is fundamentally disrespectful to the generality of the student community and severely undermines their bargaining power. The principle of institutionalised student representation constitutes an inalienable democratic right. This is the unequivocal disposition of the MCR and defines the next arena of combative diplomacy. Given the immortality of this case, it is our contention that history will clearly absolve us.

(Address also submitted as my report as MCR President for the *Postmaster & The Merton Record*, October 1993.)

28 On the Japanese experience

As part of my studies for the doctorate in robotics and mechatronics, I travel to the United States, Europe and Japan to present research papers and attend academic conferences. My first trip to Japan is of particular interest to me because of the country's stunning economic growth which is rooted in the extensive use of automation and robotics. On 24 September 1993, I express my views and thoughts after that first visit.

I left for Japan on 10 July and came back on 31 July 1993. It was an extremely exciting and educational exposure. I presented two papers about my work at two international conferences:

- Intelligent Vehicles 1993; 14–16 July; Tokyo. Paper title: 'Modular Decentralised Robot Control'
- Intelligent Robots and Systems IROS 1993; 26–30 July; Yokohama. Paper title: 'A Formally Verified Modular Decentralised Robot Control System'

The conference experience was academically and socially profitable. The presentations were cutting-edge with leading people from all over the world (United States, Canada, Germany, France, UK and Japan). My papers were well received and I benefited from extensive feedback.

In between the conferences, I managed to visit a number of Japanese universities and industrial research centres specialising in robotics and artificial intelligence. In industry, I visited Toshiba, Isuzu, Nissan and Mitsubishi. In academia, I visited the following universities: Waseda, Tokyo, Yamanashi, Tokyo Institute, Nagoya and Utsonomiya. It was enriching to see the broad spectrum of research taking place in Japanese institutions.

Socially, I managed to travel extensively. I had a one-week Japan Rail pass which made cross-country movement inexpensive. I went to Hiroshima, Kyoto, Nara, Kamakura, Hakone Nagoya and Fujisowa. The diversity of Japanese cultural heritage in the form of temples, shrines and giant Buddhas was quite amazing. I mostly stayed in youth hostels and ate inexpensively.

My socio-political agenda consisted of mixing with and talking to Japanese people, with the motivation to explore what defines them. This was intriguing. They have a uniquely proficient work ethic, an apparently submissive culture and a zest for efficiency and organisation. As individuals, they are shy, friendly and helpful, at least superficially. Their value system is distinctly different from the mundane Western one. For example, you can find a research engineer or professor staying in a dormitory or a simple apartment, with no status issues at all.

The Japanese establishment, basing its roots in a submissive culture, tends to be inflexible and insensitive. Maybe this is sometimes a necessary evil for vigorous industrial expansion. Putting it differently, individual freedom as perceived in the West is a concept the Japanese have had to sacrifice. Prime emphasis is placed on the team or group. I am not convinced that the cultural purity that I witnessed can be achieved without xenophobic tendencies. I presume there is a need for cultural opening, exchange and integration. By Western standards, the position of Japanese women is at the least dubious. It seems subordination of women is socially constructed and entrenched in Japanese culture. I could be wrong.

Capital is institutionalised and there is cross-corporate financing. This is an illegal activity in the United States. This makes it easy to invest in technological innovations, as opposed to a situation where you have to convince a bunch of rowdy and uninformed individual shareholders. There is also active government involvement in development and technological strategies. All these economic arrangements set Japan apart from most Western countries. One could call it a planned and managed capitalist economy. I am not convinced this is the best way to go, but it is definitely an extremely interesting and successful economic model.

When all is said and done, I was quite impressed by Japanese achievements, in particular in the technology arena. Despite the limitations of Japanese society, as a nation Japan is economically and socially outperforming the United States and its European allies. Maybe the so-called Third World countries have a lot to learn from the Japanese model.

29 On the 'nose brigade' phenomenon

A platform called Zimnet (Zimbabwe Network), an electronic network of Zimbabweans across the world, is set up by Dudzai Saburi, an architecture student at MIT. Members of Zimnet can share and exchange information from wherever they are in the world. This is revolutionary. Of course, we are in 1993, way before Facebook, Twitter and WhatsApp. I take advantage of Zimnet to share my thoughts on various issues and also respond to matters raised by fellow citizens. There is a big debate on Zimnet about different accents with which Zimbabweans speak English. While still at Oxford University, on 2 October 1993, I express my views on the subject.

It has been stimulating following issues on this network, Zimnet. I must emphasise that the more controversial the matter the better. It is imperative that we discuss and take positions on these issues. We should get over this naive, superficial tendency to make each other overly comfortable in a quagmire of confusion, rooted in ignorance. Rational disputation nourishes the mind and the future is built on argumentation.

On the exhausted issue of accent, I will start by stating the bottom line; the non-reducible minimum, lest it gets lost in the rumble to follow. We should accept and respect each other as we are, taking cognisance of our diverse backgrounds, most of which we did not choose. There is no proper or improper accent for a globalised (through colonialism and imperialism) language such as English. We should give each other a chance and maximally utilise the Zimbabwe human potential. This sounds easy and fashionable, so what's up? Let us walk through some social and cultural dynamics.

The phrases 'nose brigade' *(nosey)* and 'strong rural background' *(SRB)* are intrinsically derogatory, but I will use them as clinical terms to marshal a few observations. In Zimbabwe, a nosey is defined as a person who speaks the English language with an acquired white accent, while the SRB speaks it with a heavy indigenous accent. The problem is that when these two subcultures meet there is no rapport. There are ambiguous feelings characterised by mutual disrespect and discomfort. This is because these subcultures are not just about accents. They are about values. The nosey feels superior and more socially sophisticated (in the Western and white sense), while the SRB feels more authentic (meaning more African), though he or she is also intimidated in some cases. Given the fact that we live in a Western- and white-dominated world, the nosey brigade technique seems to be a trendy survival strategy. However, in the Zimbabwean context there are more people who can be classified in the SRB tradition than in the nose brigade one. What happens next is common cause. The majority coins the stereotype of nose brigades and castigates them. The reaction is that those on the receiving end formulate another stereotype: SRB, Shona-English or IsiNdebele-English. This is not how you deal with stereotypes! You do not respond by creating a counter stereotype. I have seen remarks on this network that neatly follow into this tradition.

The consequences of the whole nose brigade versus SRB phenomenon are devastating in any particular community. This was one of the tragedies of the UZ experience. People classified as noseys would not socialise across the social boundary and played certain sports exclusively or joined particular teams. The majority, the SRBs, abused their numerical strength. Most noseys were shouted down, thus being booed out of participation, academically, socially and politically. In some cases, they did not bother to participate because they felt some things were meant for the unrefined SRBs or they were just damn scared of ridicule. As a result, certain talented individuals could not play certain sports or do some socio-political work that they would have wanted to. Examples range from the sublime to the ridiculous and can be perceived without loss of generality.

How does one become a nose brigade? As has already been pointed out, this is an attitude problem. Just because you have a certain accent and you hold certain values you think you are more important than another individual. This is wrong and indefensible. There is also an empirical philosophical question on the acquisition of the accent. Before we start, let us excuse the children. Let us excuse those who naturally acquire this accent by virtue of being born or growing up in a particular environment. We should not use these cases to hide the fascinating bogus characters among us. I have a philosophical problem with fully grown individuals (16 years+) who already have an accent for English but consciously change the way they speak because they think their accent is not good enough. This inevitably leads to self-disrespect, lack of confidence, slave mentality and self-hate. I will go on to destroy the myths about the nosey accent, some of which have been perpetuated on this network. People must be themselves, identify with themselves and get on with life. Other cultures never respect imitators, more so when you imitate superficial values, such as accent.

As regards the nosey accent myths; for a start, there is no such thing as a native English accent, at least not here in the UK. Here you get the Irish, Welsh, Scottish and English people, all with different accents. Within the English folks there are different traits such as the working-class or underclass accent, the posh public school accent, the aristocratic Oxonian version and the BBC approach. In Zimbabwe, what you acquire in most of the Group A schools is a white (Rhodesian) Zimbabwean accent. You can imagine the intriguing diversity of accents at a quasi-cosmopolitan place such as Oxford University. As has already been pointed out on Zimnet, Americans, Australians and Canadians all have different accents within and across. Consequently, if your favourite pastime in Zimbabwe was copying 'superior' accents and values, then the task would be daunting for you at Oxford. Talking about accents being 'funny', quite a number of people here find the white Rhodesian accent (what the nosey brigades aspire to attain in Zimbabwe) 'distinct and funny'. Time for a change maybe!

The other myth is that adopting a nosey accent improves your communication skills, making you eloquent and articulate. These are unsubstantiated and unimaginative illusions which should be unequivocally dismissed. You can improve and acquire such attributes while still retaining a heavy African accent. I do not know how you measure these parameters, but I have seen noseys being eaten up for breakfast by SRBs in public debates, interviews, negotiations, presentations and general discussions. In fact, in my short experiences, here at Oxford and at UZ, I have not met a single nosey who is particularly eloquent, let alone articulate. But I am sure there are some.

In conclusion, the nosey/SRB divide is artificially constructed and is based on superficial and superfluous values. Neither side benefits while Zimbabwe's national interest suffers. Back to the bottom line: Let us respect each other as we are and get on with the substantive issues.

I rest my case.

(Chung, 1985) (Fanon, 1963) (Biko, 1979) (X, 1965)

30 Pontificating about Zimbabwean struggles from Oxford

Professor Masipula Sithole is quite a keen watcher, writer and practitioner of Zimbabwean politics. Another busy-body is Dr Austin Chakaodza, who is mooting the formation of a Zimbabwean political party from his base here in the UK. I receive a pleasant, but unexpected, personal note from Professor Sithole, who is on sabbatical in the United States. Separately, I get an invitation by Dr Chakaodza to work with him on his ambitious mission. Below is my detailed response to Sithole, also indicating my attitude towards Dr Chakaodza's efforts. Today is 13 November 1993.

Yep, it was a pleasant surprise to read from you. Revolutionary greetings from this bastion of British aristocracy and academia! This place is exciting, challenging and fascinating. I am doing fine. My academic work is going well. I finished the MSc in Computation in October 1992. This is Mathematical Computing Science and Computer Engineering bundled together. I attended my MSc graduation ceremony on 28 November 1992. I immediately embarked on a PhD programme in Robotics and Artificial Intelligence. I think I need a year and a month to complete it. I hope to be going home, at the end of 1994 or beginning of 1995. Academic progress will dictate.

Politically, Oxford has been extremely exciting. There is such a broad spectrum of socio-political societies and activities. This is further flavoured by the self-perpetuating Oxford myth that many happening people, academic and otherwise, perceive it as such a great place and hence come down to Oxford, oblivious of the fact that it is because they come to Oxford that it gets its reputation. Thus, the greatness is a self-fulfilling prophecy.

As an illustration, in just recent months, our student political meetings have included such luminaries as Ronald Reagan, Chancellor Helmut Kohl, Bob Hawke, Margaret Thatcher, Mother Teresa, Muhammad Ali and Mikhail Gorbachev. Of the societies, I have taken a keen interest in the Oxford Union (the oldest debating society in the world), Strategic Studies Group, Africa Society, Political Economy Society and the Politics Society. I have been President of the Africa Society and I am currently President of my College Graduate Union, the Merton College Middle Common Room. It is a hectic schedule.

No, I am still single. At the moment, I am married to activism. It is my sincere hope that this will change some day. On the Zimbabwean scene, I am still as determined, if not more determined. I can say, with neither equivocation nor ambiguity, that I feel a sense of duty and obligation to make a contribution to my country.

Now, I am extremely pleased that Dr Austin Chakaodza, based here in the UK, has taken a keen interest in active progressive politics in Zimbabwe, by way of contemplating the formation of a political party. I greatly appreciate his efforts. I have never given up or compromised on combative struggle. The major problem, however, is that I strongly believe that a viable radical popular party can only evolve from within the country as a product of active struggle on the ground. It is my disposition that all progressive forces and individuals outside Zimbabwe must get back to the country and be part of the struggle fabric. That vision puts me in an ambiguous and invidious position. Right now, as I have already indicated, I have a year and a month, hopefully, to go on my academic work. After that I will immediately leave for Zimbabwe. I am working hard on this schedule.

I am seriously committed to the Zimbabwean struggle, to such an extent that I don't want to make any false starts and get disillusioned. You see, Prof. Masipula Sithole, I am a fighter and when I get into combat, defeat is not part of my agenda. Not only am I out of the country, I am also studying. Consequently, if I were to join with Austin, my contribution would be piecemeal, uninformed and hence easy to shoot down or discredit. A contribution must be rooted in the people that it purports to serve. I don't want to play up my personal relevance, but it is my intuitive feeling that the Zimbabwean establishment or regime is quite keen to denounce, discredit and destroy me once and for all. I don't want this to happen before I even embark on any substantive action. I don't believe in half measures. I go all the way. I must be in the country to fight these guys tooth and claw, punch for punch. Given these personal limitations I feel incapacitated. I cannot actively help Austin start an organisation.

The project he is talking about is of fundamental importance. It is my strong suggestion that, for him to play any meaningful contribution in its formulation, he must immediately move to Zimbabwe and work with the fighters on the ground. Comrades such as Tendai Biti, Morgan Tsvangirai, Kempton Makamure and their organisations are essential. Committees in foreign countries are extremely secondary. On ideas, principles and programmes, let these evolve from the masses on the ground. It is important that people are able to say: 'We formed this party. It is our organisation.' Austin's outlined programme has some interesting ideas, loose ends and ambivalent positions. I won't go into details because the important thing is that he can get a 'Congress of Ideas' from the comrades on the ground in Zimbabwe, and hammer out an agenda within the country. As Zimbabweans out of the country out of choice, since none of us is in exile, we have a weak standing. We must go home, struggle with the generality of the people of Zimbabwe, and work out ideas and programmes from amongst them.

Despite my current inability to actively take up the challenge, I hope Austin will keep me posted on how he is getting on with this agenda. I am in touch, and will keep in contact, with comrades from the labour and student movements on the ground in Zimbabwe.

Please keep in touch, Professor. It will be great to meet up either here in the City of Dreaming Spires, or over there in the belly of the beast. I have two academic conferences in the United States in May and June 1994. Last summer I had two in Japan. Is your son, Chandi, still going to do some serious computing, in addition to risk management? I remember he was an enthusiastic computer hack.

How is your wife getting on with Pharmacy studies? My sister, Rosemary, is here in the UK doing a PhD in Pharmacy, at the University of Bath. Good luck with the book project, Das Tribal to rival Das Capital. I will certainly enjoy reading it. You just have to produce it! Pass my warm greetings to your family.

Yours in the struggle.

31 Social justice or free market economics?

Since the collapse of the Berlin Wall, there have been dramatic changes. In particular, Eastern Europe and the Soviet Union have collapsed. All these seismic changes have ideological implications of global significance. What does this mean for socialism? What does this mean for capitalism? How should emerging economies or so-called Third World countries respond to these upheavals? Although in October 1987 I gave up on the idea of socialist development in Zimbabwe anchored by a ZANU-PF one-party state, I still hold on dearly to the humanistic values and principles behind socialism and communism. It was not socialism we rejected in Zimbabwe. It was ZANU-PF we dismissed as a dysfunctional vehicle, incapable of achieving revolutionary transformation. This is 1994, and I still insist that the contradictions and inhumanity of unbridled capitalism render it unsustainable. While still at Oxford University, on 6 January 1994, I express my views on the Zimnet discussion platform.

Happy New Year, fellow Zimnetters! A colleague sent me a note this morning seeking clarification on my ideological orientation after the changes in Eastern Europe. In principle, my disposition has not changed. It has only been broadened and tempered by history. I am still driven by values of social justice. It is still my unequivocal contention that more people will benefit from these values than from individualistic ones. Yes, market forces should be understood but they must be used as servants and not drivers of society. They can be used for planning while subordinating them to social justice and equity.

However, my perception of socialist traditions and principles has become more critical and discerning. A central issue is the essence of democratic and humanistic values that should be inherent in any socialist disposition. It is imperative that whatever egalitarian system anyone espouses, they must win their argument in the battle of ideas. Consequently, it is people who should decide what social, political and economic system they want. If the generality of people opt for a capitalist society, the socialists should respect that and work harder to democratically convince society otherwise. There should be no ideological imposition from the top. I completely reject the notions of a one-party state and that of a single vanguard party. However, it must be noted that multiparty democracy is a necessary but not sufficient condition for socio-economic development.

It is also my submission that those on the left should be more self-critical and adopt a dynamically reflective attitude towards ideas and organisations on the political left. Individual writers and activists should never be romanticised. For example, Engels, Marx and Lenin were just three smart people who made some contributions. Of course, as human beings, with intellectual, historical, social and economic limitations, they made mistakes. No work of any intellectual or activist (right or left) should be immortalised or taken on faith. Ideas must continue to be challenged as a basis for growth and development. There is no need for anyone to be known as a Marxist, Leninist or (Adam) Smithist. Anyway, these terms mean different things to different people. Ideas and principles are more intellectually stimulating than name-labelling. Cognisance must also be taken that there are many paradigms and grand narratives about society and its evolution. Anyone who aspires to make public comment is encouraged to be exposed to as many as possible. Consequently, when they support or oppose any philosophical interpretation of the world it will be based on an informed judgement.

Given the above exposition and what we all know about Eastern Europe, it is clear that none of these countries experienced a socialist dispensation. They were failed attempts at public control. At best the Soviet Union was a degenerate working-class state. This is a controversial perception indeed. At worst its economic system can be characterised as state capitalism. There was never any worker control, management of the economy or grass-roots participatory democracy. There was a vicious central command and resources were not channelled to serve the generality of the population. The worst criminal was indisputably Stalin.

However, it is a misleading persuasion to call the whole project Stalinism. The problem was bigger than Stalin. It was historical, structural, systemic and international in character.

It is, however, instructive to note that despite the 'evil' nature of these Eastern Europe regimes, they were the only ones, including China and Cuba, prepared to give us arms to fight the illegal colonial regimes in Africa and elsewhere in the so-called Third World. The 'evil empire' backed the right causes, while the West did not! Of course, in doing so the East was also serving its own geo-strategic, economic and political interests. There was collusion of aspirations. Can one imagine Britain or the United States giving us arms to fight Ian Smith in Rhodesia or P.W. Botha in South Africa?

Weapons and military training are what we needed the most, not sanctions or self-serving and unproductive public posturing. It is clear that racist, kith and kin politics dictated Western foreign policy with respect to African liberation struggles. Of course, Africans remember, and are eternally grateful towards those who assisted them in their struggle for freedom. Shame on Western governments for their criminal inaction, gross inconsistency and lack of both morals and principles! However, the grand assistance to liberation movements in Africa cannot absolve the East of their crimes against their own people and economies.

Now, why social justice? With the implosion of the Soviet Union there is an absurd illusion that one system of values has been triumphant over another; that is, free market economics have defeated social justice. This naive simplification is not only ludicrously unsophisticated but manifests intellectual ineptitude. Yes, the economic system and political culture in Eastern Europe have been destroyed and they deserved to be dismantled. We hold no brief for them. There was nothing social or just about them. On the other hand, there is no such thing as a free market economy. It is a myth. The international market is rigged against the so-called Third World. Multinational and transnational corporations know neither patriotism nor social benevolence. The United States has no permanent friends, only permanent interests. Nations are never altruistic. They are out there to look after the interests of their dominant economic classes. Look at the problems at the GATT talks: protectionism, subsidies for French and US farmers, and tariffs against products from emerging markets. Within individual Western economies the system is rigged against small businesses, minorities, the underclass and the working class. This scenario then raises the question: Has Western capitalism delivered to the average individual?

A quick look at the United States and Britain evidences unemployment, social deprivation, homelessness, destitution and racism. The economies are characterised by a vicious recession, inflation, industrial decline, inefficiency and lack of competitiveness. These countries have never been socialist countries, and yet they have devastating problems. Thus, while we recognise the demise of the countries that claimed to be socialist, we do not see the quantifiable victories of Western systems either. The only difference is that the United States and Britain have not imploded. In essence, capitalism has had a propaganda victory over the values of social justice. It is only time which will tell where the future lies. It is interesting to note that reforms towards a market economy in Poland and Russia have produced fundamental frustrations and a crisis of expectations. Shock therapy has not worked, at least not in the short run. What beats me is why one would expect anything else, given the fact that the West, which is being aspired to, is equally plagued with problems. There are no easy solutions.

Whither so-called Third World countries such as Zimbabwe? If ever there was a weak case for unbridled capitalism, it is in these countries. Given the historical background of colonial and racial segregation, decontextualised free market economics will simply accentuate and exacerbate the economic differences obtaining at independence. A racial 2 per cent of the population control and manage 90 per cent of the national resources. Independence becomes a fraud. Land acquisition, equity in health, peasant and worker economic empowerment and education cannot be delivered by free market forces alone. It should always be remembered that colonial rule was a socio-economic system of oppression of one group of people by another. People were systematically, structurally and institutionally dispossessed and disempowered.

Active social justice is required to redress these historical imbalances. Of course, in a globalised and sophisticated economy, concepts such as market analysis, competition, incentives, comparative advantage, innovation and competitive advantage should be used to inform the economic planning process. However, unbridled free market economics should never be the overriding consideration. Doing so leads to the creation of a moribund and racial monopoly capitalist system, benefiting the resident white minority and their kith and kin resident in the United States and Europe. Put differently, the option for an unbridled capitalist economy for Third World countries is a non-existent false choice. While US capitalism benefits citizens of the United States, albeit a few of them, Zimbabwean foreign-anchored capitalism will not ostensibly benefit indigenous Zimbabweans. Fashionable slogans of deregulation, free market economics and privatisation will neither do the trick nor cut it for black Zimbabweans. Let us increase the vision, imagination and ingenuity.

This is just a thought.

(Fanon, 1963) (Jackson, 1972) (Lenin, 1961) (Guevara, 1961)

32 Youth and post-colonialism

While studying for my doctorate in robotics and mechatronics at the University of Oxford, I also participate in research seminars and conferences in the fields of social science, politics, economics and African history. The SCUSA 2nd colloquium on post-colonialism and identity is held at the University of Manchester on 14 May 1994. I present a paper challenging the foundational assumptions of the discourse, while emphasising the need to unlock the youth dividend in all socio-economic and political processes.

This paper rejects the terms of reference of this colloquium, *Post-colonialism and identity*, as essentially misconceived. The term 'post-colonial' presupposes the end of colonialism and does not give recognition to the phenomenon of neo-colonialism. It is imperative that the notions of colonialism and neo-colonialism be unambiguously understood before any post-colonial theory is contemplated.

The youth as the dominant consumers in the business of ideas demand a candid, concise and consistent analytic-theoretical framework. A neo-colonial state is one with all the trappings of political independence, and yet its economy and intellectual culture is externally controlled with the participation of an internal racial minority. These insidious activities are usually in cahoots with the overfed, brainwashed and bankrupt ruling indigenous political elite. For all intents and purposes, most politically independent countries in Africa are neo-colonial states. There has not been a different post-colonial dispensation yet.

It is common cause that the most powerful weapon of the oppressor is the controlled and polluted mind of the oppressed. Moreover, it is an irrefutable fact that the most difficult anti-colonial activity is decolonising that mind. Consequently, the state of ideas does matter. The dialectical relation between the superstructure and the economic base is well known.

Failure by this colloquium to take cognisance of the immortality of the case outlined above makes this gathering yet another Eurocentric and intellectually imperialistic project underpinning Western global socio-political-economic domination.

Anyway, what is youth? There has been neither a strict nor universal definition of this term in literature. Here, a demographic definition with a political component is ventured. The youth, or young people, are a transient group of people under the age of 30 years who are a reflection of existing social classes in any particular society. The age restriction is a flexible criterion. What is of essence is the transient nature of the youth category and how it reflects class characteristics.

Historically, the involvement of this category of people has always been critical in social, political and economic processes including revolutions. Several grand narratives can be espoused to capture the reasons why this is the case. This group of people constitutes the most dynamic societal elements, in terms of sheer energy, zeal, enthusiasm and courage. Though mostly amenable and receptive to ideas, they are critical, self-critical and experimental. They have a sense of adventure, curiosity and rebellion. In most cases, they have few personal socio-economic obligations and consequently nothing to lose.

As a result, their articulation and involvement is from a no-holds-barred disposition and perspective. A careful treatment of neo-colonial social dynamics portrays a much tighter analysis. The youth reflect the existing social classes; the bourgeoisie, petit bourgeoisie, workers and peasants. As such they have a duty and obligation to act as a barometer of social consciousness. This task is imposed upon them by material conditions and history. Since the young people come from society, they live the challenges and injustices therein. They experience the political oppression, economic exploitation and social degradation that characterise their communities. Thus, when they take positions, when they fight, they are doing so on behalf of the generality of society. This role becomes even more critical in a neo-colonial state which is characterised by a de jury or de facto one-party state culture, fragile or non-existent opposition parties, absence of separation of powers, weak trade unionism, draconian and arbitrary economic disparities, and vicious intellectual imperialism. Young people become the voice of the voiceless and the combatants of the demobilised.

In this section, concrete activities of the youth in neo-colonial Africa are explored. To contextualise these activities, it is important to note that the bulk of the anti-colonial activities were carried out by young people. This took the form of anti-imperialist guerrilla armies, village collaborators, combat forerunners and general political leadership. In post-independent Africa, the youth activities have been various and diverse. The youth have been invariably used by post-independent regimes to legitimise and consolidate their power. Examples range from the criminal Young Pioneers in Malawi, who terrorised any form of opposition to Life President Banda, to the notorious Youth Brigades in Mugabe's Zimbabwe who ransacked opposition politicians' houses after unfree and unfair elections. Similar trends were observed in Kaunda's Zambia, Mobutu's Zaire and Moi's Kenya.

Where post-independence civil wars were fought, the youth bled on both sides. The tragic cases of Mozambique, Angola and Zimbabwe are a sad but clear manifestation of this cancer. However, this is only half the story. Youth organisations – religious, non-governmental and governmental – were extensively engaged in rehabilitation and reconstruction programmes. Young people were actively involved in rural agricultural projects, teaching in the villages and grass-roots economic empowerment projects. They also challenged the despotic regimes to deliver on the promises of liberation.

However, this section of the youth consisted ostensibly of college and university students. They exposed national corruption, dictatorial excesses and misplaced government priorities committed by this elite class of tired nationalists. In turn, they demanded the separation of powers, a multiparty dispensation, media freedom, academic freedom, land redistribution and general economic empowerment. It was very clear to this section of the youth that political independence without equitable distribution of resources rooted in social justice is a fraud. Thus, the youth became the conscience of the people and agents of change. Equally unequivocal was the perception that a multiparty dispensation was a necessary but not sufficient condition for economic development. They fought for pluralistic politics as a minimum programme.

The involvement of young people in the movements campaigning for multiparty democracy is self-evident in the MMD's victory over Kaunda in Zambia, the demise of Banda in Malawi and the destruction of Mugabe's one-party state crusade in Zimbabwe. Evidence is already emerging, as the beleaguered MMD regime of Chiluba in Zambia unravels, that the youth will not be satisfied by mere liberal plural politics, but by equity, social justice and economic empowerment. Students, young trade unionists and unemployed youth have already come into vicious confrontation with the Chiluba machinery of violence.

South Africa presents a very interesting case, as it goes through transition from apartheid to political independence as this paper is being written. Angry youth demand their piece of the action. There is a lost generation of young people in SA; those who never received education because the school premises were combat zones, and are now too old to go to school.

Hence, there are young people who are unemployed and unemployable. Placing black elites in power is going to be the easy part. It will be harder to improve the material conditions of the generality of the SA people. These people need land, jobs, education, housing, health and transportation. They do not want these amenities tomorrow; neither do they want them today. They demand them yesterday. What a crisis of expectations! Needless to say, the bulk of these people constitute the youth. 'One settler, one bullet; kill the farmer, kill the Boer!' chants Peter Mokaba, leader of the ANC Youth

League. This is the language of anger and protest. There is nothing wrong with anger. It is a natural and liberating human emotion.

Of course, the angry statement above is perfectly justifiable and defensible. The essence of the statement is that the indigenous people need some land. The white settler has all the land. Consequently, there should be land redistribution by any means necessary. Mokaba owes no one an apology or explanation. Those accusing Mokaba of racism or racial violence are guilty of the most shameful treachery of making the victim look like the criminal and the criminal look like the victim.

Mokaba is the victim of 342 years of colonialism and apartheid. Hey, racism is about economic power. Clearly, even if he wanted to be prejudicial he does not have the capacity or capability to reverse 342 years of apartheid. In any case, if anyone is sincerely concerned about these outrageously angry statements, they must immediately uproot the conditions that generate the anger. Get to work and change those deplorable and degrading conditions in Soweto! The youth should never give up their inalienable and democratic right to be angry. Moreover, when Mandela becomes a sell-out, when the ANC becomes corrupt, incompetent and impotent, it is these angry youths who will have the guts to denounce and dislodge the rot.

An interesting avenue is youth and academic research in neo-colonial Africa. The question to start with is: 'Research for whom, by whom and for what intent?' Instead of being uncritical, docile and compliant consumers of research results, the youth want to be holistically involved in the construction of research ethos and ethics, methodology, terms of reference, execution and interpretation including application of such academic outcomes. There is a deplorable North-South inequitable distribution of research resources within the academic fraternity, in particular in social anthropology. Those who control the intellectual culture predetermine the future.

One of the major evils of colonialism is Western cultural and intellectual imperialism. Young people can only begin to address this quagmire by seizing and smashing intellectual imperialism and constructing their own post-colonial intellectual dispensation. All forms of cultural and intellectual appropriation by external researchers whose attraction to African studies is a sheer taste of the 'cultural other' should be blasted into oblivion. Universal principles, terms and analytic tools should be applied across cultures. A case in point is the selective use of terms like tribalism for 'uncivilised' African people and ethnicity for 'civilised' European people. Efforts should be made to use value-neutral depictions and not heavily judgmental notions as evidenced by such words as 'witchdoctor'. In any case this is a supreme contradiction in terms: How can one be both a witch and a doctor at the same time?

As young African people search for identity and the essence of being, they do not see any difference between believing in the existence of witchcraft and believing in the virgin birth. The two phenomena define equal but different belief systems based on the existence of a supernatural force. A social anthropologist should not attach preferential value judgement to either.

When all is said and done, it is a categorical imperative that the limitations of youth as agents of change and the myth of social research impartiality be emphasised. Young people are a heterogeneous and transient group. They are not a social class but a reflection of competing classes. As individuals, they have personal aspirations, which are sometimes attainable by compromising the collective agenda. Although dominant sections of the youth have potential for a radical liberating disposition, young people should never be romanticised. There is scope for serious contradictions among the youth as they reflect different interests, a case in point being ruling party youths mobilised to confront students demonstrating against government corruption. Notwithstanding these limitations, the potential of youth as a central organising, revolutionary force in a neo-colonial state remains substantive.

On extending the frontiers of knowledge, in particular constructing social theory, the researcher must come under scrutiny. There is no such thing as a neutral researcher. A researcher has views, biases and vested interests, no matter how subtle or sublime. These could be driven by political, economic, cultural and religious influences. There is nothing wrong with having such an extenuating disposition. What is unforgivably hypocritical, despicable and criminal is when researchers claim neutrality in self-serving public posturing. Academics must own up and state their biases and vested interests so that their outputs can be contextualised. Only then can research findings be useful. In a world crippled by glaring inequalities, poverty, oppression, deprivation, and general lack of social justice, the researcher is challenged to make a difference. As the guns keep blasting and the struggle for a better world continues unabated, one is either part of the problem or part of the solution. The academic researcher has an option. Distinguished scholars, what is your choice?

(Nkrumah, 1965) (Bernal, 1987) (James, 1992) (Fanon, 1963)

33 The Oxford experience: An overseas student's perspective

Being a foreign student studying in Oxford has its challenges. It is important that new students are well informed about some of the issues and that they prepare accordingly. As I am finishing my doctorate, the Oxford University magazine asks me to do an article addressing this subject, with a view to assisting new students in the future. Here is the article they publish on 14 October 1994.

Coming to Oxford from outside the United Kingdom presents various challenges, both superficial and substantive. Needless to say, it is difficult to generalise for all overseas students. However, certain issues and trends can be identified without loss of generality. The broad spectrum of experiences includes cultural and climatic changes, the unique Oxonian aristocracy, the collegiate system, competitive and diverse activities, the graduate accreditation system, and of course, the awesome Oxford myth. This is a self-perpetuating and self-fulfilling myth. Consequently, you are always caught in a quagmire of reality versus appearance.

Two major characteristics of the change in climate are absurd weather unpredictability and the devastating combination of extreme cold and dampness throughout most of the year, with frustrating severity in winter. Summers can be sunny and funny. Invariably one has to procure a good chunk of warm and rainproof clothes. Warm bedding is essential. Graduate accommodation varies within colleges but generally it ranges from expensively heated rooms, cheaply heated warm ones to cold rooms. In fact, housing can be problematic, as some colleges only provide it for one year or two. Most graduate houses have kitchens and hence overseas students can treat themselves to special delicacies uncatered for in college dining halls.

Oxford as an institution has all the trappings of British aristocracy and conservatism. This is characterised by class-based structures, overemphasis on traditional values and events, an obsession with hierarchy, denigrating official terminology and blatant disrespect for student perspectives. The best attitude is to confront and challenge this academic bureaucracy. This is the only way you get things done, anyway.

The university is evidently international, with graduate students coming from all over the world. The problem is that the geographical distribution of these students is not equitable. For example, the number of African and Asian students is unacceptably low. This is dramatically glaring for black students from Africa and the African diaspora. Whether this is reflective of the application or acceptance rates is not too clear. Whichever way it is, a more vigorous attitude needs to be adopted to encourage more applications and hence acceptances from these groups. This is an unequivocal matter of principle. As a result, at best Oxford is quasi-cosmopolitan, culturally. This does help diffuse the impact of the culture shock that hits you upon enrolling. The bottom line, however, is that most of the oversubscribed subcultures are predominantly based on Western values, which have their nauseating aspects. This leaves students from under-represented groups in cultural oblivion.

The beauty of the Oxford scene is the broad spectrum of extra-curricular activities; sporting, social and political. You cannot fail to find something that suits you. Leadership roles and participation in these organisations tend to be very aggressively competitive. Some of the societies and clubs, in addition to being informative, are academically complementary. By and large, the graduate seems comparatively less enthusiastic than the undergraduate. Within this socio-political activist fabric, overseas students should be encouraged to maintain their identity and have the confidence to engage on their own terms as equals to everyone else. They must deserve and be granted respect as such in whatever they do. There is this nefarious degeneration towards depersonalisation as one thrives to be more British than the British. The advice is: 'Stay black. Stay African. It is all good.'

Academically, Oxford is very competitive. It has the resources and the leading people in most areas. Is it really that great? In a weird way, yes! This is because everyone thinks it is. Consequently, capable students, researchers, and prominent professors and lecturers flock to Oxford. Funding agencies also self-delude and provide academic resources. External happening personalities and shot-callers trek down to give talks, mix and mingle, thinking that Oxford is the greatest thing that ever happened, oblivious of the fact that it is great because they come to Oxford. This is the exciting Oxford story: a self-perpetuating and self-fulfilling myth. The result is that, yes, Oxford University is a world-class, dynamic and competitive institution in the business of ideas, thought leadership, academia, research and self-development, arguably ahead of such places as Harvard, Yale, MIT, Stanford and Cambridge.

As a graduate, the type of subject you can study is not limited by your college. All teaching of graduates is carried out by the departments. As a result, you can invariably read for any course you want. There is this myth that Oxford is a liberal arts place. This is baseless. You can study many scientific subjects such as neurosurgery, astrophysics, VLSI design and robotics. It is possible to change courses when you are in Oxford, but the earlier you do this the better. It is imperative to always remember that making choices and decisions is a right and not a privilege. There is always the danger of thinking that one is privileged to be at Oxford. The patronising establishment usually makes you feel that way. An interesting observation is that academic standards are pretty stiff, and Oxford does not hesitate to fail those who don't make the mark. As an overseas student, there is always the fear of whether one will measure up. To compound this anxiety, the academic establishment is generally sceptical of foreign students until they have proven themselves at Oxford.

Among students, the ability myth leads to intelligence hysteria, with students acting cleverer than they actually are. Everyone is trying to define and defend the legitimacy of their presence in the City of Dreaming Spires. New entrants are trying to outdo each other in confirming that they are solidly aligned to the Oxonian tradition of academic excellence. This can be very intimidating. Manifestations range from the sublime to the ridiculous. In fact, some students suffer from a deep sense of insecurity and secretly wonder if their admission was a colossal mistake. However, they will keep these conflicted emotions between themselves and their maker. The crucial trick is to understand the intelligence and academic ability hysteria that the distinguished legacy of Oxford induces in new arrivals. As time elapses, and students become more sedate and reflective, it is then amusing to discover how very ordinary most of them are. With old-fashioned hard work, discipline, innovativeness, determination and focus, one can compete against the best.

When all is considered and the chips are down, yes, the Oxford experience is worthwhile. If one can cut through the crap and hype, you can get a reasonable education out of Oxford. The opportunities for self-development are indisputably unrivalled. The only dilemma is that you inevitably become part of the Oxford myth by either benefiting from it or perpetuating its legacy!

34 The African Mertonian: An exposition

In the entire University of Oxford, the number of black African students is scanty. The same applies to students of black British, African-American and Caribbean extraction. However, the few belonging to these groups who are here face unique challenges and hence a word or two of advice will assist. The following article on life at Merton College appears in the local and national media on 20 October 1994.

The number of African graduate students in Merton is unacceptably low. This is more so for black students from Africa and the African diaspora. Whether this is reflective of the application or acceptance rates is not too clear. Whichever way it is, a more vigorous attitude needs to be adopted to encourage more applications and hence acceptances from this section. This is one struggle inextricably linked to one's agenda as a Mertonian.

Coming to Merton from Africa involves significant cultural and climatic changes, depending on which part of Africa you are from. However, generally the winters here are comparatively very cold and damp. You will need to procure a good chunk of warm and rainproof clothes. Heating in rooms varies from expensively to cheaply heated, or cold. As a general guideline, you will need warm bedding.

Culturally, Merton is one of the most aristocratic and conservative colleges, with an overemphasis on traditional Victorian values. The best attitude is not to take this seriously. No one does. Graduate students come from all over the world and this gives the college a quasi-cosmopolitan nature. As a result, this diffuses the impact of the culture shock that hits you. However, bear in mind most of the subcultures are predominantly based on Western values, which as you know have their nauseating aspects.

As for electrical appliances, the power system is 220 volts, as in most African countries. You might find it convenient and cheaper to buy appliances here. There is a computer 'kitchen' of IBM PCs with Windows, Word and WordPerfect software. Macintosh facilities are being installed, hopefully. Extensive computer facilities – IBM, Macs, Suns and SPARCstations – are available in the departments. Laundry facilities are available within college accommodation at a nominal fee. As a graduate, you have the choice to eat in college or to cook for yourself. Yes, you can treat yourself to that special African dish!

As a graduate, the type of subject you can study is not limited by the college. All teaching of graduates is carried out by the departments. As a result, you can invariably read for any course you want. There is this myth that Oxford is a liberal arts university. This is baseless. You can study all the hi-tech subjects such as neurosurgery, astrophysics, VLSI design and robotics. It is possible to change courses when you are in Oxford, but the earlier you do this the better. Always remember making choices and decisions is a right and not a privilege. As an African there is always the danger of thinking that you are privileged to be at Oxford; the patronising establishment usually makes you feel that way. To hell with that submissive culture! You deserve to be here. Stand up and make a difference.

I hope I have given you a general exposition to Merton. Just be yourself, stay black, stay African and you can still be a Mertonian. There is no contradiction in terms.

35 Why we object to the use of the term 'tribalism'

The debates are raging on Zimnet. One particular discussion catches my eye. It is a conversation about terms that are used selectively among different races, and whether such use is innocuous and benign. Is it a big deal? One word, in particular, is under heavy debate – 'tribalism'. There are participants who are insisting that it is value-neutral. They do not seem to understand language politics and the power to define. One Zimnetter, an African-American comrade who has been quite progressive on other issues, is among those adamant that there is nothing wrong with the term. On 22 June 1996, I decide to jump into the fray and knock some heads.

Ron,

You should not insist on using the term 'tribalism'. It is pejorative and judgemental. It demeans Africans. Have you ever heard, in the Western media or literature, of references to European tribalism? Have you ever heard of them refer to how the English tribe and the Irish tribe are butchering each other in Northern Ireland? Have you ever heard a white person say, 'I belong to the Scottish tribe'? Even in Bosnia, did they ever refer to that conflict as tribalism? Yet, in the same media at the same time, a similar fight in Rwanda was described as a Hutu versus Tutsi tribal conflict.

What is the difference? The words 'tribe' and 'tribalism' are reserved for 'primitive' and 'uncivilised' groups; so-called inferior people. These terms are not neutral and are not used universally for all kinds of people. They are selectively used and are extremely insulting to any politically discerning African. Tell me a single case in which whites refer to themselves as tribes. There is absolutely no self-definition about the term tribalism when it comes to Africa. It must be rejected lock, stock and barrel. More broadly used phrases like ethnic group, ethnic conflict and ethnicity should be used. They should be applied for any kind of people. Stop accepting terms that are specifically created to describe one group by another without the defining group using the term on itself. It is like accepting the term 'nigger' or 'negro' and then trying to self-define it. It is a fruitless exercise. Selectively used terms, insulting and demeaning phrases coined by white supremacists, should be rejected without equivocation.

Lest I be accused of seeking cheap political correctness, this is serious business. Words do betray underlying prejudices and there is such a phenomenon as the power to define. Did you define yourself as a tribesman or did someone else give you that nomenclature? If it is such a scientific term, why doesn't that someone call himself a tribesman too? I would be OK with the terms tribe, tribalism and tribesperson if they are used for all groups of people on this planet. It does not matter that we have used these terms all our lives and hence they sound non-judgemental or neutral. They are not.

The most powerful weapon of the oppressor is the corrupted and controlled mind of the oppressed. Decolonising the mind and dealing with psychological slavery are difficult processes that we continually grapple with. No one can claim total victory. The struggle continues. The white supremacist, patriarchal capitalist system, its institutions and propagandists insidiously internalise these demeaning values of self-hatred and self-disrespect in us. Forget this nonsense about formal education. Who is teaching whom, what material, and for what purpose? Who are the so-called referenced authorities on African history and politics? How can a white supremacist teach us black consciousness, self-respect and self-love? Decolonising the mind does not necessarily follow from formal education. The challenge is, how do we re-educate the miseducated?

Ron, this is a general note and it is for the reflection of all Zimnetters and others. It is specifically addressed to you because of your recent remarks on the subject. More importantly, I have found your previous notes fairly solid in combating white supremacy in general and on Zimnet in particular. Consequently, I felt it is important that white supremacy does not get the best of you on this one.

Revolutionary greetings.

(Nkrumah, 1965) (Nyerere, 1983) (Malcolm X, 1965) (Fanon, 1963) (Biko, 1979)

36 The problem of white liberals in African struggles

For those involved in liberation struggles on the African continent and those engaged in black struggles in the United States, Europe and the Caribbean, there has been the age-old question: 'What is the role of whites who claim to be well-meaning, and seek to identify or empathise with the oppressed?' I see this as a potential flashpoint on Zimnet, as the discussions rage on the topical and racially charged subject of the land question in Zimbabwe. I sense some unexpressed discomfort from some black African participants over a couple of comments and suggestions from our white colleagues. I decide to broach the subject. I am at MIT as an Assistant Professor and Visiting Research Scientist in the Aeronautics and Astronautics Department. I put aside my robotic and mechatronic creations, and delve into the discourse about the challenges of involving white liberals in predominantly African struggles. The date is 3 March 1997.

There have been a lot of contributions by white folks, within Zimbabwe and from outside the country. The social, political and economic issues discussed have included the land question, political democracy, the economy, HIV/AIDS, language and education. There are obvious reasons for, and benefits gained from, the involvement of all sorts of people in struggles and issues that predominantly affect Africans. Some of these include the following: the fact that whites are part of Zimbabwe; it is important to involve everybody; reconciliation is a great idea; we gain diversity of ideas; listening to views that are opposed to yours is a virtue; integration is the way forward; we should be colour-blind; it is important to know what your enemy thinks; and, hey, we are just one big family, the human race.

In this article, I am not interested in these goodies. My focus is on the problems that arise from such involvement of white liberals in discussing issues and mapping out strategies to improve the material and intellectual condition of the indigenous Zimbabwean. Do these problems outweigh the benefits? How do we consciously budget for these problems as we continue to struggle? What are the scenarios and options?

Let us go to work right away. Given the history of Africa, and that of Zimbabwe in particular, it is no coincidence that the victims of the status quo, who are also aggressively agitating for change, are indigenous Africans. They are the victims of 400 years of slavery and 100 years of colonialism, who today suffer under the bondage of a subtle but vicious neo-colonialism. The last phenomenon is usually conveniently ignored. We are supposed to be independent. When did we obtain economic emancipation? Who owns, controls and manages land, labour and capital in Zimbabwe? Whose interests do multinational corporations serve? Who owns them and where do these people reside? Isn't there a net flow of resources from Africa to the West today? Back to the subject, for all intents and purposes, Africans were, and still are, the victims of these evils, and whites are the beneficiaries, consciously or subconsciously.

That is the subjective condition in Zimbabwe. Yes, I do understand the global problem as that of a white supremacist, patriarchal and capitalist system. This means there are at least three levels of abstraction that are critical. These identities of combat frameworks are race, gender and class. Any robust and holistic analysis should always take cognisance of the interplay between these three phenomena. Depending on the history of a particular region or people, one phenomenon might define the critical subjective condition. In Zimbabwe, race defines that condition.

It is in this context that I discuss the problems emanating from the involvement of white liberals in African struggles. The first problem is putting the African on the defence. What is your case? Prove your case. In fact, you are the wrongdoer! The African is challenged and teased by the white liberal. White supremacy has perfected the art of making the criminal look like the victim and the victim look like the criminal. The Nazi versus Zimbabwe government comparison is a good example. It is clear from the discussion on Zimnet that no indigenous African accepts that comparison. Some whites do. None of the opposition groupings in Zimbabwe will endorse the comparison, in spite of their ineptitude. How did Zimnet react to the analogy? Of course, we defended the Zimbabwe government. We affirmed our dignity.

The only problem is that such spirited defence induced by white supremacy is part of diversionary tactics. Why should we be on the defensive? We should be on the offensive. We should believe in the immortality of our case. We have neither duty nor obligation to convince a white racist or liberal of our right to land. These folks and their paper, *The Times*, compare Mugabe with Hitler. Now, some Africans actually consider Mugabe very moderate, and generally reactionary, and strongly feel that he has handled the racist white Rhodesians and the land question with kid gloves. These Africans will be uncompromising and will take no prisoners on the issue of land. They will use the same methods that were used to obtain land in the first place. So, if *The Times* newspaper compares Nazism with the current Zimbabwe government, what will their comparison be for these other Africans? Why should we even care about their analogies? Don't they have racially biased vested interests? Keep your eyes on the prize.

A further pitfall of racist-induced defence is that one becomes less self-critical. You become overly defensive, blinded by the insensitive racial onslaught. Africans need to criticise themselves for the betterment of Africans. How many of us in our response to the Nazi versus Zimbabwe government analogy went beyond defending the Zimbabwe government and our right to land? Where was your critique of the Zimbabwe government in the same response? What has ZANU-PF done wrong on the issue of land? In fact, why not include in the same article the reasons why Mugabe and his fellow travellers should be kicked out of office by Africans? What? Aha, there is the danger of playing into the hands of white supremacists. Therein lies the problem of having white liberals in these discussions. That is our dilemma. Self-criticism and self-renewal constitute the *sine qua non* for growth and development. Without them we cannot structure the way forward. We do not need meaningless accolades that Zimbabwe is a model for this and the other thing. Not many Zimbabweans believe that propaganda anyway. We have made a lot of mistakes as indigenous Zimbabweans and we can do far better than we have done so far. Now, how do we tell this to each other in the midst of folks who probably think that we are sub-human, lazy and incompetent by nature?

Another problem of white liberals on platforms such as Zimnet, and black political organisations in general, is the setting of the agenda: what is discussed and what should be done. Africans should always retain the power to set the agenda. The problem is that, sometimes, black Africans spend half their lives trying to make white people comfortable. Our virtuous and civil cultural disposition is sometimes abused or taken for stupidity. The agenda on Zimnet is pretty much set by Africans, but if you reflect carefully you will see the potential of the problematic I am alluding to. If white liberals are accepted on forums, they should never be accorded any special status. Agenda-setting liberals should be exposed. White liberals might not necessarily set the agenda, but might instead dilute the platform to the point where it becomes dysfunctional.

Then there is this talk that there are very few Rhodies in Zimbabwe. There are a lot of good and sincere white folks out there. They believe in land distribution too. What an illusion! The greatest myth of all time! Let us get this straight. Where did these good progressive whites come from? You remember the liberation war – armed Zimbabwe People's Revolutionary Army (ZIPRA) and Zimbabwe African National Liberation Army (ZANLA) cadres fighting for independence in your village with your support? How many of these cadres were white? Why not? Mr White Liberal, don't tell me that you were opposed to the Unilateral Declaration of Independence (UDI), that you were deported by Smith or that you supported sanctions against the white regime! Did you pick up a gun and shoot white racist Rhodesian soldiers in order to bring political independence and economic justice for Africans? Were you prepared to bleed for Africans and were you prepared to kill your own kind in pursuit of equal rights?

If today was 1972 would you do it? Would you join ZIPRA and ZANLA guerrillas in the war against Ian Smith? Would you even support the armed struggle? I deliberately did not define what I mean by white liberal. Now you know what questions to ask yourself and tell us whether you are a white liberal. A radical and revolutionary white person would pick up a gun and shoot his racist brother or sister to set Africans free. If you cannot pick up that gun you are either a racist or a white liberal also known as a double-talking racist, who says what he does not mean, and means what he does not say. Joe Slovo is an example of a white South African who picked up a gun to free Africans. John Brown did the same in the United States. How many white Zimbabweans are in the tradition of these heroic whites? Now, you can tell me how many good white folks we have in Zimbabwe.

By the way, there is nothing unique about the use of force in African liberation struggles. Everybody else uses force all the time. Violence is an indispensable tool in most human struggles. The American Revolution was bloody, the French Revolution was bloody and the Russian Revolution was bloody. Hitler was stopped by violence in 1945 and Saddam was pushed back by force in 1990. Back to 1996: What if it is necessary to use force to get our land back in Zimbabwe – how many white folks will go along with the programme? Why not? Given their history of not participating in active physical combat (on our side) during the struggle for independence, why should we take them seriously now? Please talk to me.

In conclusion, what is the take-home message? To Africans: Involve white liberals in your platforms or struggles if you want to. What is critical is to understand the benefits and problems that arise. In particular, always be wary of the pitfalls and consciously work out strategies to minimise their effects. It is important to understand the history of the problem being addressed, the vested interests involved and how the different groups have struggled in the past. A page of history is worth 10 volumes of logic. The bottom line is that we should be the masters of our own destiny. To white folks, Africans do not need assistance or sympathy from anyone who does not walk the talk. On matters where race is the subjective condition, if you are sincere and revolutionary, it is imperative that you commit financial and economic suicide in order for the African condition to be resolved. If you do not, the struggle will continue in spite of you. If you are not part of the solution, you are part of the problem. You will be blasted into oblivion. Africans will get what is rightfully theirs with or without the support of white people.

The struggle continues!

(Fanon, 1963) (Gandhi, 1927) (Biko, 1979) (Malcolm X, 1965) (Newton, 1973) (Jackson, 1972)

37 The state of the African continent: An imperative agenda

In the United States, as part of my thought leadership tour of duty, I give special attention to African students on US campuses. My primary motivation is to keep them connected to the African continent's agenda. I speak primarily at events organised by African student associations at Ivy League schools and Historically Black Colleges and Universities (HBCUs). I give one such address on 26 April 1999, as the keynote speaker at Stanford University during African Students' Week.

Thank you very much for coming. The topic of my discussion here today is: *The state of the African continent: An imperative agenda*. What we are trying to do today is to look at Africa and understand what is going wrong in Africa, where we have gone wrong as Africans on the continent and then try to pick up some lessons. Of course, thereafter we seek to identify possible solutions, paradigm shifts and strategies that we can deploy to make a difference on the continent. I must emphasise that this is neither a feel-good meeting nor a self-congratulatory platform. So, if you came here for some uncritical and self-indulgent programme where Africa is celebrated and touted, in pursuit of a feel-good effect, then I apologise. This is not that kind of show. You are in the wrong meeting. This is not a feel-good meeting. Here we are going to have a no-holds-barred discussion about Africa. What is going wrong in Africa? Where has Africa been? What can we do to redeem the situation in Africa? Furthermore, we need to proffer solutions; plausible and creative interventions to redeem the continent. What can we do as Africans, residing outside Africa, the African diaspora? How about those working in academia, industry, the public sector and global institutions; what can they do?

I will state up front some of the problems bedevilling the continent, to give you a flavour of what I am going to talk about, as we assess what is going wrong in Africa and what we can do about it. Armed conflict is a key issue. Africa is in a state of war right now. There are armed conflicts within countries, internal rebellions within African countries. In addition, there are inter-country conflicts, that is, wars between African countries. Africa is a war zone in the year 1999. The second challenge is the absence of political democracy. There is no political democracy in the majority of African countries. Democratic institutions are weak, while the requisite democratic culture and value systems are missing. What is the status of governance? In some cases, it is the military government or dictatorship, following a coup d'état against a civilian authority. In extreme instances, there is a coup d'état after coup d'état. Political dictatorships, de facto one-party states, and de jure one-party states characterise the political terrain on the continent. The absence of political democracy is a major problem confronting the continent.

The third matter of concern is the economic collapse, economic chaos and abject poverty. Africans are going through economic crises right now. The economic indicators such as GDP per capita, employment levels, access to health and education services, and general quality of life, tell a disturbing and disconcerting story. African economies are not vibrant. Africans are poor villagers in the global economy. Economic chaos, economic decay, and abject poverty are rampant on the African continent. That is our problem number three.

Problem number four is about leadership. There is a dearth of leadership on the continent, which has morphed into a leadership crisis. What is the calibre and quality of leaders we have in Africa in the year 1999? The calibre and quality of our leaders on the continent today leave a lot to be desired. What can we do to redeem the situation? What is the calibre of leaders that we would want to see in control on the African continent? What characteristics would we want to see in our African leaders? There is also a lack of co-operation between countries, which ties in with the whole sorry situation where some countries are actually waging wars against each other. Even if there are no wars between countries, there is no effective co-operation between countries. There is better communication between Harare and London, Algiers and Paris than there is between Algiers and Harare. Francophone countries are more connected with Paris than they are with other African countries up North and to the West. What degree of co-operation and trade do we have in Africa between countries? We do not have enough economic co-operation. There is not enough intra-Africa trade. That's the problem that we are going to look at.

Economic empowerment is central. Apartheid was an economic system. Don't tell me that apartheid ended in 1994. What shallow mindedness of us as Africans to be celebrating the end of apartheid, when it is still intact except for the name! Apartheid was about white people on top and black people at the bottom. It was about economics in Southern Africa in general, and South Africa in particular. Therefore, what we managed to get in 1994 was political independence but not economic independence. Consequently, on the African continent we have a problem of lack of economic empowerment where Africans are the have-nots. Africans are landless. When they obtained independence, they were given the crown and the whites kept the jewels. Political independence is meaningless without economic power. The crucial land question has not been resolved in South Africa, Zimbabwe, Namibia and Kenya. In fact, in most of the African countries, land dispossession was a key part of colonisation, and constituted the main grievance behind the liberation struggles on the continent.

Land is the source and foundation of all economic activities, be it agriculture, mining, commerce or industry. Colonialism was about economics. Colonialism was about land. Apartheid was an economic system. So the Africans on the continent have a problem where they have the political power to sloganeer but they don't have the economic power to provide employment or ownership of businesses, and deliver social services such as health and education. They cannot provide land to the landless and land-hungry indigenous Africans. There is an issue of economic empowerment of Africans, where what we gained after independence was political independence and never economic independence. A minority class of whites resident in Africa – in cahoots with Western monopolistic capitalism driven from the world financial centres such as New York, London, Paris and Tokyo – dominates and controls African economies. The African governments and their few elites constitute the comprador bourgeoisie, the client class of imperialism, whose primary function is to enable and facilitate the continued economic exploitation and subjugation of the generality of the African people by white monopoly capital.

Land, labour and capital in South Africa are controlled by the minority whites who constitute less than 10 per cent of the population. This privileged minority own more than 90 per cent of the economy, in particular land. These disparities and inequities create many other problems. There is a need for economic empowerment. The matter of the gulf between the haves and have-nots must be addressed. However, who and where are our dreamers today? Where are our big ideas for the economic development of Africa? Today we live in the do-nothing years. There are no African revolutionaries. There is no revolution. There are no struggles, marches or big debates. Where is the construction of redemptive knowledge and narratives? In which platforms, literature or media are we defining ourselves as Africans? Are we writing our own history, or we are still the literary subject matter for other cultures? What are our intellectual, philosophical and historiographical contributions today, in the year 1999? What are our significant additions to literature, arts and science? Indeed, these are the do-nothing years!

The Africans on the continent have not gone as far as they should in terms of jumping onto the information superhighway and taking care of business in the global economy. Technology is a weapon that we can use to empower ourselves in Africa and we are not doing enough in terms of getting connected on the information superhighway. So, the lack of progress in technology uptake is a major problem on the continent. And then, let's talk about women's rights and gender justice. What's happened to our women on the African continent? Do we not oppress our women in some of our cultural practices in Africa? Culture is dynamic. As we live African cultural traditions and practices, there is a case for both continuity and change. Where change is necessary, let us be brave enough to act accordingly. However, don't change your African culture to please or satisfy white people, the white-controlled United States or their European cousins. Change it for yourselves and your communities and for the advancement of your collective interests. The rationale for change or continuity has to be internally driven and not exogenous. For example, we can change certain cultural practices, in order to empower African women, respect their rights, and affirm their equality to men in every respect. The motivation and drive for the transformation has to be ours, as Africans, as black people. It is wrong to be overly defensive and uncritical about certain retrogressive African cultural practices. As long as we are in charge of the review process, let us be courageous, confront the weaknesses of our cultural practices and fashion change. We need to revisit our cultures and our norms in Africa to see whether we are achieving justice, in terms of gender equality and women's rights on the continent. In Zimbabwe, we have just had a situation whereby the Supreme Court has basically undermined the rights of women by declaring that women can never be equal to men. The most a woman can be is a junior man. The Supreme Court in Zimbabwe voted five judges against one for such a proposition. What a travesty of justice.

Another area of significant interest is around the issue of our values. We have internalised the worst elements of our oppressors' value system. These include obsession with power and control, crass materialism, addiction to alcohol and drugs, inordinate obsession with sex, inefficiency and corruption. What black African leaders are doing to their own people on the continent, is a terrible indictment of all of us. They are abusing, oppressing and disempowering their own. This is supposed to be what white people do to black people, not black on black. We are victimising our own because we have internalised the worst characteristics of our colonisers. It is also called self-hatred. Then there is this notion of poor timekeeping, which is prevalent even among Africans at a prestigious institution such as Stanford University. To hell with this nonsense about coloured people time, so-called *CP time*. Out also with, 'There is no hurry in Africa'. Instead, in fact, we should be rushing in Africa because we are behind in many respects and consequently there must guarded hurry in Africa.

Furthermore, we should not abuse and leverage the worst elements of our culture. For instance, when we are in trouble as a corrupt bureaucracy, an incorrigible one-party state, or incompetent dictatorship, we sometimes say, 'We cannot have two cocks in the same chicken run. You cannot have two bulls in the same kraal. In our culture, we have one chief who rules until death.' So, you are using African culture to legitimise your corrupt one-person dictatorship. If we are so attached to African norms, customs and traditions, why do we use, in our courts and Parliament, those gowns and those wigs from England? In fact, they have since stopped using these relics over there, but we stick to them. Colonial nostalgia perhaps! If we are African as we claim, why then do we aspire to Western lifestyles and creature comforts? The deadly temptation here is that Africans have conserved and kept the worst elements of our culture, while imbibing lock, stock and barrel the worst aspects from the culture of our colonisers and oppressors. We need to work on these values and see what's going on.

Now what is going on in terms of the wars? As I previously stated, Africa is in a state of war. The major war that is going on right now in Africa is the war in the Democratic Republic of Congo (DRC). At least six countries are involved in that conflict on one side or the other. This is a major problem in Africa because we have very limited resources to start with and those are being consumed by this war. Just in terms of background, the war in the DRC started sometime in August 1998 after Laurent Kabila came to power. There was a disagreement and fallout with Kabila's backers, President Paul Kagame of Rwanda and President Yoweri Museveni of Uganda. They decided to move in and invade the DRC. Then Zimbabwe, Angola and Namibia intervened on the side of Kabila. Right now, there is a war that is going on in the DRC. I am not going to go into the details of this war because it's a topic that is going to be addressed by the Zimbabwean journalist, Newton Kanhema. However, that war – as far as I am concerned, for the purposes of my presentation here – is symptomatic of our problems in Africa.

Yes, we have differences. Yes, there are borders that were created by the colonial masters, but can we not amicably resolve the matters internally among Africans? I appeal to the African in Museveni, the African in Mugabe, and the African in Kagame, to realise that we have a lot to lose in a war among Africans. In any case, in the Western world who cares about Africans killing each other? Today there is a war in Kosovo. Why are Western powers in Kosovo? It is because they are trying to prevent a humanitarian catastrophe among white communities. How many people are being killed in Serbia, in Yugoslavia versus those in Rwanda or DRC? But what we need to realise in Africa today, in the year 1999, is that black lives are not as important as white lives. You don't expect the US government to give a hoot about African lives in the DRC, Rwanda, Eritrea or Ethiopia. They don't care about that unless you and I care about it. The United States and its allies are going to intervene in Europe because those are white lives being lost. The people who are being killed look like them, so they intervene. Unless you and I take care of business on the African continent, no one is going to. We are not white; hence we are on our own.

Now it is sad that we have six belligerent countries at war in the DRC. There is a war over there in Ethiopia, the border conflict between Ethiopia and Eritrea. As Africans, we must take charge of our lives. Why the border conflicts? Because of the colonial organisation of Africa during the Berlin Conference of 1884 – that's why. It is very important that we put a little context. I am not letting the colonial masters off the hook. They are historically responsible. Yes, colonialism is responsible for sowing the seeds of discontent. But this is 1999. We are responsible today and in charge. We must take ownership of our problems. There is a need for personal agency. In 1999, we Africans are cultivating those seeds and reaping the fruits. You and I have a duty and obligation to work against the seed sown by colonialism in 1884 at the Berlin Conference, the artificial boundaries, the divide and rule, Tutsi versus Hutus, and Zulu versus Xhosa. Yes, historically, the Belgians were involved, so were the French and the English, but today we have Africans in charge of events – Kagame in Rwanda, Museveni in Uganda, Mugabe in Zimbabwe, and Mandela in South Africa. Can't we as Africans realise that it's not in our interest to fight this war? We don't have to love each other. We only need to tolerate our differences and realise that there is a bigger enemy facing all of us. Our individual conflicts and differences on the African continent should be overshadowed by this greater external threat.

Right now, in Rwanda, people are on trial for the genocide in 1994 and we have a crisis in Rwanda because you have the minority Tutsi in charge. The Tutsis are concerned about their own security while at the same time the Hutus want democracy. Now the democratic issue of the Hutus cannot be satisfied at the same time as the security issues of the Tutsis. The issue is to balance the interests between security for the Tutsis on the one hand and democracy for the Hutus on the other. These are the challenges that we have. They are not insurmountable. This can be solved except for lack of will power!

Now, we need to look at what happened in Mozambique after the war with Alfonso Dhlakama and the resolution of that conflict. Let us pick up lessons. Can Angola learn from that experience, so that they solve the issues with Savimbi? Can the DRC and Rwanda learn from the experiences in Zimbabwe? We had armed conflict in Matabeleland, during the period 1982 to 1987. Right now, there is no active civil war in Zimbabwe. It was resolved. Somalia right now does not have a national government. Can you imagine a country with no national government? That is the state of some countries on the African continent. There is no government in Somalia, only warlords. So how do you manage an economy without a national government? That is the dilemma of the African continent in 1999. In Sudan, there is some progress; Al-Bashir has indicated that he is prepared for secession and to partition the country. The people of South Sudan can go free. The war has been going on for so long. He says it is better to have two separate nations that are prosperous than a united country which is in continuous conflict.

The issue of slaves in Sudan is also of concern. I know we are very defensive about slavery because, as black people, we have been the victims of major slavery activity but, in 1999, we need to accept the fact that in Sudan there are black people who are enslaving black people. If you looked at *The New York Times* yesterday, there was an article about somebody who went out there and was able to buy 300 slaves at 50 dollars each. That 50 dollars in Sudan buys two goats. For the price of two goats, he was able to buy a human being in Africa. We need to stop being defensive and resolve these issues. If there is slavery going on in Sudan, we as Africans have a duty and obligation to face up to the situation and do something about it.

However, there is a danger of revisionism because of the Sudan slavery: 'Africans are the criminals when it comes to the whole bigger project of slavery in history.' Really? Yes, we are always participants. In the big enterprise of the transatlantic and triangular slave trade, whites were the ones carrying out slavery. There is no organised international slavery today, nothing like a slave triangle going on right now. The history of the slave trade should not be re-written by the situation in Sudan. Slavery was about Europe coming to Africa to get slaves back to the United States, to build their country. So the criminals, as far as the slave trade is concerned, are the white citizens of the United States. But we have been participants. We are guilty as charged. We participated in the slave trade by getting the beads, getting the mirrors, helping in the capturing of our brothers. But we were not the creators of the slave trade. We were participants in the slave trade, but we are not the creators of that problem. Nonetheless, let us solve the problem of slavery in Sudan. Let us not be defensive.

There is a tendency to try to make the criminals look like the victims and the victims look like the criminals. US Assistant Secretary of State, Susan Rice, on a trip to Africa with President Clinton, said, 'We cannot apologise for slavery where there were buyers and sellers.' I don't agree with that. If you say there were buyers and sellers, you are assuming that the buyers and the sellers have the same status, the same blameworthiness. You are assuming they are morally equivalent. Where is the evidence of the money made on slaves by Africans? I can show you the product of slave labour in this country. The United States was built by slave labour. Everything you see in here, starting from universities and the White House, is a product of slave labour. But when I go to Africa I don't see the structure built by the beads. I don't see structures built by the mirrors given to my ancestors. Yes, they were participants but they were not the creators of the problem. So, we need to keep it in context.

On political democracy, what we need in Africa are strong institutions rooted in a democratic value system. Institution building has not been done well in Africa. South Africa is an example of a good effort. We need strong functional separation of powers in Africa, between the Judiciary, the Executive and the Legislature. South Africa has done well in terms of establishing those three entities. The United States, with all its flaws, has a very good document, which is the US Constitution, which is going through several changes. However, at this point in 1999, I feel black people are second-class citizens. I do not romanticise the US project at all, but I do appreciate their foundational document.

Institutions are the starting point and then we have to inculcate, in ourselves and in our societies, support for multiparty democratic systems that tolerate and cherish dissent. You should believe in the right to free expression, precisely for the views that you disagree with. What's the point of having freedom of expression if you were to always agree with the other person? So, freedom of expression should be defended primarily for those views we don't agree with. Those views we do not like and do not agree with, are the ones whose expression we must protect and defend the most.

Once we have strong institutions then we must respect them. It is pointless to have a strong constitution when you don't have respect for it. That's why the issue of leaders is central. What is the calibre of our leaders? What are the values of our leaders? We want leaders who put society and collective interest before individual interest, and advance collective progress ahead of personal ambition. If we can change the values of our society, change the values of our people, then this functional separation of institutions can make sense. We need new enabling and empowering values. We need to start with the institutions and, on this, South Africa has done reasonably well. We need to see leaders who put tenure time limits on themselves and say: I have made my contribution, it's time to retire. Term limits are important. We need to see term limits within these country constitutions. We do not want people who have tenure for life. We should be dependent on institutions, not personalities. People come and go but systems always live on; that's why this US democracy is very strong because since 1776, they have had a good document. And presidents do come and go, senators do come and go, but the system remains. What kind of systems do we need to have in place? We need to have good systems in place and we need leaders who value technology, leaders who understand the importance of the information superhighway in 1999, and of course leaders who walk the constitutional talk.

Why? Because we are now in the global economy and if you do not have access to the internet you are basically disconnected from the global economy. Most Africans on the African continent and in the United States are disconnected from the information superhighway. Now if you are disconnected like that you are going to be a poor villager in the global village and you and I have an obligation to ensure that we maximally utilise technology for the betterment of our people. We can make progress if we take advantage of technology and use it as an instrument of the struggle for our survival. All these are issues that we need to talk about.

We need to address all our problems, share best practice and learn from each other. Mistakes are made but there is a need to think of African solutions and say let's sit and plan together. Museveni has done a good job on AIDS. About five or six years ago, Uganda was the epicentre of the AIDS crisis; and Museveni has done well to rebuild Uganda from the shambles of Idi Amin, from the shambles of Milton Obote, to a country that is fairly respectable on the African continent. Yes, it was with the support of the IMF, with support from the US and the World Bank. But he has done something for his own people and he has done well on AIDS. What can the other African countries learn from Uganda? Zimbabwe, my country, is now the epicentre of AIDS. Can they learn from Uganda?

I am not saying be perfect. Failure leads to success and lessons picked up from failed attempts are instructive. However, make new mistakes. There is no rational or moral reason why you should be making the same mistakes that Kwame Nkrumah made in the 1960s. We should be making progress and moving to the next level, after learning from the failures and successes of other African efforts. So Frederick Chiluba today does not seem to have learned from the mistakes of Kaunda. Why does he want a third term, and why is he harassing Kenneth Kaunda? However, we can use Zambia as an example of a smooth transition of power. In Malawi, Kamuzu Banda was defeated after a long time and then left without force. Julius Nyerere is a good example. I know Nyerere messed up his own country. I know Tanzania is one of the poorest countries in Africa. But I think we need to respect the old man for giving up power without force. I know it was after 20 to 30 years, but at least it's a good example that Africans can give up power without being shot, without force. Mandela is a good example. Mandela is better because it's only been five years. That is a better example but still we are trying to learn from very poor examples here. If Mugabe in Zimbabwe could learn from Nyerere, could learn from Mandela, could learn from Quett Masire in Botswana and give up power without being driven out by bullets, then Africa could start having progress. I know coups d'état are being linked with the West.

Mandela is in power today because of uMkhonto we Sizwe (MK), the ANC, and the Freedom Charter. Picking up the gun and shooting the oppressors to get freedom is what produced Mandela. He is president today, because of Castro, Gaddafi, China and Russia. He is not there because of Uncle Sam. The United States does not love Africans. They don't want us. Don't buy the nonsense about the Washington Consensus. If the United States was our friend, when we were fighting for freedom in Zimbabwe through ZIPRA and ZANLA and in South Africa, through MK and APLA, how come it never supported our liberation armies? How many guns did you get from Uncle Sam? How many guns did we get from Stanford University? Instead of disrespecting our enemies we are now disrespecting our friends. Castro gave us guns to fight our enemies. China gave us guns to fight for our freedom. Muammar Gaddafi gave us guns to fight for our freedom. That's why I respect Mandela defending his friendship and relationship with Gaddafi and Castro. There would be no Mandela without Castro. There would be no Mandela without Gaddafi. There would be no Mandela without the Soviet Union. I hope the United States, Europe and white people, in general, understand this.

I don't glorify these people. They have made mistakes in their own countries. But I am simply saying that, as an African, I owe Uncle Sam nothing, because Uncle Sam, the United States, was supporting apartheid under constructive engagement. The US government did not support the liberation struggles in Africa; more specifically they actually opposed the struggle for freedom against the apartheid regime. In fact, when Mandela was arrested in 1962, it was the United States' CIA that gave the necessary intelligence about Mandela's whereabouts to the South African police. So now that South Africa is free and investors are coming in from all over the world, the United States wants to appear like the best friend of South Africans. That is ahistorical and shameful. We also hear about the Washington Consensus and their prescriptions. Now what I am saying is that, in South Africa, we need to make sure that the issue of the haves and the have-nots is addressed. The people in Soweto, the landless, the unemployed, the unemployable, and the lost generation in South Africa, they must all be attended to. Mandela and the ANC should be concerned about the people who fought for independence in South Africa, the people who fought for him when he was in prison for 27 years. To hell with the hypocritical Johnnie-come-latelies from the white world.

In South Africa, there is this talk of 'take government off the people's back'. We want a small government and yet under apartheid we had a huge government serving white people in South Africa. What is wrong with using the government to level the playing field? What's wrong with using the government to economically empower South Africa? We need social justice, levelling the playing field and affirmative action in South Africa. The free markets don't build that, privatisation doesn't give you that. But yes, markets and privatisation can be used to create inclusive African businesses and empower the historically disadvantaged. What I am afraid of is that we should never be driven by the money alone. The profit will not deliver social justice. We should not be slaves to market forces. We should not be slaves to the dollar signs. We should use free markets to free our people from poverty, and create economic prosperity for all Africans globally. And South Africa is a good example of where free markets are perpetuating differences between the haves and the have-nots. My challenge to us as Africans is: Can we use free markets to level the playing field? If not, what are the alternatives?

The Europeans are realising that they are a larger market, and that they are a stronger force in the world. In the global economy, the larger the market is, the stronger you are as a force. So, Africans need to co-operate with each other in terms of building communities and markets in Africa; COMESA, an enlarged COMESA where you have SADC and the Great Lakes area – Uganda, Tanzania, Rwanda – co-operating and working together in a community; maybe they can start with trading with each other, then you can talk about common passbooks, then you can talk about common currency. People are a resource, the more people you have in a market, the stronger the market. And also, the African context is rich in terms of resources, fresh water, agricultural resources and minerals. All these are resources that we can tap to our benefit and by co-operating and trading with each other, we can actually make sure that we are recycling our resources and our dollars within the African economy. So we need to strengthen and think super national. Think big, think African. Why? Because, if we think in terms of Africa as a continent, we are talking about 800 million people. If you talk about Africans throughout the world, maybe 1.2 billion. Look at the Chinese; the Chinese have about 1.5 billion people and the Chinese in the United States are thinking about China, the Chinese in Europe are thinking about China and China today is a force to be reckoned with. I saw the Prime Minister came two weeks ago and had a meeting with Bill Clinton. It's not because the United States loves the Chinese; they have to deal with the Chinese. Why? Because number one, the Chinese are a large market of about 1.5 billion. Number two, the Chinese have a nuclear bomb, so the United States wants to make sure China is on its side. Power recognises power. Power respects power. Game recognises game.

Nobody is going to respect us as Africans in the United States or as African Americans, as long as the Hutus and Tutsis are killing each other as shown on TV. Nobody is going to respect you from South Africa or Zimbabwe, if there are conflicts and problems we have in the ghettos of the United States. The poverty dislocations, and black-on-black violence in the African-American communities reflect negatively on the African continent and its people. My charge is for a total solidarity of people of African descent – the Africans in the Caribbean, the Africans in the United States, and the Africans on the continent – so that we can become a world force and we will be like the Chinese. Let's have Africa in our hearts. The African Americans should be thinking about Africa and building bridges with Africa, organic bridges with Africa, taking their skills from the United States to Africa, taking their resources to Africa and we in Africa should be tying the knot with our brothers in the United States. Look at the solidarity and focus within the global Jewish diaspora.

The Jews in the United States, they are on Wall Street, they are in the US Government. They run and own big corporates. They are in charge of Hollywood. While doing all this, they keep Israel on their mind. Israel gets the largest portion of US aid and it disproportionately influences US foreign policy. Why? Because the Jews in the United States are a powerful force and they are looking out for Israel's interests. Why can't the African Americans and Africans in general learn from the Jewish example? No, the Africans are not thinking about Africa at all. Uncle Tom Jesse Jackson, when the United States was busy sending missiles into Sudan, what did he do? He was busy consoling Chelsea and Hillary over the philandering sick man called Bill Clinton. This is sick. Why would an African care about Bill Clinton and forget about these missiles going into Sudan? The United States is firing in missiles, killing children, killing women in Sudan and you are busy consoling Chelsea, who is a student here at Stanford by the way, and Hillary. Sick! And in any case, right now if you think about it, according to Trent Lott, these bombs that went into Sudan, it wasn't a military send-off. Trent Lott is a Republican and I quote him, 'That was not a military target'.

What can I do to bring some business into Africa? You should ask yourself that question. In 1999, there is still a strong case of Pan-Africanism; the Africans born in the United States, the Africans born on the continent, the Africans in the Islands, all have a duty and obligation to identify with Africa. Hence, we rise up and become a world power because we have about 1.2 billion Africans throughout the world and we can become a force and be respected, not out of love or out of some humanity but because when you become a force to be reckoned with economically, socially and militarily, then you can be respected. That's why we need to think about, for example, the nuclear weapons in South Africa.

What happened towards 1990, when South Africa was developing a nuclear weapon, a nuclear facility, and the United States had no problem with it? Why in 1990? But come 1993, actually after Mandela came out of prison and we were heading towards an ANC government, what happened? Then they were worried because they did not want an African government headed by an African leader to have a nuclear weapon. So, what did they do? They quickly sponsored the destruction of that facility and in some cases, some of the resources were given to the Chinese. If nuclear power is good for the United States, France, Britain and China, surely it must be good for Africa too. What do these world powers use it for? As a deterrent. Well, African countries need a deterrent too. Pure and simple. What is good for the goose must be good for the gander. I want to use it as a deterrent too. In fact, Pakistan and India now have nuclear weapons. They are doing fine in global geo-politics. Do you think if Milosevic had a nuclear bomb they would be bombing Serbia right now? They wouldn't be doing that because no one wins in a nuclear war situation. So once countries have nuclear weapons, they apply restraint and negotiate.

Power recognises power, and game recognises game. It is total unadulterated racism and hypocrisy for the United States to support South Africa and Israel to build nuclear weapons in South Africa under a white regime and then stop it when Mandela and his team get into office. This was just to stop nuclear weapons from being under a black African government. I don't believe in the notion of a rogue nation. We are scared these nuclear weapons will get into the hands of a rogue nation. The biggest rogue nation is the United States. Who gave arms to Saddam Hussein? Who gave arms to Mobutu Sese Seko? Who armed Noriega? Who killed the Black Panther Party here in the United States led by people like Bobby Seale, Kathleen Cleaver, Elaine Brown, who were in the tradition of Malcolm X? What happened to the Black Liberation Army? Why are there black political prisoners in the United States today if Uncle Sam loves us? Mutulu Shakur, Mumia Abu-Jamal, Assata Shakur is in exile in Cuba. Uncle Sam doesn't give a damn about black people in the United States and in Africa. So, when US government officials come to Africa, ask them, 'Why do you have a disproportionate number of black people in prison? Why do you have political prisoners, and prisoners of war, in this great democracy called the United States?'

As you talk about genocide in Kosovo, talk about genocide in the United States. One third of young black males in the United States are either in prison, on parole or probation. The penitentiary is black and yet the United States is only 12 per cent black, why? And once you get into prison they take away your voting rights, and other human rights. What I am saying to you as Africans is, don't take this American dream too seriously. There are problems for black people in the United States. Also, if we could realise that we are under attack in Europe from ourselves and from other people, and then we can get together and become a force. So, let's learn from the Chinese, let's learn from the Indians – Indians in the United States are embracing technology. Right now, there are Indian companies that are actually solving the Y2K problem.

They are importing labour to the United States to solve the Y2K problem – Indians are doing that. The Chinese are kicking butt, while we are just sitting down passively as Africans in the United States. By the way that is the correct term, 'Africans in the United States', not this meaningless fiction-inspired diction that says 'African American'. The Chinese, the Indians and the Jews are making moves while we are hooked to corruption, inefficiency, incompetence and self-pity even. We need to rise up and become a force to be reckoned with.

There are limitations to how you can use free markets and capitalism as a weapon of struggle, otherwise it will simply exacerbate the difference between the haves and the have-nots. We need to emphasise non-market values like community, collective economics, peace, love, self-respect and decency. These non-market values are important, in fact they are some of our values as Africans. If you go to Africa, you will find we had a lot of non-market values, a sense of community – it takes a village to raise a child, that's an African phenomenon, plagiarised by Hillary Clinton.

Now, all these values were our values and we have kept the negative ones and we are busy imbibing the worst elements from the oppressor. We need values like a work ethic. It's important that we work hard as students, work hard as professionals, and work hard as leaders in Africa. Efficiency is important. Sacrifice! These are non-market values that we tend to take for granted and don't give much respect to. We need to set up conflict resolution strategies. How can we make sure that we actually do peace-making, peacekeeping and conflict resolution, conflict prevention? Sometime you can even do conflict management, because conflict is a way of life.

The United States is a strong country because it's a large country that is prosperous. So, the larger the market, the more powerful a country becomes and we need to be co-operative at the minimum and trade with each other to move on to the next level. We need to learn from the lessons of other people who struggled. We need to get good ideas and practices from revolutionaries like Chairman Mao. We need to learn from Che Guevara. Che was an Argentinean who fought in Cuba and brought about revolution in Cuba and left Cuba and fought in the Congo and met up with my friend Laurent Kabila and wasn't impressed by Kabila – no wonder we have all these problems with Kabila in the DRC. From Congo, he went to Bolivia and was killed by the CIA. This is an example of the sacrifice I am talking about. He was a medical doctor; he didn't have to fight globally, he could just become a medical doctor but he decided to fight for freedom in Cuba, fight in Africa for freedom, fight in Bolivia and he got killed in 1967. That is the calibre and quality of a human being I am looking at. But let's not forget our own heroes like Patrice Lumumba and Frantz Fanon, who were great writers and thinkers who came from Africa and made a difference. There are other heroes, like Kwame Nkrumah at one point, and people like Du Bois, who was, to some extent, the father of Pan-Africanism. Africans should learn from Africans from all over the world. Learn about Mandela's perseverance, for example.

COINTELPRO was a systematic programme established by the FBI under J. Edgar Hoover and Bill Samuel to destroy black organisations and leaders – people like Martin Luther King, Malcolm X, and the Black Liberation Army. These are experiences of the struggle that we need to look at in history and learn from their experiences and activities. You won't be taught at Stanford University about the Black Panther Party, Black Liberation Army or that we have political prisoners – because it's not in their interests, those interests which established the school. Why would they teach you about it? If they are sincere, we should have a meeting here where we bring Geronimo Pratt, where he can talk to you about political prisoners. He can talk about Mutulu Shakur, Mumia Abu-Jamal and so on – these are Africans in the United States under fire, Africans in the United States who are struggling. We should learn from that and move on.

Our approach and view about religion must be critical and questioning. I know we had a prayer in the beginning of the presentation, but I want to be very cautious and critical about religion. Religion has been used as a weapon against black people. When the coloniser came, they had the Maxim gun and the Bible. You have to be very careful, because religion can be used to pacify you. You must instead get involved in liberation theology, where when you see Jesus Christ, you see a guerrilla fighter. By definition, a Christian should be a revolutionary. What is the colour of Jesus when you look at the 12 Apostles in that picture in your house? What do they all look like? They are white. So, you are not represented. What a pity. Was it just an oversight?

Religion must reflect your culture. Religion must reflect your values and your way of life. Religion should be about you. Every time somebody gives you a God and that God doesn't look like you, give them back their God. 'Ah! You know the colour of Jesus doesn't matter!' they try wiggle out. Really? Ok, if it doesn't matter, make him black then. 'Ah! There is no colour, anyway God has no colour.' You are also trying to rationalise your conflicted self. You are being foolish. You need to stop and think. You have been had. Either you have been duped or you are trying to dupe me. How can you say God has no colour? If the son is white, logic says the father is white too. And if colour doesn't matter, why do we find the notion of a black Jesus unacceptable? What I am simply saying is religion can be used to subjugate and pacify black people. Proceed with care.

Then we call African traditional healers witchdoctors. How can you have a witch and a doctor in the same word? It is an oxymoron. They are traditional healers – African traditional doctors. There is no difference between believing in the virgin birth and believing in a spirit medium. It's all about faith. So why would you want to patronise Africans and tell them that if they believe in the spirit medium, they are pagans when people believe in the virgin birth? Some Christians believe in the power of incense burning. All Christians believe in the power of prayer. Why are these unscientific European beliefs acceptable, and yet those of Africans are not? It is all about faith. It is the same difference. There is no superior or inferior religion. They are all the same. They must be accorded equality culturally, socially, intellectually and legally.

African culture is very important. We must have our own culture, names, religions and national attire. Just because I am not donning an African gown here doesn't mean that I don't believe that the African dress is very important. African names and languages are very important, they give us identity. However, we must clearly understand that all these symbols constitute a necessary, but not sufficient, condition for the African revolution to a peaceful, prosperous and democratic continent. It's not enough to put on an African dress and look African. It is not enough to have an African name like Mobutu Sese Seko or Kweku Appiah. Mobutu Sese Seko is a very African name, but Mobutu was one of the worst enemies of Africa. Then there was Sani Abacha, who used to don African attire while destroying Nigeria. It is not enough to don an African dress, and have a beautiful African name like Savimbi. It is not enough for you to speak an African language. You need to think like an informed, conscious and liberated African, address Africa's challenges, and put Africa at the centre of your worldview, strategic decisions and actions. That is the most important African attire and African name you can give yourself. That is the indigenous African language you should speak. This is what it means to be an African.

I want to emphasise the notion of mis-education. You think because you have a PhD from Oxford, then you are educated? No, you are not. You are not educated. What the school system gives you is that which makes you a mis-educated Negro, a mis-educated African. When you get a PhD from Stanford, MIT, or Harvard, all that you are is a mis-educated Negro or African. Education is that which you give yourself outside the classroom while at Stanford. The white universities are not going to teach you about self-love, self-respect and self-awareness. They are not going to teach you proper African and black history. How can a white supremacist teach you your own history? Given the history of slavery, the history of colonialism and the white supremacist ideology, intellectually, the African is on his own. How can you expect the school system to teach you about Lumumba, Che Guevara, the Black Panther Party and the Black Liberation Army?

Go beyond the classroom and feed your mind. Get intellectual empowerment. I am advancing the case for both academic excellence and social responsibility. Self-education is critical, because there is no such thing as universal knowledge, there is no such thing as universal philosophy. When Europeans say that this is a universal idea or universal sociology, they are patronising. Read Marimba Ani's seminal book *Yurugu: An African-Centered Critique of European Cultural Thought and Behaviour.* The book removes the mask from the European facade and thereby reveals the inner workings of global white supremacy: a system which functions to guarantee the control of Europe and her descendants over the majority of the world's peoples. You need to read broadly beyond the classroom.

Read Martin Bernal's great scholarly book *Black Athena: The Afro-Asiatic Roots of Classical Civilization*. He discusses ancient Greece in a new light. Bernal's thesis discusses the perception of ancient Greece in relation to Greece's African and Asiatic neighbours, especially that the ancient black Egyptians and Phoenicians colonised ancient Greece. Bernal argues that there is a denial by Western academia of any significant African and Phoenician influence on Ancient Greek civilisation. He gives a link between Ancient Greece and earlier Egyptian and Phoenician civilisations. Bernal emphasises African elements in Ancient Near Eastern culture and denounces the alleged Eurocentrism. He talks about 'the Western appropriation of ancient Near Eastern culture for the sake of its own development'.

Then there is George James's seminal book, *Stolen Legacy*, in which he argues that Greek philosophy originated in Ancient black Egypt. The ancient Greeks were not the original authors of Greek philosophy which, he argues, was mainly based on ideas and concepts that were borrowed, without acknowledgement, from Ancient black Egyptians. He argues that Alexander the Great 'invaded Egypt and captured the Royal Library at Alexandria and plundered it', that Aristotle's ideas came from these stolen books and that he established his school within the library. Anthony Browder's *Nile Valley Contributions to Civilization* is another great read. It is about exploding the Eurocentric myths about the origins of civilisations. It seeks to correct some of these misconceptions about Nile Valley civilisation in order to understand its role as the parent of future civilisations. Africans gave the world civilisation. If we did it then, why can we not be motivated to succeed now?

The original Egyptians who built the pyramids were black people. They were black Nubians. You want evidence – go into those pyramids in Egypt and do a melanin test. You will find that they were black Nubians. Cheikh Anta Diop did that already in his research for his book *Civilization or Barbarism*. Cheikh Diop is like the god of Egyptology, but they don't promote these ideas because they are anti-establishment. Cheikh Anta Diop was a historian, anthropologist, physicist and politician who studied the human race's origins and pre-colonial African culture.

Another scholar of the philosophy of Negritude is Léopold Sédar Senghor, a Senegalese poet, politician and cultural theorist who for two decades served as President of Senegal. Read his work. Dr John Henrik Clarke was a Pan-Africanist writer, historian, professor and a pioneer in the creation of Africana studies and professional institutions in academia. Then of course, there is the work of Marcus Garvey, Frantz Fanon, Che Guevara, Kwame Nkrumah, Malcolm X, Julius Nyerere, Steve Biko and the Black Panthers. Feed your mind. Get a primer in intellectual self-defence. That is education, not what you get in the classrooms of Stanford. Please familiarise yourself with the work of these great thinkers and revolutionaries.

There is no way you can be taught in the school system how to rebel. If, in 1999, I would want a revolution because the United States is a plantation, do you think Stanford can tell me how to rebel against Uncle Sam? But that is what we need for African Americans in 1999, because the United States is a plantation in the year 1999.

Why would the Arabs in Egypt think they are not part of Africa? It is said, former UN Secretary General Boutros Boutros-Ghali, when he was Egypt's Foreign Minister, once went down to Addis Ababa from Cairo and said, 'It's good to be back in Africa,' as if Egypt is not in Africa. Arabs who are in Africa should identify with Africa or they should move out of Africa. We need African solidarity, we need co-operation and solidarity with the Arabs in Africa and Arabs who are angry with the United States should not be planting bombs in Africa because it's the only place where they can get away with it. By killing Africans in Tanzania and Kenya, do you think you can make a point to Uncle Sam? We need to work on our Arab-African relations because right now we have a lot of problems. The Arabs must understand that the original inhabitants who built the pyramids were black Nubians.

There are various cases of police brutality that demonstrate that the United States is still a plantation for African Americans. You want evidence? Go to New York: Diallo, a black man, received 41 bullets from the police force. Louima, a black man – the police took a toilet plunger and shoved it in his behind and broke his teeth with the soiled plunger. Is that our kind of democracy? Is that justice? What kind of life is this? In Jasper, Texas, two white men dragged another human, a black man, using a truck, until they tore his body apart. He died. In Riverside, California, the police pumped 19 bullets into the body of a young woman. That is the United States for you. I want you as Africans to step back and think. Most of you are happy to be in the United States because you have illusions of the dream. Drop this nonsense of the American dream. It is an American nightmare. Drop this nonsense of, 'I am happy to be here.' You must pick up the struggle in the United States and fight for your African-American brothers and sisters, who are second-class citizens in the United States. They are sitting on a plantation. Identify with them.

The white supremacist ideology is very good at divide and rule. They want to divide the Africans from the continent and the African Americans. 'Oh! You are from Africa. You are very hard-working. You are different from these African Americans. These ones have an attitude. You are different.' Tell them, 'I am not different. This is my brother. This is my sister. It is not possible for you to respect me while you are disrespecting my brothers and sisters!' There is no way you can be respected as an African when the African American is being disrespected. In fact, it goes both ways. There is no way you can be respected as an African American when the African is being disrespected. So, don't believe the hype. You should read the infamous address delivered by a certain William Lynch to an audience of slave owners in Virginia in 1712, when he was advising them on how to control their slaves within the colony. He emphasised divide and rule: 'Pit the old slaves against the young slaves, the dark-skinned against the light-skinned, and the female against the male.' This message of control is as valid today as it was then. White supremacy uses it today. We might have our differences, but let's talk about them. Let us not play into the master's system of control, and in the process, work against our collective African and African-American interests.

As African students, even if you stay here in the United States, make sure that you are going to do something about Africa. Make sure Africa is in your mind. But we need some people to go back, to actually be on the ground and make a difference and create a new dispensation. We also have problems but we need to make sure that if we get our act together, then whoever is our enemy can become less of an enemy. The struggle in Africa demands dedication. There should be no defeat on the agenda in terms of African struggle. The struggle continues unabated. There will be no sell-outs and no compromise. Defeat, I hope, will not be on our agenda tonight, or ever.

Thank you very much for listening to me.

(Nkrumah, 1965) (Biko, 1979) (Guevara, 1961) (Fanon, 1963) (Browder, 1992) (Bernal, 1987) (Diop, 1955) (Gandhi, 1927) (James, 1992)

38 Reflections on US politics, society and culture

In the United States, I immerse myself in the national debates and discussions about politics, economics, society, black struggles, the environment, literature and culture. I communicate my evolving views on these issues with three Rhodes Scholars who are still at Oxford: Cyril Ruwende, Andre Namphy and Trina Williams. From 1995 to 1998, through electronic mail, I share with these three, and a few other colleagues from across the globe, my detailed and extensive reflections. In these pages, I present some of my messages to them, so that a sense of how I am engaging the belly of the beast is manifest. The content ranges from political to social, cultural and personal matters. Interesting antidotes include my views on books, movies, marriage, the Black Panthers, US political events, and my uncanny prediction of the O.J. Simpson verdict.

2 June 1995
Re: Population growth politics

Hi Trina,
How are you doing in Oxford? I am slowly trying to settle in this belly of the beast. Thanks for your note on your conference on population growth politics. Now that is an extremely controversial subject, especially when you consider the so-called Third World countries and proposed policies from the so-called First World. In addition to what you are reading, you have to read some radical critics who do not buy into the conventional wisdom on the subject. For a start, one cannot delink the population issues from economic empowerment, economic self-determination and fair trade between the First and so-called Third World. The reason why the Third World is 'underdeveloped',

in particular Africa, is because of 400 years of slavery, 100 years of colonialism and, currently, neo-colonialism in the form of external economic control by multinational corporations (MNCs) and Western governments in cahoots with local racial minorities or political puppets. This is the major problem in these countries and not some mythical population explosion or bouts of drought. Drought and large families simply exacerbate an already dire situation. In any case, if we solve or do something about the problem of economic disparities, then people in these countries will be well positioned to consider the issue of population growth in their own terms and definitions.

There is a lot of blatant racism and cultural imperialism in the contemporary population control theories. This has led some radical critics to propose a very interesting counter-attack, what I will call here the 'critical population mass theory'. This theory argues that although Western powers (whites) are in charge of the world because of their military, economic and technological supremacy, there is a critical population ratio of Caucasian/non-Caucasian that has to be maintained in order to sustain that control. This, they argue, is the central motivation behind these population-control theories backed by the World Bank and IMF. I know this counter theory might at face value sound spurious. However, they have a lot of data to back their case. At least they show that there is nothing altruistic about the Western population control crusade. It is driven by Western self-interest, period.

If anyone is seriously concerned about the impact of population growth, they should be equally concerned about the economic conditions of the people in question. You cannot propose a green or environmental agenda nor prescribe a birth-control technique to a starving peasant. He or she needs to feed first. In fact, I have a sneaky suspicion that when Western pundits talk about saving the environment or the world, they are talking about saving it for white folks. If we talk about consumption of resources, who consumes more, the Third World and their large populations or the Western countries and their small populations? The rich 20 per cent of the world (the rich countries) consumes 80 per cent of the world's resources. So, who needs to reduce their population size? What is wrong with equitable distribution of world resources?

Anyway, my motivation in saying all this controversial stuff to you is just to emphasise that you are not dealing with some benign, neutral and common sense driven subject.

Cheers.

7 June 1995
Re: Personal plans, affirmative action

Hi Trina,
Uh-m thanks for that long response. It is good to read those thoughts of yours. I must say it was all pretty deep and informative. As for me, I would like to be married by 35, at the latest. I am 29 right now and that gives me six years. Now, within these six years I need to achieve some professional

and personal financial security. By the end of the six years, I should have embarked on my lifelong career of some sort. I am not too sure what this is going to be. Also within these six years I hope to get to know somebody special. However, I will take my time.

Marriage, to me, is a partnership, characterised by growth, accommodation, shared ideals and goals, love and respect. I believe that love between two people can grow and be developed. I do not believe in instant chemistry, but rather, developed chemistry. I have no inflexible core values. Rather I am always ready to learn from my partner. In addition, marriage should not be a barrier to our individual ambitions, but rather part of our shared ambition. It is essential that marriage be taken as the third person, an equally important party to the partnership. Hence, rather than always asking what is good for me or my partner, the issue should also be what is good for the marriage.

The debate on Affirmative Action (AA) rages on. As you might know, Governor Pete Wilson recently signed a decree outlawing most AA programmes in California. The Republicans have made AA and welfare reform 1996 campaign issues part of their 'Contract with America' deal. Recently, the Supreme Court ruled a Black Scholarship Scheme at the University of Maryland illegal – now that is a serious precedent. On the other hand, President Bill Clinton has at best been ambivalent; at worst, he is part of the AA-bashing bandwagon. He has ordered a review of all AA programmes. He speaks with a forked tongue through both sides of his mouth on this issue.

There are some blacks, mainly those of a Republican disposition, who argue that AA demeans them as inferior to whites. They argue that whatever blacks achieve is undervalued by AA. This is a simplistic treatise bereft of intellectual rigour and tenacity. Here is my argument. AA was put in place for a purpose: to redress historical inequities produced by slavery, exploitation, colonialism and racism, as well as other forms of past and present discrimination. AA is a modest attempt to achieve equal access, a level playing field and some degree of social justice for everyone. The US society is still inherently racist. The conditions that lead to the introduction of AA have not changed.

Those pushing for the scrapping of AA are guilty of trying to make the victim look like the criminal, and the criminal look like the victim. I am prepared to consider AA reform as long as the motivation is to make AA more effective. In other words, I would be happy to embrace an alternative strategy to AA which seeks to resolve the problems that lead to the prescription of AA in the first place.

For someone working on her exams, this is quite a mouthful for you, so I will deal with the Hollywood moral responsibility issue in my next note. Hey, who is the Rhodes Scholar working with you on the exams? I will also give you some exam tips next time.

Cheers.

25 September 1995
Re: Books, O.J. Simpson, race issues

Hello Andre,
Thanks for your note. It is good to hear that you are back in Oxford. I was out of town. I was up in DC for an NSF-organised workshop on Controls and Dynamics. It was great. By chance and arrangement Trina was in DC as well, so we spent some time together. In fact, we tried to call you from my hotel room on 19 September 1995 to wish you happy birthday. Trina told me about it all, but we could not get you at your New Jersey number. Anyway, have a happy belated birthday.

Now let us go to the issues. Thanks for the book 'reviews', I had already browsed through some of them and I will check out the ones where I have not done so. In particular, Steinberg's one will be a good breakdown. I have seen Marcus Mabry's 1995 book *White Bucks and Black-Eyed Peas*. In fact, I saw him talk about it on TV recently. It is an interesting book. There was a lot of excitement about Dinesh D'Souza's *The End of Racism*. I have not read it yet. I need to do that pretty soon. I would not mind a brief summary of that one. I have been checking out the biographies, Colin Powell's, Newt Gingrich's, and Andrew Cuomo's.

O.J. Simpson. I have been following this one pretty closely as well. By now I am sure you are behind the issues. That is what it means to be in poor ole England. The closing arguments are tomorrow. I agree with the drift of your argument. The major problem is that the jury did not hear, officially, the damning stuff about Fuhrman and Vannatter. The only way they will hear about this stuff is maybe through the so-called pillow talk. However, as you say the jury is not dumb. It would have been better to have the whole scenario unequivocal. Another issue is that O.J. Simpson is a celebrity. He will need more than an acquittal. He will need vindication that he did not do it. I am sure he will be acquitted but I am not sure whether he will get vindication. I checked out one of those Phiatto brothers on Larry King's show. He looked macho and insisted that he was seeing that Denise Brown. However, he was very sceptical of the way the defence was trying to use him.

On race, I refuse to accept that Mark Fuhrman is an aberration. Furthermore, I am not prepared to address the question of whether he is typical of the LAPD crew. That is the wrong question. He is a typical white citizen of the United States, period. I found it so outrageous how most white folks express astonishment about Fuhrman's remarks and yet most black folks were like, 'This is everyday life.' Typical US hypocrisy! Did it strike you why that journalist woman never found Fuhrman's remarks offensive, when she recorded them? It has nothing to do with a journalistic mode. What a load of garbage! It was and is usual lingua between two white folks talking about blacks in their absence.

Did you see Spike Lee host Larry King's show? It was interesting. He forced some of those white folks masquerading as experts to address some of the pertinent racial issues about the O.J. Simpson saga, by asking the right questions. How about Colin Powell on the King show? What do you think about this big Uncle Tom's views and chances for the top job? Ross Perot has just announced the formation of a third party, the Independence Party or The Reform Party. They are starting in your favourite state, California.

The struggle continues next time. Cheers to the Oxford crowd.

2 October 1995
Re: US politics, O.J. Simpson

Yo Andre,
Thanks for your informative note. I enjoyed reading it. I checked the Skip Gates article in *The New Yorker*. That is pretty interesting. I think Powell's best chances for the top job are to make noises about running but then not run. However, in the process he could make himself an indispensable VP candidate, to say, Dole. Then in 2000 or 2004 he will have a shot at it from a vantage point if the ticket wins in 1996. I don't think the right wingers in the Republican Party are ready for him as yet. They are already shooting him down as too liberal, what they actually mean is that he is black ... However, I must emphasise that his getting the presidency, if he gets it, will only be useful for its propaganda value to black folks. I do not expect him, with his Uncle Tom views, to make any substantive difference to the black condition. Clinton and the democrats can do more.

Thanks for the breakdown of D'Souza's book. This guy is something else. The problem in the United States is that of bounding debate on one side of the spectrum. The establishment allows this bigoted racist to preach his gospel while permitting only Uncle Toms to engage him. I agree that his views are an expression of white supremacy. We should unequivocally reject everything he says and the premise of his thesis. Engaging them the way the Uncle Toms do only serves to legitimise such views. We should force the establishment to allow radical combat of these racists. I am sure you realise that the few effective sentences that you proposed will not be acceptable to the white media in this country. Freedom of expression in this country is so superficial. The United States has a very effective way of ignoring radical views and rendering them impotent. Check the way they completely ignore the NOI and Farrakhan and vilify those who associate with such groups, sometimes using market forces.

I am glad you were tracking the O.J. Simpson scene. I watched all the closing arguments. This is fascinating stuff. Those prosecutors Marcia Clark and Chris Darden were fairly effective in both their closing arguments and final rebuttals. However, I think the show belonged to Cochran. I think he managed to convince those jurors. Apparently one of them was in tears. I thought those 15 questions were a smart move, although the prosecution tried to ignore them in their rebuttal. Did you see that Fred Goldman outburst! That was completely out of order. The media has not sufficiently criticised this man. I did not see anything unethical about Johnnie's comparison of Mark Fuhrman and Hitler's views.

The white media is going on about those NOI guards that Cochran had. Yet no one is talking about the hate mail and threats that he has been receiving. How hypocritical! Did anyone expect him to get security from the LAPD? Other pundits are criticising Cochran for apparently threatening jury nullification, when he told the jury that by convicting they will be endorsing a conspiracy.

Yep, Cochran has shown reasonable doubt all over the place. However, why can't O.J. Simpson produce the gloves he wore during those matches? Where are the shoes and clothes he wore on 12 June? I know the defendant is not obliged to prove anything. Nonetheless, such grey areas do not help his case and the prosecution capitalised on them. In fact, vindication will surely depend on clear answers to these questions. However, I am sure he will be acquitted. The worst-case scenario is a hung jury. However, vindication won't be forthcoming. The situation is worsened by the white press that has already tried and found him guilty.

Bye for now.

3 October 1995
Re: The O.J. Simpson verdict

Hi Cyril,
I am sure you have heard the exciting news. The verdict has been reached. It will be announced today, Tuesday, 10am PT. After the events at the courts today most pundits are convinced that O.J. Simpson has been convicted. Their major reason is the fact that the jurors requested Parker's evidence and that the jurors did not look O.J. Simpson in the face.

There is an unequivocal consensus in the media that O.J. Simpson has been found guilty. Cyril, I think these pundits are 100 per cent wrong! These are mainly white pundits who have always thought that O.J. Simpson is guilty. Consequently, they are interpreting the events to suit their own predictions. I am so certain they are going to eat their words at 10am. Even if the Parker evidence is true and incriminating it is not sufficient to convict. In a case like this it takes less time to acquit than to convict. You cannot convict in four hours when you know that the case will definitely be appealed.

Not all the nine African-American jurors would convict given the reasonable doubt and racism characterising the case. You need only one juror to get a hung jury. The jury said they have a unanimous decision. It can only be an acquittal. The pundits have got it wrong over here. The fact that the jurors did not look at O.J. Simpson or that one of them had a very sad look, means what? Aha! This is where the white pundits have been duped by a smart jury! These jurors were trying to hide their decision, by concealing their emotions, in keeping with the principle of being dispassionate. Why?

Because they knew there was going to be a long waiting period between attainment of verdict and its announcement.

I even suspect they might have actually discussed the strategy: 'Let us not betray our decision or emotions. Don't look at O.J. Simpson.' So they sent the opposite signal, which fooled all the pundits including O.J. Simpson. He looked very upset, but he will have a pleasant surprise at 10am PT. Inside their hearts the jury was excited and happy for O.J. Simpson but they did not want to show that. To say that they were sad and did not look at O.J. Simpson because they had convicted him is seriously undermining the shrewdness and cleverness of this jury. It does not take any stroke of imagination nor ingenuity to avoid eye contact with O.J. Simpson because you have convicted him.

This is a confident and shrewd jury that took only four hours to do what every pundit predicted would take more than 10 days! People have been massively duped by this jury. They are in for another surprise at 10am PT. I know my reasoning is going against current conventional wisdom but I am so excited because I know I am right. I am going to laugh at these naive pundits as they eat their words at 10am. I know they will start attacking the jury, Johnnie Cochran and others.

Cyril, please drop me a note before 10am PT and tell me what you think about my interpretation. What is your prediction? I hope you read and respond to this note before 10am PT (1pm ET). If I am wrong, I will humbly eat my words. I hope no one will laugh at me. However, defeat is not on my mind. This is the kind of thing I would bet on. O.J. Simpson is going to walk.

Cheers.

3 October 1995
Re: Enough respect!

Hi Cyril,
The verdict has been announced! I got it right. My prediction of the outcome was on point. I am so excited and I will give you a call soon. I must emphasise that O.J. Simpson has been legally found not guilty. I still have my doubts as to whether he is actually innocent. He got an acquittal but I am not sure whether he will get vindication. As a celebrity, he needs both an acquittal and vindication. The latter you do not get from the courts.

For me the issues are: Where are his gloves that he wore during those commentaries? Where are the clothes he was wearing on 12 June, in particular those expensive shoes? Why can't O.J. Simpson produce all this stuff? However, in the US legal system all this is unimportant and can be ignored. The defence does not have to prove anything. They only need to show reasonable doubt. They showed plenty of that. The DNA evidence is problematic because of the possibility of planted evidence.

Anyway, I will talk to you soon.

19 October 1995
Re: Oxford, Million Man March

Hi Andre,
Thanks for your note. So, Oxford is kicking, I miss that place. What were Davidson's main positions on 'Television and Africa'? Any interesting questions asked? Two of my colleagues, fellow Rhodes scholars, are back in Oxford for their DPhils: Chris Landsberg (South Africa 1991, my year) and Adekeye Adebajo (Nigeria 1990). You might have met them by now. They did the MPhil in International Relations and then left Oxford, Ade for Tufts (did an MA) and Chris for SA (where he was doing some research). Now they are back at Oxford. I took over the Presidency of the Africa Society from Ade and Chris was on my committee, as Social Secretary. Chris should be an extremely useful contact for your SA research. His number is 510491. Tell him I referred you to him.

It is a pity that you have such a bunch of uninspiring freshmen (and *freshwomen*). That is sad because as I have always said every generation of Rhodes scholars define what it means to be Rhodes scholars. Now it seems these folks have a skewed definition. But you guys must keep organising and doing political work, maybe they might get inspired.

The Million Man March was extremely successful. I am sure you watched it from that side. Farrakhan was great. He is the major black voice that white power structure in the United States does not control. Whether one disagrees with certain aspects of his utterances, religion or agenda is immaterial. The United States needs public voices that do not suck up to Uncle Sam and his fellow travellers. Most of the so-called black leaders are too concerned and preoccupied about what the white-controlled United States thinks. Black folks all over the world spend half their lives trying to make white people comfortable whereas white folks never give a damn.

One could argue that Farrakhan says the kind of stuff that most black folks privately agree with, but would never publicly acknowledge because they would lose acceptability, influence, favour, or even jobs from those that control the mainstream (white) United States. I taped most of his speech at the march. So, if you missed any parts of his speech, you can always get it from me at some point. I was very upset with Larry King that evening, Monday, when he had Farrakhan. He was not interested in having Farrakhan at all. He was absent-minded and essentially went through the motions of interviewing Farrakhan. He only gave the guy 20 odd minutes, most of it spent on phone-in questions and commercials. Press freedom in the United States, what a sham! It is the manufacture of consent, the beauty of white financial control of the media, the genius of incision. On these issues, Noam Chomsky's analysis is unassailable!

Cheers for now.

30 October 1995
Re: Mixed races, Black Caucus

Hi Trina,
I am glad to hear that your meeting with your supervisor went well. Keep working on the research, so that when you meet him next time you will be more pleased with your output. A good approach would be to actually prepare the material in advance (at least four days), so that you give yourself time to reflect on the issues and then polish the substance and presentation. Try to kick that last-minute habit. However, I am confident everything is going to be alright. Last year was your first year in Oxford, so don't judge yourself too harshly on the basis of last year. Nonetheless I am glad you are learning from your previous experience. That is what characterises growth and development.

Mixed races: So, there is a Zimbabwean of mixed race this year at Trinity. What is her name and what is she studying? Did she go to UZ prior to landing in Oxford? The perception of mixed races in Africa is very different from that in the United States or Europe. For example, in the States anyone with black heritage or blood is considered 'black'. In Africa, the identities were constructed differently by the colonial masters. People of mixed races were called 'coloured' people or mixed race. They were put in a different category from blacks, that is, indigenous Africans without any white blood or heritage. These categories were used to determine the degree of subjugation one was subjected to. To show you how ridiculous these definitions can become: my friend Chris Landsberg, whom you have met, is actually classified as 'coloured' in SA because of some white heritage from his mother's side. Black as he looks you could hardly tell this from his appearance.

Invariably, in the hierarchy of oppression, 'coloureds' suffered less oppression than blacks. They had more civil rights while having separate and better residential areas. They were preferred to blacks for jobs. This was a very divisive phenomenon whose impact continued even after the attainment of independence in these African countries. Although these definitions were imposed, some black, coloured and white people internalised them and accepted them. As a result, even after independence there is still an observable cultural barrier between 'coloureds' and blacks in Zimbabwe. There is not enough socialisation between the two groups. Why is this the case? There is enough blame to go around on this issue.

In particular, the major accusations against 'coloureds' are that they have a superiority complex towards blacks. They do not make an effort to learn from their black heritage. They neither speak indigenous languages nor embrace indigenous cultural practices. They want to identify with whites and their participation in the liberation war and in progressive struggles was (is) thin on the ground. They benefited from colonialism and they are not prepared to pay the price of redistribution. Of course, not all 'coloured' people are guilty of these crimes. On the other hand, some blacks are guilty of a cultural inferiority complex towards 'coloureds', not being open-minded about differences, intolerance of cultural diversity and internalised racial prejudice. Although there is a significant population of 'coloured' people in Zimbabwe, they are more of a subculture than a culture. I think the divide between 'coloureds' and blacks was artificially created and that the 'coloured' identity is superfluous. These two groups of people should politically self-define themselves as black, close ranks and work for the betterment of all humanity.

It will be interesting to find out whether your Zimbabwean colleague speaks any indigenous languages, that is, Shona or Ndebele. If she does not, one wonders whether she has any good reasons. Since she is of mixed race, does she equally understand, appreciate and live the mixed cultures in equal measure? If she is culturally more white than black, what rationale does she have for that? By the way, it is also pretty common to find 'black' Zimbabweans who do not speak indigenous languages, out of 'choice'. However, that choice is socially constructed by a colonial legacy based on self-disrespect and rooted in cultural imperialism.

Now, one has to be careful in faulting Black Caucus for asking her to leave. Firstly, we must accept Black Caucus as it self-defines itself. There are good reasons why it exists. If one is questioning the basis of its existence that is another debate. There are probably only good reasons why they asked her to leave. Firstly, they might have made a genuine mistake and thought that she was completely white. In which case, she should have unambiguously indicated her status and self-defined herself as black. I am sure Black Caucus would have allowed her to stay.

I disagree with her when she says by doing so she would be choosing a race. This line of thinking shows that she does not understand the political definition of black. By refusing to say she is black, she is creating an artificial and meaningless dilemma. Has she, or someone like her, been discriminated against, in any way, by the white socio-political-economic power structure because of heritage or racial background? If the answer is yes, then she is black, period. Secondly, if she does not politically define herself as black and simultaneously questions the existence of Black Caucus, then Black Caucus had every right to ask her to leave. As you walk through my thoughts bear in mind that I do not have all the facts, I am just working on the few facts you gave me and using my own instinct.

The FSU African Student Association has been virtually inactive. It had a dormant committee. They have not had a single event this Fall Semester. At the meeting, we had about eight people show up. The current President tried to rationalise the inactivity, but you can guess whether I would allow him to get away with it. Anyway, we discussed strategies for resuscitation, possible events and structural changes, and called for elections of a new committee in 10 days. Everything is in their hands, as the faculty member in charge I was just an enthusiastic adviser.

I hope you made progress in the Bodleian Library. Good luck.

Cheers.

TOP: *Author attending the Merton Ball with Charlotte, Merton, Oxford, 1993*
BOTTOM: *Author getting down during the Merton Ball, Merton, Oxford, 1993*

Merton Ball, Merton, Oxford, 1993

TOP: *Author at the Merton Ball, with E. Moore (MCR Committee member) and J. Nivens, Merton, Oxford, 1993*

MIDDLE: *In the shadow of C. Rhodes, at the Rhodes Ball with M. Mooki, Rhodes House, Oxford, 1994*

BOTTOM: *Merton MCR social event, Merton, Oxford, 1993*

Merton MCR social event, Merton, Oxford, 1993

Merton MCR Mad Hatter social event, Merton, Oxford, 1993

TOP: *Author as President of the OU Africa Society with A. Bell, Oxford, 1991*
BOTTOM: *Author as President of the OU Africa Society with T. Abdul-Raheem, Author, T. Okwonko, A. Mohamed Babu, C. Landsberg (Africa Society Social Secretary), Oxford Union, Oxford, 1994*

TOP: *The OU Africa Society committee – M. Hornsby, C. Landsberg, L. Schröder, Author, St Antony's, Oxford, 1994*

BOTTOM LEFT: *The OU Africa Society event – A. Adebajo (former President OUAS), Author, C. Landsberg, D. Keen, St Antony's, Oxford, 1994*

BOTTOM RIGHT: *Author displaying the champagne won as best speaker in the Oxford Union debate on the environment, Oxford, 11 November 1992 (Does not drink it!)*

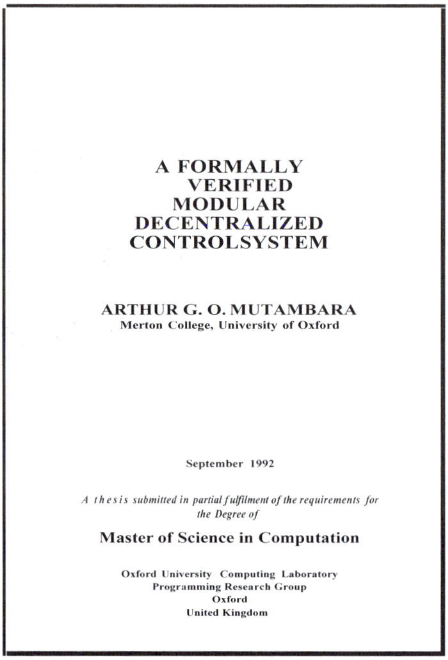

A FORMALLY
VERIFIED
MODULAR
DECENTRALIZED
CONTROLSYSTEM

ARTHUR G. O. MUTAMBARA
Merton College, University of Oxford

September 1992

A thesis submitted in partial fulfilment of the requirements for the Degree of

Master of Science in Computation

Oxford University Computing Laboratory
Programming Research Group
Oxford
United Kingdom

TOP: *Author in the French Alps on an intellectual retreat with fellow Rhodes Scholars, France, 1994*

BOTTOM: *Author's MSc dissertation, Oxford, September 1992*

TOP: *Author at the 21st Century Trust Conference, in the French Alps, France, 1994*
BOTTOM: *Coming out of the tough MSc Examination (dressed in sub fusc for the occasion!); Author and S. Utete, October 1992*

BOTTOM: *MSc graduation, Author with C. Landsberg and R. Mutambara (Author's sister), Oxford,*
28 November 1992
TOP RIGHT: *Author, MSc graduation, Oxford, 28 November 1992*

UNIVERSITY OF OXFORD

THIS is to certify that it appears by the Registers of the University of Oxford that

Arthur Eugeni Oliver Mutambara

Merton College

in Trinity Term 1992 *satisfied the Examiners in*

Computation

in the Examination for the Degree of Master of Science, and having, in accordance with the Statutes of the University, kept the prescribed residence and passed all the necessary examinations, was on 28 November 1992 *formally admitted to the Degree of*

MASTER OF SCIENCE.

University Offices, Oxford.

28 November 1992

R.O. Hughes

Assistant Registrar

Author's MSc certificate, Oxford, 28 November 1992

TOP: *MSc graduation with G. Peffer and D. Botsman*
BOTTOM: *Author in laboratory office, Oxford, 1993*

Author with mobile robotics colleagues, Oxford, 1994

TOP: *Author with a mobile robot*
BOTTOM: *Author at PhD graduation, Oxford, 4 March 1995*

UNIVERSITY OF OXFORD

THIS is to certify that it appears by the Register of the Ancient House of Congregation of Doctors and Regent Masters of the University of Oxford that

Arthur Gugeni Oliver Mutambara

Merton College

having submitted a thesis entitled:

Decentralized Estimation and Control with Applications to a Modular Robot

and having satisfied all the conditions prescribed in that respect by the Statutes of the University, was on the Fourth *day of* March 1995 *duly admitted to the degree of*

DOCTOR OF PHILOSOPHY

As witness my hand this Sixth *day of* March 1995.

Assistant Registrar

Author's PhD certificate, Oxford, 6 March 1995

PhD graduation guests – O. Mooki, R. Mutambara (Author's sister), T. Williams, Author, R. Haynes. Seated: L. Zigomo, I. Haynes, Oxford, 4 March 1995

TOP: *Graduation ceremony with Merton College Dean, T. Braun, 4 March 1995*
BOTTOM LEFT: *Author, Las Vegas, 1993*
BOTTOM RIGHT: *L. Madhuku (left) and Author, Cambridge, 1994*

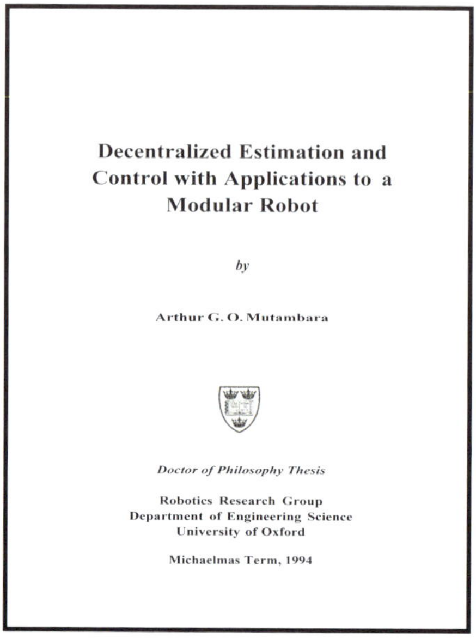

Decentralized Estimation and Control with Applications to a Modular Robot

by

Arthur G. O. Mutambara

Doctor of Philosophy Thesis

Robotics Research Group
Department of Engineering Science
University of Oxford

Michaelmas Term, 1994

TOP: *Author's PhD thesis, Oxford, December 1994*
BOTTOM: *J. El-Nabhas, Author, T. Williams, J. Namphy, A. Namphy, lunch at Oxford, 1994*

TOP LEFT: *Cyril Ruwende, Author, Atlanta, 1995*
TOP RIGHT: *Sharon, Author, Cyril, Jim, Atlanta, 1995*
BOTTOM: *Author, C. Munjoma, C. Munjoma, C. Ruwende, E. Chitate, Atlanta, 1995*

TOP: *Author with Cornel West, Harvard, 1996*
BOTTOM: *NASA Cleveland, 1997, Author's base that year*

TOP: *Author, R. Mabuwa and O. Mutukudzi, Boston, 1999*
BOTTOM: *Author and F. Mawindi, DC, 1999*

TOP: *Author and F. Ruwende, New York, 1999*
BOTTOM: *Author with M. Mawere, Florida, 1997*

TOP: *Author with R. Mugabe, Florida, 1997*
BOTTOM: *Author with M. Mawere, Florida, 1997*

Author attending MIT graduation as faculty, June 1999

TOP LEFT: *Attending FAMU graduation as faculty, Author and S. Peterson, June 1998*
TOP RIGHT: *Author attending MIT graduation as faculty, June 1999*
BOTTOM: *Author attending MIT graduation as faculty, June 1999*

Author attending MIT graduation as faculty, June 1999

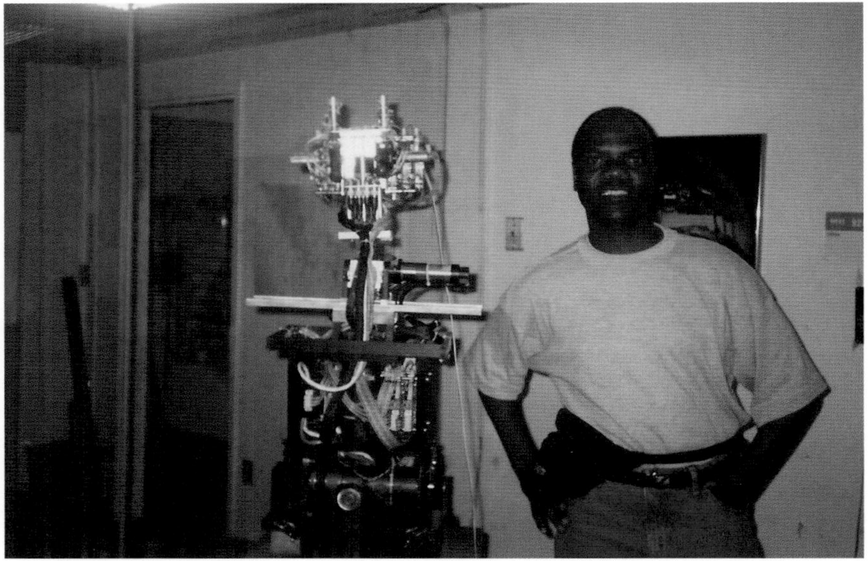

Author with a humanoid robot, AI lab, MIT, 1998

TOP: *Author with a humanoid robot, AI lab, MIT, 1998*
BOTTOM: *Author at McKinsey, Chicago, 2001*

Author at McKinsey with colleagues, Chicago, 2001

TOP: *Author at McKinsey partying with colleagues, Chicago, 2001*
MIDDLE: *Author at McKinsey with colleagues, Chicago, 2001*
BOTTOM: *Author at McKinsey with colleagues, on Lake Michigan, Chicago, 2001*

TOP: *Author with V. Maiswa and C. Munjoma, Harare, 2001*
BOTTOM LEFT: *Author with Michael Porter, Johannesburg, 2002*
BOTTOM RIGHT: *Author with P. Chimbosva, Johannesburg, 2002*

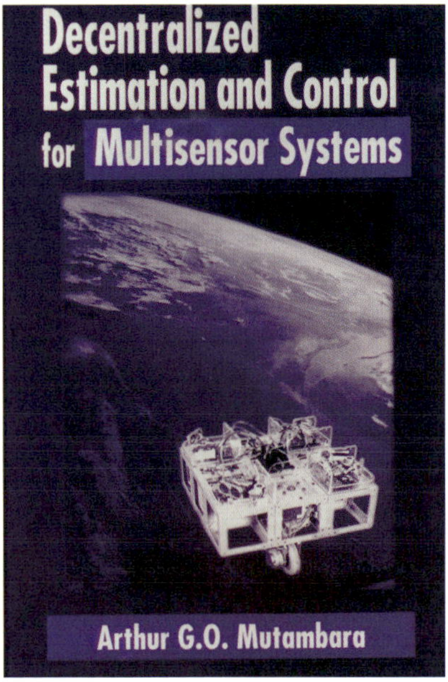

TOP LEFT: *Author in 1995*
TOP RIGHT: *Author in 2002*
BOTTOM LEFT: *First book, 1998*
BOTTOM RIGHT: *Second book, 1999*

25 November 1995
Re: Timekeeping issues

Hi Trina,
Thanks for the messages. It was good to read a lot of material from you. I appreciate it. I found your response to Randy's two articles very thoughtful and interesting. In particular, I like the case you make for institution building as opposed to personality cultivation. Furthermore, you raised the critical issue of self-interest versus the collective interest. What is even more important is the challenge you make: 'What can we do right now?' This is essential because there is always the danger of paralysis by analysis where people do a lot of talking without any concrete actions. This has always been your position and I have always admired you for it.

Of Randy's two articles, I had seen the first one. I think someone has been circulating them. I enjoyed reading the second one. It belabours the importance of grass-roots action as opposed to dependency on so-called charismatic leaders. Point taken – however, in any national struggle, leadership has its place. We need both effective grass-roots and effective national leadership. The article borders on overstating the case for local action over charismatic leadership.

Commitment to too many activities or people is one of your major challenges. You asked for my suggestions. I have said something about this to you a couple of times. The problem is that if you spread yourself too thin on the ground, you compromise the quality of all the things you do without exception. At the end, you are exhausted but with no outstanding activity that you have achieved. In particular, you might actually seriously compromise things that are important to you by clouding them with an array of interesting but non-essential activities. You need to keep focused on the critical things such as spiritual development and academic work while learning to prioritise and being able to say 'no' to events or invitations.

Sometimes people appreciate it better if you say 'no' than when you say 'yes' and then fail to meet their expectations. Similarly, no one is pleased if you just go through the motions of fulfilling an obligation when you are completely ineffective because of exhaustion. As a result, you will superficially know a lot of people, without knowing any of them well enough. You end up short-changing the people who try to get closer to you and know you better. They end up displeased, although you are not intentionally hurting them. With friends, I think the quality of time spent with friends is more important than the quantity of superficial acquaintances.

That was a long note, wasn't it?

Take care.

25 January 1996
Re: US politics, Clinton address

Trina,
Hi
Thanks for the survey. It looks pretty penetrating and interesting. In some cases, it is very bound, that is, a narrow spectrum of options. The following framework will suffice to illustrate the bounding of debate in the United States.

Do I consider my political views to be a Democrat, Independent or Republican? Alternatively, do I consider my views to be liberal, moderate or conservative? It is hard for me to place myself in such analytical frames or boxes. Anyway, this is typical of how debate is bounded in this country. However, given that it is just a survey, with limitations thereto, that there is good motivation behind it and that the results can be put to good use, I will definitely respond to it. Thanks for forwarding this stuff to me. In fact, as per your suggestion I have already subscribed to BOBC. It is a source of good material on black issues.

Bill Clinton gave his State of the Union address on Tuesday. No big deal. He was essentially pandering to the Conservative agenda, a kind of pre-emptive all-encompassing speech. Issues that he raised included the end of the era of big government, the need for welfare reform, v-chip for parents to control TV programmes, one strike you are out, the prospect of uniforms for kids (if necessary to curb violence among them), praised Dole et al for WW2, attacks on bad movies … He also defended his foreign policy and his positions in the budget impasse. The whole speech was marked by a charade of clapping and standing up after every sentence or so. People were simply going through the motions of showing support and solidarity. This looked extremely superficial and I think it further undermined the sincerity of the whole event. The US 'democracy', in particular, the separation of powers, has a lot going for it. It does not need this farcical charade. In fact, I could not help but wonder whether this event was any different from scenes from George Orwell's *Animal Farm*.

O.J. Simpson gave his first public interview to BET on Wednesday night. He has already done a video for sale at $29.95, so he was not saying much. He did not talk about any of the evidence. He simply referred to his video and civil case depositions. It turned out to be more a publicity stunt for his video than anything else. They talked about general matters surrounding the issues: race, O.J. Simpson's life, the media, and the kids. The most interesting aspect of the interview was that O.J. Simpson tried to play down the fact that white-controlled United States has spurned him (as evidence by most whites believing that he is guilty, the hate campaign in the media, denying him access to most forms of the media, blocking the adverts for his video, neighbours asking him to leave, graffiti saying 'killer or murderer', views expressed on talk shows by pundits and ordinary whites, being turned down by some clubs or companies).

He does not believe that a disproportionate number of whites believe that he is guilty. He said he does not believe in the polls. He vouches that the generality of the white populace believes he is innocent. His appreciation of the support he received from the black community is lukewarm. O.J. Simpson is in self-denial of colossal proportions! It is scary. Even if it was a publicity stunt to lure white support or empathy, that is a worse manifestation of denial. It did not work anyway.

He expressed extreme anger at the media for its renditions, flat lies, misinformation and distortions about the case. What he failed to ask himself was which press he was talking about and who owned that press. Unfortunately, the interviewer did not press this point. On closer examination, it was going to be clear that it is a predominantly white media, manned, managed, controlled and owned by white folks. This is the media that was dogging him. That same media is trying to stop him from earning a living. It viciously denounced BET for giving him airtime. They even questioned the journalistic abilities of the black man who carried out the interview.

The irony of the whole iguana is that O.J. Simpson has the audacity to show ambivalence or ignorance about race in the United States on a BET interview, after mainstream white media houses such as CNN, NBC and Pay-Per-View would not have him. He avoided directly answering questions about his practice of exclusively dating white women, associating with whites and working for top white companies. Essentially, O.J. Simpson appeared as the same ole O.J. Simpson before the murders, oblivious of the role of race in the United States, pandering to the humanity of white folks and naively asking for a share of a colour-blind and universal American Dream. The brother disappointed many black folks.

However, all those black people who phoned in, although disappointed with his views on race, still maintained their belief in his innocence. Most whites who were interviewed prior to the BET interview said that they were not going to watch it. Of those that watched, very few bothered to phone in afterwards. Those few that did phone in simply reaffirmed their position that he is guilty. Oh, poor O.J. Simpson! One wonders what it would take for him to publicly acknowledge the role of race in the United States.

Well, that was a mouthful. By the way, I recorded both the State of the Union address and O.J. Simpson's interview for you. You can watch them when you want. How did your supervisor's lecture go? Are you still running?

Bye.

25 January 1996
Ref: Bill Bradley, US politics

Hi Trina,
It was pleasing reading from you. Things are kind of kicking up there in Oxford, heh? I am glad your work is going well and that you also find time

to relax a bit. That helps you improve your efficiency and renew your focus. I know everything will work out for the best. Thanks for the breakdown of the issues surrounding the employment trends between women and men in the UK. I did not follow the Super Bowl closely enough to appreciate the controversy about the interceptions.

Not much has been happening to me recently, the same old routine. I gave out some homework last week which is due this Thursday. It was pretty tough, but I gave the students hints and ideas about how to solve some of the problems. This class consists of the better students (it is a graduate course) so they should be able to handle the material. I am trying to keep a consistent gym routine (three times a week), mainly running. I am glad you enjoyed the rowing outing. I did some rowing for one term. I was not that good, but I enjoyed it though, in particular the training sessions. We lost the competition I was involved in.

I watched Bill Bradley on Larry King's Show the other day. He had some interesting things to say. He is leaving the Senate after 17 years and has written a book about his experiences and ideas. He wants to be involved in what he calls the next stage of US politics and for him to be effectively involved in this endeavour he has to free himself of his other obligations. His major issues are serious campaign funds reform, in order to politically empower the ordinary citizen. He feels that the millionaire's millions should not be the substitute to the poor person's soap box. Another issue he feels strongly about is that the government should be able to use public power against private power in the interest of the public. He is not impressed by the Clinton regime's prevarication and he has not ruled out running as an independent. He also feels strongly about the need for racial healing and feels more should be done in this direction. He is not convinced that Colin Powell would be the answer to this one. He feels everyone in the United States should do it for themselves, talk about and do something about racism, even at the risk of offending the other party. He says he learnt a lot during his basketball days. He feels either party could implement his agenda if they wanted to. His strategy is to go around the country and talk about his ideas and then change them in accordance with the received feedback. He would then go back to the people for further consultation.

Although some of the Bradley ideas and methods at best sound naive and simplistic, they go a long way to show how the traditional democratic agenda has been betrayed and how the political spectrum in this country has fundamentally shifted to the right. Even moderate liberals are disillusioned. His contention is that if neither party takes up his ideas, he would consider running as an independent. I do not think he will run. However, by not ruling it out, he hopes to keep sufficient media interest on himself. Presumably, if Clinton fails in 1996, Bradley may go for it in 2000.

Forbes is giving Bob Dole a run for his life. Forbes has established himself as the close second to Dole and the Dole camp is getting uncomfortable. His success is primarily due to his concentrating on one penetrating issue, the flat tax. His millions' ability to buy airtime of course has facilitated the intensity of his focus. I think, in the final analysis, Dole will get the nomination but he will be mortally wounded. Consequently, he will be clobbered by Clinton, the man who knows how to get elected and nothing else.

That is a mouthful. Bye for now.

Sunday, 28 January 1996
Re: Job trends …

Hi Trina,
Thanks for your messages. Yes, I received your last email that covered your views on the State of the Union address, some comments on O.J. Simpson and remarks about your supervisor's lecture.

Maybe what you meant was I did not comment on your supervisor's lecture on job trends in the UK. Well, what I found interesting, which I was not aware of, is the job acquisition trend between men and women in the UK. So, more women are in jobs than men? I did not realise that the situation was that distinct in the UK. I am still digesting the sociological basis for this phenomenon. I am familiar with similar trends among the African-American community, here in the United States. In this case, the sociological explanation is that in the racist US socio-economic-political system the black woman is viewed as less threatening and, hence, she is preferred for jobs, rather than the black male. This is further compounded by a criminal justice system which is biased against black males as evidenced by one third of the US black males being on probation, parole or in prison. Although this is a simplified rationale for the trend, since there are other factors that affect people's life chances, it is a fairly robust point of departure for analysis.

Although the old Don's question was a large one, my response to it is fairly simple. Yes, many things have changed since WWII, including school selection, access and the examination system. However, the reason things change, the way they change, the change itself and those that bring change can still be understood and interpreted within the same general paradigms predicated on gender, race and class analysis. People's life chances are still affected by these factors. What is different is the complexity and sophistication of the analysis now required, given advances in knowledge, epistemology, technology, the way people live, information communication technologies and, in particular, institutions and changes in local and global relations.

There might be new variables in today's analysis but no one can argue that education or any societal activity for that matter is now devoid of the prejudices or influences of gender, race and class. What is more instructive is to look at the interplay between the new and old variables, then determine which variables are more significant in a particular environment. The Prague conference sounds pretty interesting. Although you should be primarily working on your thesis, you could do with a break over Easter. You don't want to work flat out through Easter. You could carry some material with you. What makes the conference a good idea is its agenda and the fact that it is fairly inexpensive. However, look at how much progress you would have made on the thesis.

Be honest with yourself, if you feel you really need to work through Easter in order to produce a good thesis, then simply forget about the trip. Keep focused and remember that this is your critical time at Oxford. You had your share of parties, trips, knowing people, and college activities. This is simply not the time for most of these activities for you, at least not this Hilary and Trinity. You are the best judge of your supervisor's expectations and your academic progress (or lack of it). That takes precedence. The trip is very secondary.

I hope you had a good weekend. What did you do? Did you watch the Super Bowl?

Cheers.

2 February 1996
Re: Catching up

Trina,
It looks like you are focusing on some penetrating matters in your thesis, around the issues of school effectiveness. It will be very interesting to find out what answers you come up with to those micro processes' questions. I think your approach is pretty cool, because for a thesis you need to zero in on a specific and narrow agenda and thoroughly address it. By the way, that is why doing a thesis is not the best way to learn and acquire knowledge. In fact, for a thesis the narrower the terms of reference, the better.

Always remember the objective of a thesis is to say something new; that is, make a contribution to knowledge. This is easier if the focus is intense on one particular set of issues. What might be interesting at some point in analysing your findings may be to question the validity or limitations of delinking the micro and macro processes. It will be interesting to discuss the nature of the dialectical relationship between the micro and macro processes. This will be just a discussion which will show that you are aware of the interconnectedness of the issues and hence the limitations of your approach. It is always good to give a critique of your approach, methodologies and findings.

Thanks for the Magic Johnson article. Actually, I had not read it before. That was a very interesting angle from the NYP. It is well reasoned, but I wonder what the writer's real motivation is. Well no one ever knows that!

Good luck in your work, keep focused and work hard. Always remember this is supposed to be a stressful but temporary period in your academic career.

3 February 1996
Re: Catching up

Hi Trina,
It was good talking to you last night.

Well, later on that evening I watched the Magic versus Jordan game. It was quite charged and was very exciting. Magic played OK and scored some wicked shots. However, he was not as good as he was in the Tuesday game against Golden State. He was mainly frustrated by Dennis Rodman. Jordan was very good and faster. However, the best player of the match was Pippen. Rodman also did pretty well with those outstanding rebounds. The Bulls won with something like 99-85. I taped most of the game for you.

I woke up pretty late today. I went to the gym and I did my usual running. I ran for 25 minutes, I wished you were there to run with me. Afterwards, I was very exhausted but I felt pretty good. I then cooked myself a good meal of broccoli, eggs, lettuce and rice. I also had some fruit. I think today I will just kick back, listen to music, watch TV and chill.

Did you guys like the movie *Heat*?

5 February 1996
Re: Malcolm X, movies, timekeeping as a value

Hi Trina,
This is another good day. Thanks for your message. It is great the guys liked *Heat*. It was an OK movie to me. I liked the interplay between Robert De Niro and Al Pacino as well. My main contention is that, given the hype and the presence of these two great actors, the movie was not outstanding. In particular, I did not find the plot fascinating, there was not enough suspense. Although there was excellent dialogue, in particular by Al Pacino, the movie was fairly predictable. I like a clever plot, I want to be outwitted and surprised by the storyline. One part that touched me the most was De Niro's rule to 'Never do or get involved with anything that you cannot walk away from in 20 seconds.' For sure, despite his love for that woman, which I thought was fairly genuine, when trouble came he walked away from her. She looked at him walk away in disbelief. That was very emotional to me. I like a movie that touches my iron heart!

The rest of the weekend went alright. As you know, this month is Black History Month. There are a lot of programmes on TV to commemorate this theme. I watched *Malcolm X*, the movie, on TV for the second time. The first time I watched this movie, in around 1993, I was not that impressed because of my extensive familiarity with actual TV footage of Malcolm X and literature on him. Also, somehow, I felt that Denzel was not convincing enough as Malcolm. Only Malcolm can be Malcolm. Other criticisms of the movie we have talked about, including the tough Bell Hooks critique. However, this time around the movie had a powerful impact on me. Maybe

I watched it with a less critical mind. In particular, I found the portrayal of his last days very effective; the disagreements with the NOI, the threats, the wire-tapping, the strain on his family, the fire bombs, plots, the build-up to the assassination, 'Now is the time for martyrs,' and the actual assassination. The eulogy was so impactful. The other stuff with Mandela and the kids shouting I still thought were over the top (OTT).

I am glad you made it to church on time. Timekeeping is important, Trina. I think what you need to do is to internalise it as a value beneficial and important to you, not so much as something you have to do for people you are interacting with. Try to make a conscious effort to do most of your activities on time as part of your personal self-discipline.

When interacting with people, there is nothing wrong with being upfront with those you are dealing with at a particular moment about your next obligation or next scheduled appointment. You can tell them at the beginning of the event how much time you have, or midway you can say how much time you have left. You should resist the impulsive instinct to please people by being with them at the expense of another important activity or person(s). You will be simply stealing from Tom to pay Dick. There is no achievement. At the end of the day if you really care about people, and more importantly, respect yourself, you will be disappointed.

Even if people are disappointed that you have to leave early, you can imagine the extreme disappointment of that person you might have stood up or let down by being late. People will respect you more if you are upfront with them as to how much time you have available and when you try to keep your time. Overcommitting gives instant superficial gratification which eventually leads to frustration, despair and ill feeling when appointments are broken.

Relationships and productivity are compromised and endangered. People react differently to being stood up or to a missed appointment. In general, there is always a bad feeling. 'Why is this happening to me? Does she have a good reason for the sloppy behaviour? Is she trying to say something to me? Now, if she does not have any good reason can I ever trust her to keep her word when we make another appointment? Can she be trusted on critical matters?'

These questions become important when people you care about are involved, such as family, friends and people you fellowship with. It is very hard for people you care about to accept, or at least painful to accept, that you can stand them up or be late and give a reason that you were spending time with other people or give some other flimsy and avoidable excuse. People, as flawed as they are, start to read into your behaviour. 'She tries to please everyone which is a sign of low self-esteem or insecurity. You can never trust her. Never emotionally invest in her. Just be superficial with her. She does not sincerely believe in our mission. If fellowshipping with us is important to her, why can't she make time for it?'

These are the kinds of conclusions and interpretations that might make the rounds in people's heads depending on the nature of the interactions involved. More importantly, for you to optimally benefit from your pursuits, activities, fellowships and efforts, timekeeping is a good value. You will be happier and more productive. Consequently, you will be able to self-actualise and self-transcend better.

Arthur

6 February 1996
Re: Success in Oxford

Hi Trina,
One thing that is so important to me right now is your success at Oxford. I wish that your academic work at Oxford comes to outstanding fruition and that everything turns out the way you want it to. Just stay focused, make sacrifices if necessary and always remember that it is a taxing but temporary period. If it is not stressful you might not be doing something right. It is better to spread your thesis work evenly than to work frantically at the end. I suggest you look at past MPhil theses in your field, check out the required general standards, formats and structures. Start asking yourself how you are going to specifically satisfy all the requirements and give yourself time frames. You might have done all these things already. In that case just bear with me, I am trying to be helpful. In a sense, MPhil and MSc theses might be even more nightmarish because of the submission deadlines. You can never put together your best thesis in a rush or at the last minute.

There will always be things you could improve upon given more time. Just take my ramblings as the remarks of someone concerned, but detached and away from the battlefield. Is there any news or feedback about the McKinsey interview and your Olympics applications? Let me know how everything goes.

Cheers.

12 February 1996
Re: US elections

Hi Trina,
Campaign 1996 is kind of heating up. The events are centred on the GOP presidential candidates. The Republicans are really in trouble. Bob Dole as an alternative to Clinton is not a very strong candidate. The disarray and frustration for them is primarily because they feel that 1996 should be their year, given the Republican revolution of 1994 and other factors. Forbes has been doing pretty well and beating Bob Dole in some polls. His key thing is concentrating on one penetrating issue, the flat tax. His millions are furiously working. Buchanan's victory over Graham in Louisiana was interesting. There are a lot of Christian right wingers in that area. Bob Dole did not participate in that contest. There are a lot of public attacks and

sniping among the GOP candidates. Pundits are saying this is unusual for the Republican Party. It seems everyone is breaking old Ronald Reagan's 11th commandment, 'Thou shall not publicly speak ill of fellow Republican brethren'.

News just in, the Iowa Caucuses' results are out. The pack looks as follows: Bob Dole, Pat Buchanan, Lamar Alexander, Steve Forbes, Phil Graham ... then the rest. Interpretation of the results is kind of equivocal. Some pundits argue that the Iowa Caucuses are more of an anomaly than anything else. They argue that in recent history no one has actually won the nomination after winning Iowa, except Jimmy Carter in 1976. Others argue that if a lot of people participated in Iowa, the Caucuses can be viewed more as a primary. This makes the outcome more significant. Pundits are trying to establish some correlation between the results with what might happen in the upcoming New Hampshire primary. In the end, I think Bob Dole will get the nomination, but his candidacy will be fragile. Consequently, he will be clobbered by Clinton, the man who knows how to get elected and nothing else. It is interesting that one of the Democratic Senators, Bob Kerry, recently called Bill Clinton an unusually good liar! The White House was not amused.

I hope your focus on the academic agenda will be effective and fruitful.

Cheers.

21 February 1996
Re: Movies, US politics

Hi Trina,
I am glad your work is progressing well and that you still keep yourself intellectually engaged in other activities. That is good. Did Joseph Rotblat say anything interesting? The kind of discussions and ploughing through in the 'School Effectiveness' debate are critically important, in particular when it comes to contextualising your own contributions to the field. I am very keen on the fact that in your work you seriously engaged the sociological critique. In other words, your own conclusions and findings should at least take cognisance of the Marxist critique. This is of particular interest when you discuss the significance of your findings in the broad ideas spectrum and big societal picture, characterised by the multiplicity of variables, both internal and external, affecting the school product. You should make your work fairly impenetrable and robust to cheap shots.

Things have been kind of interesting for me, actually. This term I have met a lot of interesting people and I am doing some exciting things with them. This past weekend I watched the new movie *The Juror* with Demi Moore, Alec Baldwin et al. It is a pretty good film, with a good story and excellent performance by Demi and Alec. My small criticism is one sex scene which I felt was completely unnecessary and did not add anything to the movie. I dislike movies that take advantage of cheap sex scenes and mindless violence, in the absence of a good storyline and good acting.

The disappointing thing was that the film had essentially stayed away from unsophisticated sex and violence scenes except for this particular incident.

Also over the weekend I watched and taped my best Malcolm X documentary to date. It was on GPTV. Trina, it is excellent! Maybe you have already seen it. It is called *Malcolm X: Make it Plain*. It came out in 1994. It is more than two hours long, has extensive footage and commentary from people who knew him.

My work is going well. I have just graded my second homework and I am giving a test on Thursday. There are some good students in the class. The material is fairly tough and I usually take no prisoners. Yep, politically things are kind of heating up over this side of the Atlantic. The New Hampshire Primary results are out! This primary is very interesting because it is the first primary and hence in a way it sets the tone of the rest of the primaries. Yes, historically it has also been predictably accurate. Since 1952 no presidential candidate, after losing New Hampshire, has gone on to win the nomination.

The surprise result today is that Pat Buchanan came top with 27 per cent of the vote, beating Bob Dole who came second with 26 per cent! Lamar Alexander came in third with 23 per cent. The margin is the closest since Ford defeated Reagan in 1976. The results have been damaging to Dole and a lot of excitement and heat has been generated. The pundits are trying to read into the results. The key consensus interpretation, it seems, is that Buchanan is too right-wing, divisively conservative and protectionist, hence unsellable to the general public. Consequently, it looks like he won't get the nomination and if he does he will definitely be defeated by Clinton. However, there is going to be a vicious debate for the soul of the Republican Party. The prediction is that Bob Dole will get the nomination. The issue is whether he will be immortally wounded. The problem with Bob Dole is that he is thin on ideas and the vision thing.

His case is predicated on the fact that he, and his fellow travellers, feel that he deserves the nomination more than anyone else. Why, because he is the oldest, the most experienced, was injured in WW2 and has been running for the Presidency since 1976. What a flimsy basis! Buchanan's victory is being attributed to the solid and unequivocal support he is receiving from the small but active Christian right. Lamar Alexander's chances are being dismissed because he has neither the name recognition, money nor the big idea.

The primaries have been front-loaded, so there will be a lot of them in the next few weeks. This is going to apply excessive pressure on the financial resources of Pat and Lamar. Dole is financially robust. Money has made the entire US democratic process farcical and meaningless. The Democrats are basically licking their chops. Bill Clinton was unopposed in New Hampshire. About 100 000 people came to vote for him, which is more than what Reagan received when he was unopposed in that primary in 1984. The Democrats have never had it so good.

Cheers.

Saturday, 4 May 1996
Re: Zimbabwean writers, books, Black Panthers

Hi Andre,
I am sorry for the break in communication. I took some time off after the end of the semester. Now I am back on summer research and travel. I will be in California between 29 June and 11 July (San Francisco then Pasadena). I am doing a conference in Frisco and then I have a research visit with NASA (JPL) and Caltech. I am glad you had a good feel of the political situation in Zimbabwe and what the progressive folks and forces are up against in the country. That is what we struggled against as students and also what I am thinking intensely about as I contemplate my next move on the Zimbabwe scene. It is hard but not insurmountable. My ideas are still vague, but we will talk.

Tsitsi Dangarembga is a very perceptive and insightful writer. *Nervous Conditions* is a good illustration of this. Her major problem is that her experience with the rural Zimbabwe culture is very peripheral (not her fault). She was born to a very successful high school headmaster and teacher (both UK-trained graduates). Incidentally, her father was my headmaster and her mother my English teacher. Tsitsi's life was basically sheltered from the onslaught of poverty, a rural life experience and the social experiences of the average Zimbabwe woman. She left for college education in the UK after high school. Anyway, in spite of all these limitations of her life experience she writes very well. She is, in fact, one of Zimbabwe's better-known female authors.

Chenjerai Hove is great; excellent prose and poetry. I attended a writing workshop with him when I was still in high school. I have always liked his writing, in particular the satire about the liberation war in Zimbabwe and the post-independence experience. He is incisive and entertaining. In fact, last year, when Mugabe gave his annual address, Hove gave a very bold alternative address. His major problem is that he is not ideologically thoroughly developed, nor is he robust. He is essentially a nationalist with a conscience. Other interesting Zimbabwean authors are Charles Mungoshi – he is the master – Musaemura Zimunya and Dambudzo Marechera. Dambudzo is the *baddest* brother ever! He died in 1987, a smart dude thrown out of Oxford, New College, in the mid-1970s. Legend has it that he wanted to burn up the Bodleian Library.

The new book by Cornel West and Henry Louis Gates, *The Future of the Race*, is not that outstanding. They are basically looking at W.E.B. Du Bois's essay *The Talented Tenth*. They then look at the role of black intellectuals and the middle class in resolving the situation of black folks in the United States. They look at the question separately and using different approaches. Gates was the most uninspiring; he does not write very well. I am still to read *Coloured People*. Is it a good book? On his part, he basically concentrated on his experiences at Yale, very uneventful days if you ask me, and his colleagues from his time. He kind of traced their life experiences. Cornel basically trashes the essay and Du Bois's life experience and insights as inadequate. West's scholarly skills are more persuasive than his intellectual sincerity.

I am back with the Black Panthers. I really like these brothers. This is the most radical black politics ever got in this country (1966–1974). I have just read through *Soul on Ice*, *Seize the Time* and Elaine Brown's biography, *A Taste of Power*. This biography is awesome. I literally could not put it down. I just ploughed through it. I am sure you have read it; the confrontation between Huey P. Newton and Farrakhan was dramatic. I really have tons of respect for Huey. The expulsion of Bobby Seale was another dramatic event that grasped me. Huey's rage was getting the best of him. He got Bobby disciplined (20 strikes) and threw him out of the party and out of Oakland that night. I appreciate the fact that Huey made a lot of mistakes in the end, his rage, expulsions, and cocaine. I still salute the brother. I have not gotten hold of Angela Davis's biography. I have read *Women, Culture and Politics*. I have also looked at *Soledad Brother*, by George Jackson. I am going to watch the movie *Panther* again.

So how is good old Oxford? I understand O.J. Simpson is coming to Oxford. Keep in touch.

Cheers.

8 May 1996
Re: Black Panthers

Hi Andre,
Thanks for your note. It was good reading from you. Yep, it will be good to meet up in California. I am looking forward to that. The Panther stuff is very fascinating to me. Yep, I have since gone through *Assata*, *Soledad Brother* and also David Hilliard's recent biography, *This Side of Glory*. I am still waiting for my order of Davis's biography and I am searching for *Blood in My Eye*. Over the years, I have seen about 40 per cent of the *Eyes on the Prize* series (I and II). Just recently I watched the *Black Power* one that covered the Panthers, King's assassination, Carl Stokes (Cleveland), SNCC and other groups. The series is excellent.

In fact, I had placed an order for all 10 videos through Blockbuster Videos, for my collection. Unfortunately, they told me that they are not being produced anymore. I am going to call Blackslide in Massachusetts and try to make a direct order. I will definitely read *Coloured People* at some point. I guess my bias against Louis Gates's writing is political. I find his ideological ineptitude and clumsiness irritating. This is coupled by his lack of political commitment, clarity and incision. I have listened to him a couple of times on TV. I am not convinced that he intellectually understands what the issues are; neither do his strategies for the way forward fire my imagination. He strikes me as the kind of docile black person these white folks would like at Harvard – the *House Nigger*, that Uncle Tom who does not rattle the feathers of white supremacy.

I have just started reading *The New Yorker*, 29 April to 6 May 1996. I miss the intellectual vibrancy of the Oxford scene. Keep me posted on the David Kennedy discussions on immigration. Thanks for the *Primer on US Immigration* that you forwarded. What's up with that O.J. Simpson Oxford Union meeting?

Cheers.

15 May 1996
Re: O.J. Simpson at Oxford

Hi Andre,
Thanks a lot for your notes. Well, well, that O.J. Simpson meeting must have been so exciting! I really wish I was still in Oxford. That Black Power salute was right on. I am glad the brother acknowledged. His utterances and responses to questions are getting better with time. Although, ostensibly, he is still in denial, I am sure the brother is learning. Thanks for the details about the meeting. I really enjoyed reading the note.

That was a very cheap shot on the part of Amy Wakeland. I wonder why she chose to decontextualise your comments, while making insidious remarks and at the same time hiding her true baseless conviction that O.J. Simpson is guilty of murder. What I find objectionable are people who for whatever reason believe that O.J. Simpson is guilty of murder, but then hide this opinion. Usually they betray their feelings by dramatising the spousal abuse issue at the expense of, and insensitivity to, other socio-political variables involved in the whole drama. I share the concerns of people who genuinely respect and accept the NOT guilty verdict, but who also want to address spousal abuse. That is a fair and good discussion. I hold no brief for patriarchy or male domination. However, the point of departure should be that O.J. Simpson was found not guilty of murder. All these racist charlatans, masquerading as champions of women's struggle, together with their fellow travellers, the self-hating un-black blacks, I viciously despise.

I take no prisoners on this one.

Bye.

Sunday, 2 June 1996
Re: Netanyahu, US politics

Hi Trina,
I hope you had a nice weekend and did a good amount of work too. How was the worship service with James Njonjo? Give him my regards. As indicated in earlier communication, he was a Rhodes Scholar from my year, but could not handle Oxford and was thus forced to leave. This is his second bite at the cherry. I hope everything goes well for him this time around. I wish him good luck.

I guess you received my Friday note, covering the Stand for Children March. It came and went yesterday. There was not that extensive coverage of the march. It was not even on C-SPAN. I saw bits and pieces of it on CNN. However, it was very successful and well organised. At least the White House will take cognisance of the issues raised. The criticism from right-wing think tanks continued. Their arguments are essentially those described in my last mail.

Yep, Benjamin Netanyahu is the new Prime Minister but it was so close, less than 1 per cent difference! He is a very interesting character. He went to MIT (BA, MS), served in Israeli special forces, was Ambassador to the United States, opposition leader, and now Prime Minister. He is an extremely articulate and effective speaker. In fact, he came to the Oxford Union (1992–1993) and I shot one or two questions at him. He responded well, I enjoyed the meeting. His victory in these elections is very significant. After Rabin was assassinated, one would have expected a lot of sympathy votes for Peres. Netanyahu succeeded in spite of this. I think he has no choice but to continue with the peace process; however, the emphasis will be different, the price for peace renegotiated and the terms of peace adjusted. Given his narrow victory margin, he cannot effect any dramatic changes. The US government will also put pressure on him to pursue peace. I do not see the elections in Israel directly impacting on the US elections. The voters in Israel were responding to very specific issues in their country. US foreign policy has in general been bipartisan; this is more so towards Israel. However, that bipartisan policy might be slightly reshaped in keeping with the new rulers in Israel. There will be no fundamental changes, though. The US elections will be predominantly fought on domestic issues that clearly distinguish the Republicans and the Democrats. However, Bill Clinton is making this hard by claiming most Republican programmes. He has occupied the centre-right platform.

I will send you some stuff on the 1996 Olympics soon. Good luck in those exams.

Cheers.

Monday, 3 June 1996
Re: Books, Stand for Children March

Hi Andre,
Thanks a lot for the interesting and well-written article about Bernstein's talk at Oxford. I enjoyed it immensely. Guys like Bernstein are solid theoreticians and executioners of revolutionary thought. It must have been a great talk. Over here we are battling with the Spring Semester. I was in DC recently attending a National Science Foundation (NSF) robotics review panel. I met up with Trina, Jonah, Munro, Adekeye Adebajo and Cyril Ruwende. I have been doing quite some reading, *The Bell Curve* and Stephen Jay Gould's recently republished *The Mismeasure of Man*. It has a new introduction

and five more essays directly addressing *The Bell Curve*. The guy writes so sharply. I have also been reading William Julius Wilson's books *The Declining Significance of Race*, *The Truly Disadvantaged* and his new one, *When Work Disappears*. He has since moved from Chicago to Harvard.

The Stand for Children March came and went. It was both well organised and attended. However, it was not as broadly covered in the media as I thought it should have been. It was not on C-SPAN. Ms Marian Edelman, chair of the Children's Defense Fund, has been explaining the purpose of the march and why it is important at this juncture. In particular, she was emphasising the hypocrisy of talking about the importance of protecting and providing for children while massively cutting welfare funds. She is also emphasising that the march is non-partisan. Critics of the march say it is an opportunity for people who believe in big government to push their agenda of a wasteful extensive welfare programme. They also argue that it is a partisan march for big government engineered by the Democrats. The Clintons are close friends of the Edelmans, but they did not attend the march as it was supposed to be non-partisan.

I think the stand was definitely a worthwhile effort and also an effective platform to raise issues affecting children. It served as a reminder of the obligation of active governance and social justice in redressing social issues. This is critical given the misguided and misplaced euphoria about the so-called end of the era of big government championed by the Republicans and spinelessly echoed by Clinton. As a front for a specific agenda for children, the march was a success, and I think the policymakers will respond, although the response might be passive. However, it is important to adopt a holistic approach which addresses the entire spectrum of social-political-economic problems bedevilling this country. The whole canon needs to be looked at, since issues affecting children cannot be resolved in isolation from this spectrum.

I am going to MIT on Tuesday night. I am doing a robotics laboratory visit. I am in the process of setting up my Mobile Robot Laboratory here. A cousin of mine is also graduating from Harvard with a Master of Theological Studies degree on Thursday, so I will get a chance to attend your old school, Harvard's graduation ceremony! In fact, Cornel West is addressing one of the Wednesday alumni events. I am definitely going to attend that one. Keep me posted on Arafat's visit to Oxford. I will be checking my mail from MIT. I will be back at FAMU-FSU on Sunday.

Cheers.

28 June 1996
Re: Catching up

Hi Zano,
Thanks for your note. Yep, it is almost 10 years since our grand CPA essay competition on the one-party system. Enock Chikweche, now Munyaradzi

Gwisai, is still definitely on the Left. He was Secretary General on our SRC committee (1989–1990). He came to Columbia, did an LLM and is teaching at UZ. Another guy is Lovemore 'Briggs' Zano. He is still strongly on the Left too. Well, as you know I have been doing some serious reading of all kinds of material, Left, Right and Centre. Oxford was such a great and unequalled experience.

Since I came to the States, I have read tons of material and engaged some interesting US public intellectuals. Just recently I was up at Harvard's alumni and graduation week. We had some serious discussions with some interesting folks such as Cornel West and Louis Gates. I have reread the African-American history from the abolitionists to today. I closely follow political issues in this country and watch a lot of documentaries about the United States. The effect of all this has been to broaden my exposure and experience, while deepening my intellectual roots. I am still solidly on the left and robustly so, given my thorough exposition. Sure, I appreciate the role of the market.

The details of my views are in that article I did during our interaction in 1993. It is very representative. There are some serious right-wing intellectuals, academics and politicians that I do respect and not Mickey Mouse simplistic minds or most of the unthought-through right-wing utterances that make waves on Zimnet. I think most of this intellectual ineptitude is because people just do not read, or they simply lack sophisticated analytical skills. I am extremely contemptuous of right-wing views or pro-capitalist views that lack intellectual rigour.

I am off this Saturday, 29 June, to California. I am doing a conference in San Francisco and will be a Visiting Research Fellow at Caltech and NASA (JPL) in Pasadena. On 11 July, I fly to Seattle and take the train to Vancouver! It will be my first time in Canada. I am looking forward to it.

Let us keep in touch. As I travel I am always checking my email. Take care and keep in touch. Greetings to your family. How big is it now? Mine is still just me.

Cheers.

26 February 1997
Re: *Rosewood* – A good black movie

Hi Trina,

How are you? Thanks for your recent notes.

It is always pleasing to hear from you. Sorry for the delay in communications. I am glad you guys had fun skiing, I have never tried it. I will look for the book by John L. Mason, *Let Go of Whatever Makes You Stop*. In fact, I think I will be able to look around today.

Last weekend I watched the new movie directed by John Singleton, *Rosewood*. It is a great movie, I strongly recommend it. This movie challenges and corrects the stereotypical message: 'The good white liberal is the saviour of black folks'. If you think about it carefully, you will realise that this message is pervading in greatly vaunted black movies such as *Biko*, *Mississippi Burning* and *The Ghosts of Mississippi*. The life and family of the good white liberal is given disproportionate significance and emphasis. Blacks are correctly portrayed as suffering all kinds of socio-political-economic oppression. However, they are portrayed as playing a secondary role, if any, in their emancipation. The good white liberal is their saviour! What a racist falsehood perpetuated by patronising Hollywood directors and producers.

Rosewood unequivocally demolishes this myth. The storyline basically centres on an African-American community destroyed by their white neighbours. In this movie, the role of whites and blacks in the history of racial strife is done justice. Black folks are their own saviours. They stand up to oppression and they are the principle agents of change. In the context of racially based subjugation and confrontation, the notion of a 'good' white liberal is in fact a myth. White people are not capable of being good, being human or having a conscience when it comes to race. For a start, ostensibly, all the white folks are guilty of racial crimes directly (most of them) or indirectly (a rare few). When they do help blacks fight racial abuse they do it as a last resort. They do it begrudgingly; sometimes they do it for the wrong reasons. In most cases, they do it for themselves. A good example in the movie is when a white shop owner says killing blacks will deprive him of customers. 'Mind on my money.' That is what pricks his conscience to help blacks from being massacred.

The same 'good' white man had been using a black woman as a sex slave. He is forced by black heroes to save some black women by taking them into his house. In a dramatic scene – respect must be given to director John Singleton – he saves some of the women and categorically refuses to save his sex slave because his white wife was in the house. He did not want to damage his relationship with his wife so he decided to let his black sex slave die. What a great white liberal! Guess what? His wife, another white liberal who bravely defended the house full of black refugees later in the movie, witnesses her husband refuse sanctuary to his sex slave and does nothing about it. 'Let that black woman die, how dare she sleep with my white husband? However, I will go ahead and protect some black people.' I guess that was what was running through her head, without any sense of irony or duplicity. What kind of conflicted conscience is this?

The main event that led to the massacre of black folks was when a white woman was raped and beaten by a white man. She then decided to lie and said she had been raped by a black man. Sounds familiar? This movie is charged. John Singleton gives an unapologetic portrayal of white supremacist activities in the South and how blacks fought and made strides.

This is the best movie I have watched in a long time. But, as you have probably guessed, white folks are not watching it. No one is talking about it in the white media. The only discussions about it are on BET and other black media houses. I watched it on opening night; the place was 99 per cent black. White folks could not be bothered. Please do watch this movie and then we will talk. I have only given you sketches about the movie, so not much has been spoilt. This movie is the bomb.

Cheers.

17 March 1997
Re: An update from this front

Hi Jonathan,
Thanks for your prompt response. It was good to read from you. No, I am still single. I have not crossed that bridge yet. I hope to get married in the next three to five years, back in Zimbabwe. I have met some interesting African-American women. One of them we met at Oxford, and is a Rhodes Scholar from the United States, but there are too many complicated cultural differences. In particular, I am not prepared to compromise my intention to settle in Zimbabwe nor my Zimbabwean agenda in any marital arrangement. Consequently, my ideal woman is a Zimbabwean woman. I have just been playing dating games with these African-American women, an educational process indeed.

At the moment, I am concentrating on the professional front – research, publications, conferences, research contacts and teaching. I am also trying to cushion my entry onto the Zimbabwean scene, financially. I am trying to save some money so that at least my personal finances are reasonable enough in terms of such needs as housing, transport and other basics, in order to jumpstart my Zimbabwe activism. The bottom line is that I must be able to survive in spite of the system and the bureaucrats back in Zimbabwe. Coming out of school one is generally financially vulnerable and hence the tendency to bastardise one's views and positions to those of the system. Personal financial wilderness also makes one more susceptible to the corruption games that characterise our polity. I am trying to be strategic and tactful, without being too careful. I also have to avoid the paralysis-by-analysis syndrome.

Another important front I am concentrating on is my intellectual and political growth. I have been reading extensively on politics, economics and sociology. In particular, I have been recently concentrating on African-American history, politics and struggles, from W.E.B. Du Bois, Booker T. Washington, Joseph DeLaine, the civil rights era, through the Black Panthers to current struggles. I am particularly fascinated by the Black Panthers. They were the closest to my political inclination. In fact, their era was the most radical black politics ever got in this country; no wonder there was such intensification of the Counterintelligence Programme (COINTELPRO). The way they were destroyed and self-destructed is amazing. Of the contemporary public intellectuals, I am currently ploughing through the work of Cornel West, William J. Wilson (the Chicago poverty expert who has moved to Harvard), Henry Louis Gates (that Harvard Uncle Tom), John Henrik Clarke, Bell Hooks and Stephen Jay Gould. I am also trying to build a very extensive personal library, so I buy all the books I read, including classic texts. The idea is to make my library bigger than yours! Anyway, the point is that if everything fails in Zimbabwe, at least I can always sit under a tree in my rural village, read a good book and feel content.

The Banana saga: This issue has derived so much currency primarily because of Mugabe's embarrassing, homophobic and bigoted utterances. I appreciate the fact that most African cultures are very conservative on the issue of homosexuality. For his part, Mugabe was being opportunistic and hypocritical. He is showing no leadership acumen while abusing public office to express his personal narrow-minded views. If he had such strong views about homosexuality how could he allow a homosexual rapist to serve as President from 1980 to 1987? He was clearly aware of Banana's activities. As a nation, we should decriminalise homosexuality, while not necessarily encouraging it as an alternative lifestyle. Those predisposed to homosexuality should have their rights protected by law. As for Banana, the law should take its course. He should be prosecuted; if found guilty of homosexual rape he must do time.

However, the most important lesson from this episode is the need to have strong institutions; that is, the Executive, Legislature and Judiciary, with functional separation of powers. It is an opportunity to evaluate our institutions and do some effective institution building. How can a citizen be abused and raped and háve no recourse to justice? His abuser tells him he is the 'last court of appeal', the victim informs the Police Commissioner General and the Deputy Prime Minister, but still cannot receive justice. The more interesting question is: What other abuses of state power went on and still go unchecked in our system fraught with the monopolistic politics of patronage characterised by a one-ruler, one-party culture?

Keep me posted on your plans of moving to South Africa. What is the status of your appointment with UZ? I am also forwarding an article I did for Zimnet last summer, my last to the newsgroup, on the problem of white liberals. Your comments will be greatly appreciated. I hardly write to Zimnet at all. They are neither serious nor scholarly. They are mostly a bunch of bankrupt attention-seekers playing around with unthought-through soundbites. I however subscribe to the Zimnet platform, primarily to read the raw information from or about Zimbabwe. We get a bit of this from time to time. How is the Great Lakes Conference?

Cheers.

(Gates, 1997) (D'Souza, 1996) (Brown, 1993) (Powell, 2003) (Seale, 1991) (Gingrich, 1997)

39 Africa technology and science strategy

Realising that technology is the great equaliser that affords Africa the opportunity to leapfrog in social and economic terms, we put together a vehicle, the Africa Technology and Science Strategy (ATSS). Its strategic pay-off line is: 'Innovative paradigms and solutions for Africa'. I present the following speech at ATSS's launch at MIT on 15 March 2000.

The company will engage in profit and non-profit activities that will facilitate the transformation of African countries into successful and sustainable 21st-century economies through the application of cutting-edge technology, science and medicine.

This mission is predicated upon the premise that there is no unique science or technology for poor communities or countries. Science and technology are universal engines for economic growth, poverty alleviation, economic empowerment and social justice. Consequently, there is nothing that precludes the application of current cutting-edge science, technology, skills and innovations to the problems afflicting the African continent. The categorical imperative for that application is customisation and adaptation of the science, technology, skills and innovations to the African context in ways that take cognisance of the needs, history, culture and values of specific African communities.

In addition, new technology and science-based-education curricula have to be developed in Africa, while in the economy emphasis is placed on information technology, export-based investment, added-value exports, research, design and manufacturing. These efforts will provide a robust strategy through which the economic gap and the digital divide between rich and poor countries can be arrested and eventually closed. Far from being impediments, the lack of extensive industrialisation and infrastructure development in most African countries actually facilitates the application of some of the current cutting-edge technologies and aspects of the knowledge economy. Unconstrained by infrastructure sunk costs and old technology compatibility issues, many African countries will find it easier to adopt innovative technologies such as renewable energy (in particular, solar power), wireless digital communication, portable computing, information technology products, satellite systems, biotechnology and advanced medicine. Thus, these technologies and the growth of the knowledge-based global economy provide Africa with a unique opportunity to run where others walked.

Objectives

The company has four specific but related and overlapping objectives. The first two objectives are ostensibly non-profit while the last two are profit-based. All four objectives derive from the central organising paradigm of employing science and technology as the primary means for resolving African problems.

1. Technology advocacy: This objective involves lobbying policy makers, industrialists, entrepreneurs and academics, in both Africa and advanced countries, to accept and engage the central role of cutting-edge technology, science and medicine as a means for solving African problems and needs. The work will be based on extensive study and research into the needs of African countries and identification of applicable technologies, innovations and adaptations. This activity will generate specific and tangible recommendations that marry African needs and cutting-edge technology. These will then be actively disseminated to institutions in advanced countries and those in Africa for adoption and implementation.
2. Technology policy and education: Activities in this arena include research into the development and formulation of technology, science and health policies and programmes for both private and public institutions in Africa. This will also include proposals to establish new tertiary institutions of technology, develop new technology and sciences-based education curricula; and postulate a value system and culture that are supportive of effective implementation of the technology, science and health policies. Specific products of this activity will include technology and education policy and programme documents that are for adoption by governments, corporations and educational institutions in Africa. Although lessons will be generated across countries, the policy formulation will be country-specific.
3. Opportunity and capital matching: This objective entails identifying venture capital to invest in the established areas of need in Africa. This will be the core of the company's profit-based activities. The company will develop detailed investment proposals based on the results of extensive research into the needs and problems of specific African countries. Emphasis will be placed on matching that involves the

transfer of cutting-edge technology to Africa from advanced countries. These company activities will also promote and buttress efforts such as foreign direct investment (FDI), export-based investment and added-value manufacturing.

4. Consulting and advisory service: This objective involves providing an expert science and technology consulting and advisory service to both public and private institutions involved in the activities deriving from objectives one to three. The consulting work is, however, not restricted to these specific activities. It will also include technology and science policy and programme evaluations, needs assessments, and environmental impact analyses for proposed projects. It will be extended to governments and other public institutions, non-governmental organisations involved in development work in Africa, private corporations and individuals seeking to establish new ventures, as well as those already doing business in Africa.

Company financing

There will be two types of company financing: foundation funds such as soft money, grants and donations; and venture capital from corporates, investment firms and banks.

Foundation money (soft money) will fund the non-profit activities arising from objective one and two. These include:

- internal development of organisation;
- extensive study and research into specific African needs, problems and opportunities;
- research into, and identification of, the matching cutting-edge science and technologies;
- exploration and formulation of the required innovations, customisation and adaptation;
- establishment and delivery of tangible and implementable recommendations.

Venture capital (VC), incubators and other sources of investment will fund the implementation of most of the proposals from the non-profit research activities. Thus, VCs are sheltered from risky research activities, while the results from foundation money find usefulness and value in profit-based implementation. Hence the non-profit for profit paradigm is achieved. Other recommendations from the research activities will be adopted by public and private institutions such as corporations, governments and community-based organisations. The company consulting and advisory services will be provided for both the non-profit research activities and the profit-based activities (opportunity-capital matching and the implementation activities). The consulting fees will be lower for the non-profit activities. The long-term strategy for the company is to be self-sustaining and independent of soft money.

40 Crisis in Zimbabwe: An imperative and exhaustive agenda

My last public engagement in Zimbabwe was in 1991 during my graduation from UZ. In March 1995, after obtaining both my MSc and my PhD from Oxford, I went back to Zimbabwe but I kept a low profile. The year is now 1999, and I am visiting Zimbabwe from my academic base at MIT. In addition to giving robotics and mechatronics research presentations at UZ, NUST and SIRDC, I decide to deliver a public lecture on the political situation in Zimbabwe. It is organised by the SAPES Trust in Harare on 6 March 1999.

Thank you for this opportunity to share with the people of Zimbabwe. Today I seek to discuss an imperative and exhaustive agenda that embraces and respects the constitutional debate, while emphasising that it is not enough to talk about the content of the new Constitution and the processes of drawing it. Furthermore, it is not enough to talk about political democracy and how to remove the Mugabe regime from power. We need to move beyond constitutionalism and the regime-change agenda. We need to talk about what we are going to do differently and more effectively in the economy. A people-driven and democratic Constitution is a necessary but not sufficient condition for economic success.

Consequently, my discussion is structured into three levels that characterise an exhaustive and imperative agenda for Zimbabwe in 1999:

1. Building an effective institutional framework;
2. Developing a functional political democracy;
3. Crafting economic programmes and platforms.

So, what is the nature of the Zimbabwean crisis? There is a deadlock in the Constitution-making process. There is a crisis in terms of unemployment and poverty levels. Over 55 per cent of our people are unemployed. Inflation is above 60 per cent, interest rates are between 45 per cent and 65 per cent, while unbridled price increases and shortages of basic commodities characterise our economy. All these issues have to be resolved. These are bread-and-butter issues that I want us to discuss today. Hence my platform today is for all political parties: Zimbabwe Unity Movement (ZUM), United Parties (UP), Movement for Democratic Change (MDC) (which is in the process of being formed) and ZANU-PF. Yes, I want the ruling party to confront these issues too. Civic society organisations, workers, students, teachers, farmers, the business community and the entire citizenry must all work together in a concerted effort to resolve our national challenges.

Building an effective institutional framework

Now on the constitutional debate, I do not want to belabour issues that have been extensively debated in our nation. I take a very clear and unequivocal position. I support the National Constitutional Assembly's (NCA) position on the two areas of disagreement with the Constitutional Commission (CC) established by Robert Mugabe: The need for a clear Constitutional Reform Act; and the demand for an all-party Constitutional Convention at which the composition and mandate of a commission is to be decided.

These are very reasonable demands. My question to Robert Mugabe and his regime is this: 'Tell me one thing that can go wrong if the Zimbabwean government were to embrace these two sticking points?' Why can't Mugabe be magnanimous and show leadership by reaching out to the NCA? Magnanimity is a function of power. ZANU-PF is in charge today and hence Mugabe should show magnanimity by accommodating and compromising with the NCA. This will allow our country an opportunity to go through an all-embracing, people-driven and democratic process of crafting our rules of governance. There is a need for compromise and flexibility in pursuit of the national interest. In any case a Constitution has to be a compromise document. How can you have the same Constitution for peasants and millionaires? How can you have the same Constitution for poor black farm workers and rich white farmers? So, by definition, a Constitution has to involve trade-offs and painful concessions. Consequently, the ball is in the court of the Mugabe regime.

I can tell you what can go wrong with using the Presidential Commission of Inquiry Act. Theoretically, the President has the powers to disregard the recommendations or to manipulate the findings in the commission. He is constitutionally provided with those powers to do so. Even if it is most unlikely for him to do that, why should we trust him? Worldwide, constitutions exist because the governed should never trust their rulers. We should never depend on the governor's benevolence but rather on institutional frameworks such as a national Constitution. If we trusted our rulers or if the rulers were to be trusted, there would be no need for a Constitution. Consequently, there is no rational basis for the people of

Zimbabwe to respect and trust Mugabe by assuming that he won't abuse the powers legally provided for him.

At the end of the day, a Constitution is a document that every citizen should embrace and defend, irrespective of their political persuasion. How can you come up with a Constitution through a process in which major sections of civic society such as the workers, churches, the students, farmers and the business community are not effectively represented? The NCA represents a very significant and powerful component of civic society in Zimbabwe. It does not make sense for Mugabe and his cronies to unilaterally come up with a partisan constitutional document, irrespective of its beauty and eloquence. It is a travesty of our national dignity for them to impose such a document on the people of Zimbabwe.

While I support the NCA, I would also like to proffer a critique of this group and other civic organisations. I do this fully cognisant of the tendency of the ZANU-PF press to just quote my criticism of the democratic forces while ignoring my vicious attacks on the inept and bungling Mugabe regime. The NCA must put their house in order. There is lack of coherence and strategic alignment. What is the NCA's Welshman Ncube doing appearing before the CC to give evidence, when there is an NCA decision of total disengagement with the illegitimate CC? Furthermore, the NCA must also understand the limitations and weaknesses of their position and strategy. I am going to be straight up and take no prisoners. Let us consider the scenario where the NCA succeeds on its own, with the exclusion of the ruling ZANU-PF government and its associated CC partners, and comes up with a Constitution. The fact that respected civic society activists like Lupi Mushayakarara, Ibbo Mandaza, Jonathan Moyo and Erich Bloch have been seduced into the CC is of significance and consequence. Despite our disdain for, and dislike of, Mugabe's politics and orientation, we must give him credit for his Machiavellian skill in dividing the progressive and democratic forces by enticing some of them to his side.

Put simply, I am saying that if the NCA goes ahead without a ruling government and some significant sections of both the civic and business community, they will also have a legitimacy problem. More importantly, they will have a major implementation challenge.

How do you adopt a Constitution without the participation of ruling government? Consequently, with a rigid NCA strategy you cannot even begin to address the economic crisis bedevilling our country. There has to be a compromise between the CC and NCA approaches.

It is also interesting to note that there are efforts to disguise the partisan nature of the CC. If all members of the commission are bona fide, why are most of the CC committees headed by independents like Lupi Mushayakarara, Jonathan Moyo and Erich Bloch? The regime has stuffed the CC with party functionaries and it is common cause that the Constitution-making process can be influenced by partisan interests. By using the independent commissioners as chairpersons, Mugabe is trying to hide his devious intentions and establish a superficial sense of justice. We are not fooled. Those dominating the committees will make the decisions, period. If you are a democrat you must go along with committee democracy, that is, collective decisions. Hence if you are a chairperson and the committee is dominated by ZANU-PF, you have no choice but to go with the majority on the committee. This is why it is absurd and irritating when some of these chairpersons start complaining that the issues they are raising are not being put in the questionnaire. They should have seen through the ZANU-PF illusion of impartiality and predicted their own fate.

In terms of the content of the Constitution we desire, there is general consensus among democrats. We want clear functional separation of powers between the Executive, the Judiciary and the Legislature. A serious scaling down of the powers of the Executive is a categorical imperative while fundamental empowerment of the Legislature is essential. By providing elected representatives with legal authority, office infrastructure, research capacity and draftsmen they can initiate both legislative bills and economic policies. We cannot have all bills originating from the Executive. The Legislature must be enabled so that it can be an effective player in the tripartite constitutional arrangement. Legal provisions are necessary to ensure that judicial officers are protected from both political and economic patronage by the Executive. The objective should be an independent, enabled, enhanced and progressive Judiciary, with limited judicial activism. There must also be a strong and clear provision for gender justice in our constitutional framework so that women are full citizens in our country. Women's rights are human rights.

When all is said and done on the Constitution, it is imperative that we understand the limitations of a Constitution as the framework that determines and prescribes citizens' endeavours and actions. We should appreciate that a Constitution is a bourgeois document that provides a democratic environment for all citizens: farmer, worker, employer, student and entrepreneur. For each class or interest group what is important is then to come up with clear programmes and platforms which best serve its constituency's agenda. However, there are limitations. What if, for some of us, the desired solution is a social revolution, meaning that our objective is to seize and smash the entire exploitative system in Zimbabwe? How can you provide for a total revolution in a Constitution? Revolutions, by definition, overthrow systems. They do not recognise laws. The American Revolution in 1776 was not constitutional to the British rulers of the rebelling colonies. The French revolution of 1789 was not constitutional. The Bolshevik Revolution in 1917 was not constitutional to the prevailing order in Russia. Our heroic war of liberation was not constitutional to Ian Smith and his Rhodesians in this country. All these historical experiences illustrate that where unjust and undemocratic circumstances exist, revolutions might occur, overturning and disrupting both constitutionality and constitutionalism. Sometimes the effective solution consists of extra-legal and unconstitutional methods and strategies. So, don't be carried away with worshipping the Constitution as if it is the Alpha and Omega of human existence. We are probably so fed up in this country that we are prepared to tear up any Zimbabwean Constitution, revolt against the system, and create a new egalitarian and equitable order. We don't give a damn about a Constitution if people in this country do not have food to eat, accommodation, a living wage and access to health. These are basic and fundamental things.

So, people of Zimbabwe, make sure that when we have this bourgeois document we come up with clear programmes to empower people, so that they can feed themselves. It is imperative that the fight for a new Constitution translates into the resolution of bread-and-butter issues. The workers, peasants and poor people of this country demand that their material conditions be improved dramatically. It is important that we acknowledge that the challenges of colonialism and neo-colonialism are also economic, not just political. Hence it is important that we address the issues of the haves and have-nots.

Developing a functional political democracy

Let us assume that the NCA and CC come up with a compromise that is amicable to both parties leading to a new Constitution of Zimbabwe. I want to show you the political limitations of that document in terms of delivering political democracy. If we have an election in Zimbabwe and one party, say ZANU-PF, wins the Presidency and dominates the Senate and House of Representatives, what are the implications? Let us assume that the President violates the Constitution, a very good people-driven and democratic Constitution for that matter; the impeachment of the President will be very difficult if not impossible in a political environment inordinately dominated by one party. The dominant party will control both the Senate and Parliament Judicial Committees. It will have the numbers to block any impeachment vote in both legislative houses. So, who is going to impeach whom using the beautiful Constitution?

This dramatises the challenges of a monolithic political system which will not be solved by a new Constitution alone. Zimbabwe has the problem of a socio-economic-political patronage system based on a dominant ZANU-PF monolithic party. The hegemony of one party is felt in all sectors of life including the economy, social organisations and the media. This is not consistent with the pursuit of democratic values and principles. How do you destroy the monolith?

The new Constitution helps by allowing groups to organise and work towards this task. However, a good Constitution is a necessary, but not sufficient, condition for the establishment of functional political democracy. In addition, you need a strong independent press, a vibrant civil society and viable opposition parties. A serious opposition party should be able to win elections and effectively run the country. It must have a shadow government with well-developed foreign, economic, land, monetary and social policies.

An effective opposition party is good for both Zimbabwe and the ruling party. A dynamic opposition has the impact of increasing the competency and performance of the incumbent party, which is driven towards increased efficiency by criticism and competition. They are kept on their toes by an effective shadow government. It is okay to steal good ideas from the opposition. In any case, who wins when this happens? Zimbabwe does, and the incumbent government too. Thus, a good opposition is beneficial to both ZANU-PF and the country.

A wise and strategic opposition must look beyond the upcoming election. When you form a party in 1999, your target should be 2010. I strongly support Tsvangirai and the upcoming MDC. However, what I am saying is that when you form the MDC, you should be saying, 'We are going to be building and fighting for the next 10 years,' so that when you lose in 2000 you don't crumble like ZUM. You don't disintegrate like FORUM. You need to learn from the mistakes of the previous opposition parties. So, when I say we must have a long-term vision, I am trying to be constructive. If you target 2000 and lose you might disintegrate into oblivion. That is not a good lesson. If you win in 2000 I will be happy for you. We will say more power to you. I will be more than happy because Mugabe's regime has lost legitimacy through mis-governance, corruption and political intolerance.

The question is whether the opposition can win. How can they win? There is a need for party-building initiatives, membership drives, social mobilisation, civic education, political organisation and voter education. Civil society must be organised and active, while the media must be strong and independent. There is a difference between independent and anti-government media. As an illustration: if Mugabe takes a good position on land, the independent press should support that position, while the anti-government press will obviously not give him any credit. One must be able to separate the message from the messenger. We need to distinguish and delink the messenger from the message. This requires skills and tenacity.

Say I agree with the Mugabe position on land but I have no faith in Mugabe, the messenger, because of his record of failure and deviousness. Robert Mugabe has had 20 years to address the land question. While we appreciate the constraints of the Lancaster Constitution up to 1990, beyond that year he has had a pretty much free hand. He has acquired some land over the past 20 years, but who did he give that land to? This land went to ministers, permanent secretaries, army generals and other ZANU-PF sycophants. However, the immortality of the case for a land revolution should not be disputed.

The other reason most opposition parties do not succeed is that, on paper, Mugabe is closer to the peasants and workers. A Zimbabwean opposition party cannot win elections in Zimbabwe if it is to the right of ZANU-PF. The have-nots consisting of peasants and workers are the majority of our people. Hence, a political platform for the elites will not win elections in this country. ZUM, UP, ZUD and FORUM were all to the right of ZANU-PF. They had no ghost of a chance at the polls. This is why I support the MDC because its origin includes the labour movement and progressive civic society. There is potential for the MDC to ideologically position itself to the left of ZANU-PF. That is why I was incensed by *The Sunday Mail* for insinuating that I was attacking the upcoming MDC in my speech at the Ambassador Hotel last week. I did not say the trade unionists are misguided. No, I did not say any such thing. The MDC is the best thing that has happened in this country in the past 20 years.

However, we want to make sure that the MDC is a sustainable political party that survives victory or defeat in 2000. More importantly, we want the MDC to deliver on the basic bread-and-butter issues for ordinary Zimbabweans, while charting a new political system for our country. We want to see a revolution of values in Zimbabwe. The MDC, ZUD, UP and FORUM must have a different set of values from those of ZANU-PF. If you have autocratic and corrupt tendencies just like Mugabe, how are you going to run the country differently? I do not want to see a Chiluba situation here in Zimbabwe. What is the difference between Chiluba and Kaunda? We need to be focused so that if the MDC comes to power tomorrow and Tsvangirai is President, Zimbabwe is protected from his excesses and those of his successful party. Just as we currently need checks and balances to the ZANU-PF monolithic political system, we need restraining and stabilising measures against any new order. We must always cherish the idea of a strong opposition to whoever is in power. No one should ever be given a blank cheque. This should apply to every political leader, including Tsvangirai. This is the kind of thinking we should ingrain in our society.

It is so fundamental because, in 1980, we gave Mugabe a blank cheque because we thought he was our saviour. How wrong we were! There should always be robust opposition to whoever comes to power. We should never depend on an individual's assumed goodness, no matter how popular, talented or smart they are. Instead, we must build strong institutions and value systems and depend on these instead. If I come to power, Zimbabwe needs protection from me. There are no holy cows in this forum today. People of Zimbabwe, this is a no-holds-barred and no-prisoners-taken platform!

A great leader thinks about legacy. What kind of legacy is Robert Mugabe going to bequeath our nation? Is he going to be in the class of Mandela, Nkrumah, Nyerere, Lee Kuan Yew, Jefferson, Lincoln and Washington? It depends. If he goes the Mobutu way, he will not be buried at Zimbabwe's Heroes Acre. There will be no such honour for him if he is kicked out of power as an egocentric despot. There will be neither respect nor nobility extended to a disgraced dictator, or an unrepentant egomaniac. If he was to die today, do you think people would mourn him the same way we treated Joshua Nkomo? No! Would people feel sad, or remorseful? For what? For the unemployment, the shortages, the hyper-inflation and the institutionalised and pervasive corruption? No, there would be celebration in the streets of Harare instead.

Mugabe has the audacity to say he knows his ministers are getting a 10 per cent bribe in deals. He makes a joke out of such a grave matter. Why does he not fire them? Corruption is a serious and unpatriotic offence. Who is naive enough to believe that Cabinet ministers can take bribes while Robert Mugabe is not doing the same? We say this to Robert Mugabe: 'In the year 1999, we are not blind, deaf and dumb. You are the chief looter of our national coffers and the grandmaster of endemic corruption. We will hold you personally accountable. We are not fooled by your gimmicks and shenanigans.'

Due to the power of patronage occasioned by the ZANU-PF political monolith, members of the opposition, or just ordinary citizens, cannot win government and public sector tenders. You have to be a James Makamba, a Philip Chiyangwa or a Leo Mugabe to get anything done in this country. Why is this so? Joshua Nkomo was a voice of reason. It is not my intention to romanticise Umdala Wethu at all. However, we must give credit where credit is due. He was an old and tired nationalist like the rest of them and made mistakes too. The difference, nonetheless, is that Nkomo was prepared to sacrifice his own political career in pursuit of the national interest. He compromised in order to put an end to the genocide in Matabeleland. He was prepared to sacrifice his political party in order to bring the unity that ended the massacres. He was the voice of reason within a cruel, corrupt and intolerant bunch. Do you remember his intervention during Strive Masiyiwa's struggle for a cellphone licence? 'Award the young man the tender,' he demanded.

If Mugabe cares about this country, he must make sure he is part of the process of developing an all-inclusive Constitution. He is undoing the contributions that he made in the liberation struggle by overstaying in office, promoting endemic corruption and presiding over a brutal and undemocratic regime.

Developing a functional democracy is much harder than building a constitutional framework. This is because democratic values are not legislated but developed over time. These are values such as transparency, respect for the rule of law, belief in and practice of equality, social justice, gender justice, equity, fair play and accountability. For example, how are you going to solve challenges of ethnicity in this country? You cannot address them through a Constitution. You just have to use education, social mobilisation and leadership by example to destroy this cancer. Ethnicity is endemic in our society and its organisations be it government, business, trade unions, student unions, civic society or the churches. A functional political democracy which is vibrant and effective is the answer.

The media has a role in exposing evil and illegal activities such as corruption. It is not enough to talk about corruption without coming up with major institutional designs to combat corruption. We must have vertical institutions to combat corruption. These are interventions from within organisational systems and structures. We must have horizontal entities to combat corruption. These are entities that are external to the organisations. We are so obsessed about the people who are getting bribes, the 10 per cent. That's well and good, but what about those who are giving the bribes? It takes two to tango. Let us look at some of the international banks who are giving the ministers and government officials the bribes. The giver of bribes is as corrupt as the taker of bribes. Hence as we tackle corruption using vertical and horizontal institutions, we should also take cognisance of the role of the giver of bribes.

We also need an independent Anti-Corruption Commission whose members and mandate should not owe their allegiance to Mugabe, Parliament or the Judiciary. Members can be nominated and subjected to public hearings for confirmation.

Another aspect is the independent auditing of public accounts. We need to get private companies to audit such institutions as the Ministry of Finance, Ministry of Foreign Affairs, Ministry of Local Government, Ministry of Mines and Power Development and the Reserve Bank of Zimbabwe. Corruption is systemic and pervasive in this country and we need to have institutional designs to combat it. The rule of law itself must be imposed and leveraged. So, while a good Constitution will help to combat corruption it must be complemented by institutionalising and internalising the respect for rule of law, adherence to constitutionalism, all rooted in a new value system.

The political question is not easy because you can't legislate for success. You cannot legislate for values to come into existence. We as a nation have to slog away. You have to work on the ground and you have to convince people that the workers' programme is the best programme, if that is your persuasion. I do not believe that it is just or democratic for you to impose your agenda as the so-called vanguard party. The workers must win in the battle of ideas; that the ideas of ISO are the best ideas for Zimbabwe, the ideas of MDC are the best ideas for Zimbabwe; the same applies to UP, ZUD 1 and 2, and so on. I have work to do in this country to mobilise people and convince them that my programme is the best programme and, therefore, win in the battle of ideas.

Also, why are people splitting and then accusing ZANU-PF and CIO for their problems? My question is: Are you blind, deaf and dumb? Didn't you know that the CIO would infiltrate your party, or that ZANU-PF would infiltrate your organisation? You must be cleverer than that. Given 20 years of experience in Zimbabwe, you don't have to support the ZUD or MDC to be upset if the ZUD or MDC programme fails, because the failure of one group in Zimbabwe, where there is a political monolith, is indicative of the failure of the entire opposition ranks. If MDC or ZUM splits like that before elections, when you and your colleagues form a people's party, why would people take you seriously? Opposition politics would have lost credibility. How different are you from Makamure, they will ask. The precedent is terrible. We are talking about building a functional political democracy where change is possible.

Crafting economic programmes and platforms

Now with stage one and two accomplished, we need to move to stage three: crafting economic programmes and platforms. Here we assume that we now have both a good Constitution and a functional democracy in place. An opposition party like the MDC could actually be elected into power. The third challenge is then the need to have clear economic programmes and paradigms to solve bread-and-butter issues. What will a victorious MDC do on the economic front? Remember, my topic is for an exhaustive agenda for all political players in the country. Let us have a discussion on how we are going to grow this economy, how we are going to address the issues of unemployment, our infrastructure, high interest rates, the cost of money, inflation and the land question. What kind of land policy are we going to embark on? I am challenging the opposition parties to have a debate among themselves – MDC, UP, ISO and ZUD – on the economy, technology, land and industrialisation. What is the role of technology and the information superhighway in 1999? The debate that we want to see in Zimbabwe is about solutions. I don't want this platform to degenerate into a gripe session, or a pity party. We want answers. It is great to talk about a Constitution. It is great to talk about how to use a democratic dispensation to get into power. But the question is: 'Get in and do what?' We have a national AIDS crisis in this country – what is the opposition's strategy to combat the HIV/AIDS pandemic?

How are we going to take advantage of the issues that are brought to the fore by regional integration within the context of globalisation? For example, economies of scale – the bigger the market, the more successful the region gets, which is evident from Europe and the European Union. Do you think the British and French like each other? They don't like each other, but they are coming together to form a powerhouse, the European Union, that competes against Japan, the United States and Asia. That's the idea behind the EU. It now has a common currency, the euro. Do you think the United States loves China with its billion people? It does not, but a geographical area with a billion people means a huge potential market for US goods and corporates. It is not love but sheer economics.

The United States does not have permanent friends, only permanent interests. All you need to do is to discern what those interests are. So, when you find the United States giving China 'most favoured nation' status, it is because of the potential market that is envisioned out of a billion people. Also, China has nuclear weapons. Power recognises power. Game recognises game. There is no way the United States can use their military to attack China or Russia like they did with Milosevic, because both nations possess nuclear weapons. Hence there is a balance of terror. Yes, terror, unfortunately!

The war in the DRC must be stopped immediately, but I do not throw any cheap shots on this one. There is enough to blame around that war. I know people don't like Mugabe. I don't either. However, let us get real,

Kagame had issues. You cannot attack Mugabe in the DRC, without talking about Kagame and Museveni, and their own crimes in the region. There is a clear case of patriotism on Rwanda's side because Rwanda is concerned about its own security, but the question is, security at what cost?

On Museveni, he is not an ideal leader anyway, given his democratic deficit. People tend to confuse their national problems with regional issues. You cannot attack Mugabe only on this affair. I do not completely agree with the participation of our national forces in the DRC. Yes, Mugabe made mistakes, he was taking our money unnecessarily; but what we need to realise is, we need to stop that war and acknowledge that Kagame and Museveni have issues to answer as far as that war is concerned. I am appealing today to the African in Kabila, the African in Mugabe, the African in Museveni and the African in Kagame, to immediately resolve that conflict. Why are we busy fighting over territory when we know that there are people who hate us more than we hate each other? Our shared and historical enemies can only rejoice while we slaughter each other. What do we have in the global economy? Why don't we resolve that war? We don't have to love each other to resolve this matter.

SADC, regional integration and economic blocs are the way to go under globalisation. SADC, the Common Market for Eastern and Southern Africa (COMESA) – you put the two entities together and you are talking about 360 million people. With those kinds of numbers, you can go and negotiate serious Pan-African deals with the EU, China and the United States. SA is insane to be negotiating bilateral deals with Europe. You have to put your house in order and build up trade between Zimbabwe and South Africa, Botswana and South Africa, SADC and COMESA, into a sub-regional integration – good old-fashioned Pan-Africanism in terms of economy – because in the global economy, we need to make sure we have strong markets and strong economies that are based on integration between African peoples in the sub-region.

On the issue of export-based investments, I am only talking about possible ideas. I don't have a monopoly over these issues. I just want to ignite a debate on how to grow the African economy. I want to see a debate on solving unemployment, on solving these three economic animals: inflation, exchange rates and interest rates – the cost of money. We must come up with programmes that can resolve these problems. Export-based investments are where you can go and attract foreign investors to come and work in partnership with local investors and produce valued goods and services in Zimbabwe and sell them to the United States, to Japan and to Europe.

Export-based investments are key, because we are currently importing too much in this country. Our problem is that we produce what we don't consume and consume what we don't produce. We are churning out raw materials and selling them at cheap rates to the United States and Europe. And then what do we do? We import teaspoons and nails made in Japan, teaspoons made in Malaysia. What does it take to make a teaspoon? So, we want to have our own production that can create employment for our people through export-based investments, and then export to bring foreign currency in Zimbabwe and also those products being manufactured in Zimbabwe will be available to our own people. So, we need to be creative in our exports and imports. We are importing too much and we need to be producing and exporting refined products, that is, the issue of competitive advantage. What are we good at producing? What can we do better than DRC, better than SA, and then, concentrate on that and sell to the region, to Europe. We need to really sit down, reflect, discuss and identify where we can be competitive in the global economy. The global economy is about technology. What is the role of technology in Zimbabwe, high technology, and what is the role of the information superhighway? What is interesting is to remember that we are now talking about the number 3 item of our agenda today – that is, the crafting of economic programmes.

Number 3 won't work if numbers 1 and 2 are incomplete or not resolved, because who wants to bring money to Zimbabwe when there is no macroeconomic stability? Who wants to bring money to Zimbabwe when there is no political stability in Zimbabwe? Who wants to bring money to Zimbabwe when journalists are arrested and harassed with impunity? So, the political climate affects your economic programmes and paradigms. The constitutional framework affects the kind of economic activities you will carry out and, also, if your people are fed and healthy and if they can debate better on building a better Constitution. How can a starving peasant discuss the key elements of a new national Constitution and the lofty ideals of constitutionalism? How can a starving peasant in Tsholotsho or Dotito discuss functional separation of powers? So, discussions and enlightenment are fundamental so that people know what the issues are both around the Constitution and economic matters. We need a clear agro-industrial policy, a clear manufacturing policy, and a living and vibrant social contract between labour, government and industry. We need to make sure, when we come up with that contract, that the interests of the workers and the rights of the workers are enshrined viciously and strongly within that agreement, because the majority of the people in Zimbabwe are either workers or peasants, so the economic interests of this majority are fundamental and pervading democratic rights.

Women's rights are fundamental human rights. The right to education and the right to a job – all these are human rights. So, the social contract must take cognisance of the aspirations of the generality of the people of Zimbabwe. And also on technology – we need a tripartite science- and technology-driven strategy that is anchored by the government, academia and industry. Industry must support the university. Ideas from the university must be implemented in industry. Commercial businesses must put money into academic research – both basic and applied. The government must create the enabling environment while also injecting resources into research and university education in general. The government must leverage the expertise and knowledge of our researchers and intellectuals at UZ, the Scientific and Industrial Research and Development Centre (SIRDC) and the National University of Science and Technology (NUST). We want to make sure our best brains are utilised in formulating macroeconomic policies, technology strategy, manufacturing plans and industrialisation strategy.

A good case study of the tripartite science- and technology-driven industrialisation strategy that I have just described is what occurs in the United States. Industry, the academy and the US government work closely to drive science and technology research and development as a basis for industrialisation. If you go to the White House website there is an Economic Advisory Committee made up of professors from Harvard, Berkley and MIT advising Clinton on the US economy. There is a Science and Technology Advisory Committee full of professors from MIT, Stanford and Caltech advising the President on technology. So, if you see US President Bill Clinton being clear, knowledgeable and articulate about the economy or technology, he has been advised by the best in the United States.

What do we do in Zimbabwe? We say: 'The University of Zimbabwe is full of enemies!' How can you say the University of Zimbabwe is full of enemies? It is like saying the country is full of enemies. If the country is full of enemies what are you doing in government, running the affairs of your enemies? You must be smart enough to know what you don't know.

Government leadership must be able to consult lawyers, economists, scientists, engineers and entrepreneurs from the academic and research community so that it is able to develop and implement programmes and paradigms that can solve our economic woes in this country. When a leader is given advice, the public and sundry will not know where the specific idea comes from. You will get the glory as Robert Mugabe, or as the Minister of Finance. Nobody will know the source. The glory will go to you as the politician while Zimbabwe benefits. So, this culture where there is no respect for Zimbabwean intellectuals, where there is no respect for industry experts, is detrimental. Let us leverage the wisdom of all Zimbabweans. Also, let's make sure that we consume our own products in Zimbabwe. Why don't we buy 'Made in Zimbabwe'? Why do we want 'Made in Malaysia', 'Made in the United States' and 'Made in Japan'?

When we have problems in industry, where do we go? Do we consult Zimbabwean intellectuals or do we go to SA? Do we not go to England or the United States? Let us make sure that we take advantage of our own expertise in our different industry sectors such as the Zimbabwe Electricity Supply Authority (ZESA), PTC and Hwange Colliery. This will enable us to grow this economy from our own indigenous capabilities. This is crucial if we are going to make it in the information superhighway. The information superhighway is very interesting.

Remember, I said we have three levels to our discussion today. Number 3, the economic agenda, is heavily influenced by technology, in particular high technology, specifically the unfolding field of ICT. ICT technologies are not compatible with dictatorship. Autocracy and technology do not go hand in hand. Why, do you want evidence?

Just imagine you are Robert Mugabe and your idea of democracy is that when the labour union goes on a strike or stayaway, you shut down ZBC, you shut down *The Herald* and *Sunday Mail*, and prevent all these from covering these protests. Now, is this practical in the age of the information superhighway? No, because all you need within the context of the information superhighway are three things: a computer, telecommunications and power. With these you can broadcast and share information.

So, we need to make sure that as we come up with our agro-industrial policy, we accelerate our approach in bringing power to Zimbabwe, telecoms to Zimbabwe and computers; because with these three things you have got the internet. If you are not on the internet you are basically disconnected from the global economy. Most Africans are not on the internet, and most African Americans are not on the internet. So, these communities are effectively disconnected from the global economy.

Now, what do you think would happen if there was a benevolent donor who says to Robert Mugabe: I want to give you computers, I want to give you telecommunications and power so that 70 per cent of Zimbabwe is on the internet? Given his culture of autocracy, given his culture of dictatorship, a culture that seeks to control information dissemination, will he agree to that free package? For purely political reasons – because his idea of political democracy is control and more control of what citizens have access to – Mugabe would reject the offer. If you have access to the internet, criticism or denigration of Mugabe can occur as far away as Japan or the United States, and you can get to know about it in a second.

So, the culture of our leaders – who are petrified by democratic values, who are petrified by information dissemination – has to be changed. Dictatorship and autocracy are not compatible with the information superhighway. You can never fight technology; all you can do is use technology to further your interests, to make people's lives better. The superhighway today, basically the internet, is a critical weapon of struggle that we can use to further the interests of the generality of our people and we cannot fight technology but embrace it for common benefit.

That is a critical juncture in this country. We need to also think of the minority. There are two types of the psychology we should be aware of – the oppression of the majority by the minority and the oppression of the minority by the majority. Like in Zimbabwe on the matter of Zapu2000, I don't buy the argument today that Zapu2000 is ethnic at all. Why don't we ask ourselves why Zapu2000 is being formed today? Are there issues in Matabeleland to be addressed? Why do you think Zapu2000 is ethnic, why didn't you help them and solve those problems in Matabeleland so that they don't have a platform? It is important in our Constitution and in our political democracy that we protect the minority from the tyranny of the majority. It is very easy for us in Northern Zimbabwe, in Mashonaland,

Masvingo and Harare to forget that there is a minority who are potentially being victimised by the majority. Think about the Gukurahundi atrocities in Matabeleland from 1982 to 1987. How many of us talked about it from 1982 to 1987, or acknowledged that people were being killed by the 5th Brigade in Matabeleland? Where was the labour movement, where was the student movement – my favourite organisation? Where were they from 1982 to 1987? Where were the civic society and the media? Where were they when people were being butchered by Mugabe in Matabeleland?

The psychology of the oppression of a minority by the majority – we need to take cognisance of that. We need to make sure we put in place institutional structures to protect the minority from the tyranny of the majority. We must be cognisant of the potential victimisation of the minority by the majority. We did not speak out in the Students' Union, in student movements in 1985. Don't talk about it now, where were you in 1986? Where was Edgar Tekere in 1985? Where was Edson Zvobgo in 1985 about the Matabeleland atrocities? And now Edson wants to offer an apology today? How shameful! We need to make sure that we think about the minority.

Another example I can use is that of the United States. Black people constitute just 12 per cent of the US population. Working alone as a minority group, this makes democracy a limited weapon or tool for them. In the United States, with its 12 per cent black population, the majority can vote democratically to throw all the black people into the sea. So, democracy becomes a flawed weapon when you are a minority oppressed by the majority. In fact, in the United States they do that every day. They are voting to throw the black person into the sea all the time, because 12 per cent of the population in the United States is black people, and yet 50 per cent of the inhabitants of prisons are black. What is going on? In the United States, one third of young black males is in prison, on parole or on probation. In the year 1999, the United States is just another plantation, as far as I am concerned; a plantation worked by enslaved black people. Black people are justifiably upset and angry because they are treated as second-class citizens in the United States.

The psychology and philosophy of the oppression of the minority by the majority with impunity!

All these matters are what I want to see discussed and interrogated; and remember, the platform here is a platform that is exhaustive. The debate on the Constitution is a very powerful, persuasive and robust debate. But remember, once you have a damn good Constitution, it allows you to organise and win in the battle of ideas, but it doesn't guarantee you are going to win. Once you win, it doesn't mean you are going to feed Zimbabwe using a good Constitution. *Hazvidyiwe* (you do not eat a good Constitution). At best a good Constitution is an enabler of productive economic activities. What you need to do is to come up with clear, unequivocal economic programmes and paradigms to solve bread-and-butter issues.

Let us get the debate going in terms of what we do when we get into power as the opposition. What do we do as ZANU-PF when we win in 2000? My platform, my programme, my issues are for the entire Zimbabwean citizenry across the political divide. It is for the entire civic society, and for all political parties. Zimbabwe, which way forward? Let us embrace an imperative and exhaustive agenda.

The struggle continues.

(Ushewokunze, 1984) (Nkomo, 2001) (Fanon, 1963) (Chung, 1985) (Gandhi, 1927) (Mandela, 1994) (Soto, 2003) (Porter, 1998)

41 The case for both academic excellence and social responsibility

One of my major concerns, right from our UZ student activism days, is the issue of the balance between academic excellence and social or political activism. We have cases of very radical and brave student leaders who are, academically, pathetic performers. Some never finish their degree programmes, while others are forced to repeat courses and graduate at the bottom of their class. This bothers me. On the other hand, we have some razor-sharp whiz-kids who get all the distinctions and come top of their class, but show zero appetite for any type of social or community involvement. Neither group of students impresses me. I want to see outstanding academic excellence and robust social responsibility rooted in community engagement, in the same person. I now take this message on a crusade throughout US campuses. In particular, I target black students' unions at Ivy League schools. On 8 February 2000, I give just such a motivational speech to the Black Graduate Union at MIT.

Thank you very much for coming to this discussion. What we are going to talk about today is the case for both academic excellence and social responsibility. At elite institutions, such as MIT and Harvard, we understand very clearly the essence of academic excellence. However, sometimes we tend to underestimate the equal importance of social responsibility. Social and political consciousness is essential to a high achiever.

What I am going to do today is to demonstrate to you beyond any reasonable doubt that you need both weapons of struggle in your life – academic excellence and social responsibility. I am going to discuss some of the problems that we need to address as people of colour, or black people in the United States, in the year 2000 and beyond. Why is this essential? It is because, in spite of the superficial manifestation of success, we have not arrived yet. We have serious problems and hence we want to diagnose what those problems are, and understand our role in resolving them. What can you do now, while you are still a student? What can you do when you graduate from MIT into the world?

You must make sure that, in these years at university, you take time to sharpen your tools and prepare yourself to make a difference in society once you graduate from college. Now why is it important that you have these two tools of academic excellence and social responsibility? If you are going to be a great engineer or technology educator, you need to understand how society works, you need to understand how the economy works. This will enable you to be effective as an engineer or a scientist. You need to embrace social responsibility as a tool of understanding and impacting the social, political, economic dynamics of your work environment. As a scientist, you don't work in a vacuum. You are going to work with other people, people who look like you and people who don't look like you. So, it is imperative that you understand where you are coming from, where you are right now and where you are going. All these are critical and important matters for you to understand.

In any case, you also become more effective if, in addition to your technological or scientific expertise, you also understand society, master economics and grasp the essence of the law. That's how you become an effective chemical engineer or mechanical engineer. In any case, caring about the communities we come from is something we owe to those who came before us. Why are we here at MIT? Why is MIT now accommodating a good number of black students – 2 per cent – when there were not that many 30 years ago? How did it happen? It is because people who came before us fought to level the playing field. It is not because there were no smart black people 50 years ago. It was because of the inequity within society, which still exists today. We are here because others chose to struggle and sacrifice themselves in the 1950s and 1960s. We owe it to them to be socially responsible so that we can also create a better environment for those who will come after us. Maybe we can move up from 2 per cent and achieve a 12 per cent black student population at MIT. That will be quite an achievement. However, if you think about it, given the national demographics that is where the numbers should be. So actually, something is systemically wrong with MIT and the United States. The conditions at MIT must be made more conducive and enabling for all students.

Furthermore, there is a gap between ability and performance. Once you get into MIT, what kind of performance do you produce? What are the retention numbers? What percentage of black students who enter MIT graduate on schedule? How does this compare with other population groups? Maybe there is something that needs to be changed in this environment to make black students more productive. We recruit and get very capable black students here at MIT but do we get performance that is commensurate with that ability?

Back to the subject of excellence and social consciousness, you have a unique opportunity as scientists and engineers to be all-rounders. I have always argued that as scientists or engineers you can actually master both worlds of science and the humanities. Just imagine as you study Chemical Engineering or Mechanical Engineering, you can go into a History lecture and understand what they are talking about. You can do the same with English Literature, Philosophy and Economics. You can boost your knowledge by reading these subjects on your own. With some preparation, you can go into a Sociology or Business seminar and understand the discourse. You can cross over to the Law School at Harvard and easily master one or two things. Of course, you need to read the law on your own and prepare. All this cannot be said of a student studying History, Classics or Law. A student with such a major cannot easily walk into a class on Control Systems, Finite Element Analysis, Power Electronics or Calculus of Variations. It is harder for them to cross over from sociology to a class of electronic systems or chemical dynamics. So, as a scientist you are in a unique position to actually master technology and science, on the one hand, and socio-political and economic issues on the other. However, you have to work extra hard, to be that master of both worlds. You have to realise that it is important that you acquire the skills of analysis. You ought to realise the essence of both reading and writing cultures.

Being based at MIT, it is quite easy to master both worlds. All that is required is for you to be active here at MIT. Go to Harvard across the road and attend some of their seminars, go to Boston University, or attend events at the University of Massachusetts. You can easily attend all these intellectual events and feed your mind. That is what we call intellectual empowerment. This is how you attain a primer in intellectual self-defence. Consequently, when you are done with MIT you are armed with both a science or engineering degree and an intellectually empowered mind. As a result, you can go into the world and become an effective engineer or scientist. Having proximity to multiple sources of intellectual activities is the beauty of being at MIT, in the heart of Boston.

Studying and learning outside the classroom is essential, because if you are not careful you might end up being formally educated without being knowledgeable or possessing efficacious and operational excellence. Okay, let us imagine you come top in your class at MIT with a perfect 4.0 GPA, are you sure you can go and become the head of Boeing, GM, GE or NASA? Remember, the United States tells you the sky is the limit but you and I know the sky is not the limit. My argument is that the smarter you are, the more you get angry with the United States. The more talented you are, the angrier you get with the United States because you realise the sky is not the limit. If you are mediocre or average and you can't become President of MIT you can rationalise it by saying, 'Maybe I wasn't good enough.' What if you are more than good enough, and those great doors do not open because of the colour of your skin or gender? A politically conscious mind will help you deal with your predicament.

Just look at the elite white schools such as Harvard, MIT, Yale, Princeton and Stanford. How many of them have been headed by a woman? White or black I don't care. None. How many of them have been headed by a black person? So what does it take to become President of MIT, beyond academic ability? Why is that quality only missing in black folk? Why have we always had a male President at this institution since it started on 10 April 1861? Are you telling me there is no woman or black person who could have headed MIT throughout its long history? What is it that is required to run this institution that a woman or black person does not have?

What happens is that as a black person in the United States, although you can do extremely well, the sky is not the limit. Even as a superstar graduate from MIT you are going to meet your glass ceiling. When it happens to you out there, you must know why it is happening and you can work around it and mobilise. Pick up the struggle and work with others. In any case, you owe it to those who didn't make it to MIT. You and I have a duty and obligation to do something about the conditions in New York, LA and Boston, because racism is still with us in the year 2000. Institutional racism, scientific racism and social racism, all these forms of racism are with us today. What I am challenging you now to do is to master your chemical engineering and, at the same time, master the understanding of white supremacy, the understanding of the system. When I say system, I mean race, class and gender.

Look at the issue of prisoners: Why is it that a third of the young black males are associated with parole or probation or prison? Even if it's not one third, the point is that the number is disproportionate to the national demographics. Why is it that they are associated with parole, probation and prison? Also, of the prison population, 40 per cent of the prisoners are black, and black people are 12 per cent of the population. In some cases, the prisons are 50 per cent black. These are people who look like you. Why not ask yourselves, as MIT engineering students, what is going on? We need to talk about prison because young black people are locked up. Why are they being locked up?

There are two reasons we can fashion. We could say black people are predisposed to criminal behaviour. It is in our genes. That is one interpretation. Alternatively, we could say it is a social problem. There is something wrong going on in our society that leads to the incarceration of a bulk of young black males. Of these two schools of thought, only the latter makes sense. US society must reform. Surely you can't justify the racist genetic theory. We have to address the issue of our society. We need to be looking at the causes of crime. Why are our people committing crime?

What are the social causes of crime in society? That is one aspect we should investigate. However, we first acknowledge that some people are actually locked up not because they committed crime. They would have been set up by crooked cops, working for the anti-black socio-economic and political system. You have read about the case in Chicago about a black man who was locked up for 16 years and was released last year when a lawyer and a bunch of students investigated the case and showed that he did not commit the crime. New DNA techniques are freeing a lot of locked-up innocent people. There are many black people who were locked up who did not commit any crime at all. It could be you next time.

Don't think if you are at MIT or Harvard, you won't get locked up for no reason. Then there's the LA situation in California where the institutions are coming up with information, that the institutions have people, these people could be anybody and could be you. The issue we need to talk about is that they are political prisoners, such as Mumia Abu-Jamal, Mutulu Shakur. Geronimo Pratt was in prison for 27 years and only released in 1997. Why was he locked up? It is because he was set up by a snitch called Butler. He was 600 miles away from the murder scene in California at the time the crime was committed. Why was he set up? Because he was a member of the Black Panther Party. He was released after 27 years, just like Mandela, and no one talks about him.

And so, we are not making false allegations because the state agrees that there was a violation of his right. He did not commit a crime and he came out after 27 years. The movie *The Hurricane*, how many of you have watched it? It is a depiction of a true story. Hurricane was locked up for 20 years, again he had not committed the crime. He was set free to go after 20 years in prison. What can you do?

The other problem of prison is disenfranchisement. When you commit a felony and you come out you can't work anymore, and you cannot vote. You are disenfranchised. Many young black males are getting disenfranchised. I want you to learn about black people, facts about the prison system and political prisoners. Read your history from W.E.B. Du Bois, Malcolm X, Martin Luther King, the Black Panthers and The Black Liberation Army. I want you to read a book by George Jackson called *Blood in my Eye*. Read books by the following other Panthers: Huey P. Newton, Bobby Seale, Ellen Brown, Eldridge Cleaver, Kathleen Cleaver, Fred Hampton and Kwame Ture.

Why I like the 1960s is because we had young people like you – 18-, 19-, 20-year-olds – who were active. When I see Fred Hampton, at 20, and Kwame Ture at 22, speak and I compare them with yourselves, you must be ashamed. You are at MIT and Harvard, and your knowledge of the world does not even compare. Their sacrifice and courage put you to shame. These young people in the Panthers and SNCC were as smart as it gets. However, they chose revolution.

So, what are you doing in the year 2000 here at MIT? Are you standing up to power? Yes to academic excellence. Indeed, you must be intelligent, but also active in society. You must be doing well in your classroom but you must also be agitating for change. This period of inactivity in the United

States is what we can call the 'do nothing' years, if you compare them to what was happening in the 1960s. There is no movement, organisations or serious agitation for change. There is neither a revolution nor revolutionaries. It is a terrible indictment of all of us.

We need to come up with a programme to solve the issue of Boston but we want to make sure we learn from the mistakes of the Panthers, and the strength of the Panthers. Don't reinvent the wheel. We need to learn from the history of activism of the 1960s. I would like to urge you to read and empower your mind. A page of history is worth 10 volumes of logic. Go back to Joseph DeLaine, Booker T. Washington, Marcus Garvey, Frederick Douglass, right up to the hip hop nation. The white-controlled United States is so scared of heroes like the Black Panthers and the Black Liberation Army, because they were using guns. The United States seems to abhor violence as an instrument of struggle, but my position is if you dislike the use of violence change those conditions in the ghetto that make me want to revolt and shoot somebody.

Our heroes who came before us put their lives on the line, Fred Hampton was killed in Chicago at 20 years old by the police. People are still in prison now because they are members of the Black Panther Party and Black Liberation Army. All these activities are what we need to feed our minds with that knowledge. What I am suggesting is that we understand where we are coming from, starting from the capture into slavery in Africa, the Middle Passage, through slavery on the US plantations, into the civil rights movements, right up to the United States of today. How do we relate to those so that, as engineers and scientists, we can organise ourselves, by getting knowledge and making a difference in society?

Also, if you look at the Abraham Maslow hierarchy of needs. The needs start from food, shelter, clothes, and move up; I want you to get to self-actualisation, and go beyond it and bequeath a legacy. This final stage is called 'self-transcend'. If you think about it, begin by saying I came from MIT, got a degree from MIT. What happens when you are gone? Let's say your name is John Dexter – when you are gone, what is John Dexter's legacy? We know the Malcolm X and Martin Luther King legacies. When you are gone, you want us to talk about the John Dexter legacy. Self-transcend, live a legacy, go beyond the self, beyond the PhD from MIT and be satisfied and help somebody else. Can you make a difference in society? Can you self-transcend and leave a legacy?

I will talk about the hip hop nation, today in the year 2000 there is more progressive material coming from hip hop music and black people like Janet Jackson. Why? Because the young people involved in the hip hop nation have a potential for revolution, there is potential to conscientise people through artists like KRS-One, Public Enemy and the Ghetto Boys. If you just listen to Tupac Shakur's *Dear Mama*, *Brenda's Got A Baby*, *White Man's World* and *Keep Your Head Up*, you see the wisdom coming from hip hop. They are poets with minds. Now these are messages coming from young black men with no high school diplomas. They are high school dropouts. Yet, they effectively talk about the white men's world. They talk about black sisters who are left with children by these men, talk about women who are raped by people and are left alone. These are messages that are coming from Tupac. In fact, Tupac says, 'I am like a flower growing out of concrete.'

If you see a flower growing out of concrete you don't say this flower is rough, rugged and raw. You must be happy that a flower is growing out of concrete, because flowers don't grow in concrete. So, the United States should be happy that Tupac Shakur could achieve 2 per cent of what I accomplished. According to the United States, he was meant to fail. The United States failed Shakur as a high school dropout, the same for Malcolm X. He had to remake himself after coming out of prison to come out on fire. Now, you tell me, when you see Malcolm X speak, when you listen to Shakur's lyrics or see him in an interview, are you not impressed by these two's natural intelligence and inspiration? Malcolm X is a genius. Tupac is a genius. So, the United States is failing our best. My question therefore is, if the United Sates is failing our best, what about the not-so-great, our average people? How about our people below average? It's a total travesty.

Let us talk about work ethic. You are at MIT, you know something about working hard. Now you tell me how much time it will take you to do three movies and 150 songs in one year? Tupac Shakur did just that in his last year of his life on planet Earth. How many hours do you think he slept? Not only was Tupac extremely bright and creative, he was a workaholic. He was the ultimate superstar. Can you as students at MIT and Harvard compare yourself to Tupac? Are you as smart? Are you as enterprising? Do you work as hard? Just try to do three different Bachelor's degrees in four years. Then we can put you in Tupac's league. Read the book by his bodyguard, titled *Got Your Back*. Tupac used to sleep in the studio working hard, dropping hits and tunes. What I am saying is that even in the hip hop nation we saw progressive values such as solid work ethic, creativity, focus and determination. This is in addition to the social consciousness in the critique of society that is found in their lyrics. These young people in the hip hop nation are distinguished poets with minds. They are revolutionary poets and wordsmiths.

Yes, there are also these bad aspects in the hip hop culture, such as the disrespecting of black women, crass materialism and the worshipping of money. Of course, there is the commercial side. Young people are trying to get paid. All this speaks to the limitations of using hip hop as the only arena and framework of struggle. The revolutionary poets must complement revolutionaries. Unfortunately, in the year 2000, there are no revolutionaries in the United States. How sad! In hip hop, a special place of honour is reserved for artists who sell lots of records, while pushing positive messages. These artists include Tupac, KRS-One, Public Enemy, Ghetto Boys, Common, Ras Kass, to mention but a few.

If you have the temptation to think that you are going to be the lucky one – 'I am going to blow up, and become a superstar in the United States' – I am going to give you a counter-example in the form of Arthur Ashe. What did he say when he contracted AIDS and was dying? I will quote him: 'The burden of race in the United States was heavier than the burden of AIDS.' Every time I quote this, members of my audience are shocked and they say, 'Did he say that?' They think that because he was getting all this glamour, cash, fame and glory, he was happy. No, he was not.

He was still a black man in the United States. He still carried the burden of being black in the United States. As a result, he was still upset. Look at the biographies of Gladys Knight and Oprah Winfrey. They have lots of money but are still angry with the United States. Bill Cosby's wife gave a terrible indictment of the United States when their son was murdered. People were shocked. They thought just because they had fame, success and money, they were happy with the country. As I said before, in the United States, the more talented you are, the more upset you get because you really see that the sky is not the ceiling.

Clarence Thomas is sitting on the Supreme Court bench. Surely if he is sitting there, he must have some academic excellence, but I don't see the social responsibility. He is trying to kill affirmative action. He is trying to destroy the bridge after crossing it. That's the temptation with white supremacy. It is easier to attack black people by using a black face. It's like: 'No, I am black, too, but I don't agree with you.' White supremacy will use Clarence Thomas and his like to further the white agenda at the expense of black people.

There are examples of people who have some academic excellence but no social responsibility. There are many Professors who are in that category. Don't get carried away and say because you are a black Professor, then you are progressive. You might be a miseducated Negro. Who taught you how to be black and who taught your teacher, Mr Black Professor? Trace back and you find a white master. A white Professor cannot give you black consciousness. When you see a black Professor next time, ask them, 'Professor, what are you doing about miseducation?' If you are not careful, a PhD from MIT or Oxford will make you a miseducated Negro.

What you need to be an educated man is self-education. What I am saying is read the original sources of knowledge of black staff that they won't give you in the school system. Why would they equip you with such tools of education? It's not natural. You need to teach yourself, through studying black books, about our own history, self-love and self-respect. You can also attend progressive meetings at Harvard or Boston University. Actually, you are in a unique and privileged position here at MIT because you have renowned universities like MIT, Harvard, Boston University and the University of Massachusetts. I have been here just for two seconds and I have received messages about events taking place at Harvard.

Colin Powell, he is interesting because he has taken a position on some affirmative action in the community and so on, but I will give examples of how you are forced to choose between making it and identifying yourself with your people, between making it and doing what is right. Henry Louis Gates of Harvard interviewed 13 African-American men for his book *Thirteen Ways of Looking at a Black Man*. In his interview with Colin Powell, Colin Powell said he knew that Bush and Reagan were racists. Then he goes and takes a picture of Reagan that was autographed by him and is written, 'Colin Powell, whatever you say goes.' Then he says to Gates, 'Look at this. This is what President Reagan was saying about me. So, you want me to attack Reagan?' My question is: 'Are you prepared to sacrifice the black community because of an autographed picture?'

Are you prepared to sacrifice the black community because of the job at McKinsey or GE or at MIT? You are going to be forced as black people who are shot-callers, you are going to be forced to make a choice, make a decision between getting paid and doing what is right. We all need to be paid, I also need some Benjamins (money), but sometimes you need to draw the line to what you are not prepared to do. Don't sell your soul. In the hip hop nation, this is what you sometimes see happening when, because what the artists want to do is simply sell records, they go with the music to the recording companies without the powerful and scathing messages because they will be trying to get paid. People are selling their souls to get paid. That is very unfair because many people of colour are going to be forced to make decisions and choose between what is right and getting paid. All you have to do now is to be active in the BSU, BGSA, NSBE or Black Women's Association at Harvard. Organise a joint event between the groups, Latino groups and African Association groups. We have the same enemies and our destinies are intertwined together.

We don't have to be collapsed into one organisation but we just need to work together, organise common agendas, common issues, agitate for change together, go and support the Black Women's Associations at Harvard, go and support the black cause at Boston University, University of Massachusetts and so on and so forth. Challenge yourself – if all you are doing at MIT is to go to class and make good grades, then challenge yourself to say I am not doing enough, I can do more. Please be able to get that 3.8 or 3.6 GPA but, at the same time, feed your mind. Be active in BSU, support the event, and be part of the committee. Why? Actually, it's also good for you, professionally, because when you get into corporate United States, when you work at McKinsey & Company, when you work for these companies, the leadership skills that you would have mastered while working for NSBE will stand you in good stead. The organisational skills will come in handy. Your social skills will come in handy so whatever you do – even getting paid, social responsibility and social activism will help you.

This is the time that you have opportunities as young people. Seize them! Take advantage of them! Once you start working out there you are going to have social and economic obligations. You will be constrained by political and family commitments. You won't be able to do what you can do right now. So, as a student, it's a unique opportunity for you to feed your mind and grow intellectually and socially so that you can make a difference in your society. There are two things you do yourself, discipline and feed your mind, and then you need to join other people and socialise and fellowship to make a difference. Remember, if there are things which are not right at MIT you need to advocate for change. If there are things you know are wrong in the United States, you need to advocate for change. Whether we are talking about regime change, systemic change or institutional change, it is always carried out through some form of organised structure and you need to be a part of those formations – at the forefront of change.

At the same time, as individuals we need to be responsible to make sure that we can become better people and we can actually make a difference in our own lives and in society. Your health is the most important thing you have. Take care of it by eating well and exercising. Why? Because your health is the only vital thing you have in a struggle. Most of our heroes have been taken away by health problems. With Kwame Ture, it was cancer and some even suggested it was an FBI-induced cancer. Louis Farrakhan is ill now with cancer as well. I don't know how he is progressing over there in Chicago. We wish him well.

So, we need activists. Some who came before us were shot. Malcolm X was shot. Dr King was shot. At least we are not putting you in harm's way. We are pushing for consciousness, intellectual empowerment and making a difference in your different communities. Join organisations where you can discuss survival techniques and find ways to survive in this stressful environment such as MIT.

It is very critical to show personal and social solidarity to each other and so, the next thing we need to discuss, is how we portray the issue of culture. Remember we talked about hip hop. The problem with hip hop is that we actually do not own these recording companies. So they can dictate what you can't say and what you can say. He who pays the piper calls the tune. I respect the Jews for taking care of business and making sure that they get reparations and making sure that their people know about their story. Now you and I have a duty and obligation to make sure that our story is told the right way by ourselves and again it comes with economic empowerment, running our own business, the movie houses and record companies. We need to represent ourselves worldwide because, as long as somebody else is in charge, they can dictate and portray it their way.

So again, what we are saying is he who controls the money dictates the terms of reference, dictates what cannot be said and what can be said and we are just basically trying to get paid and running around when we don't control the business. We need to own our own businesses and all institutions in our communities. Remember ownership was never part of a slave's mentality or psyche. A slave or enslaved person was supposed to be owned. They were never supposed to own things. It is not in the nature of a slave to own things. We need to break this cycle and start owning things, own our businesses, own our own schools, so that we can make a difference and rightly portray ourselves.

Education is another critical thing. If you are to look back in history, the worst crime a slave master would commit was to teach his slave to read and write. You could beat up your slave, cut their fingers, no problem. However, if you taught your slave to read and write, that was a major crime. Why? The crafters and managers of the slavery system realised that an educated and mobilised mind could lead to a rebellion by the slave. It gave the enslaved person a primer in intellectual self-defence, a weapon of struggle. When the African is educated, he is conscientised. Then he can start questioning issues, start defending himself, and the potential for revolt increases. Remember the black African was never meant to be educated or informed. The education that we are getting we are being afforded grudgingly, and by default, not by altruistic design.

That is why you need to make sure that you go beyond the formal curriculum. You must go beyond what they teach you at MIT. Beyond this, I am emphasising solidarity and collaboration between Africans in the United States and Africans on the continent. There are also Africans in Brazil. Remember people of African descent, wherever they reside, must unite. We are all the same people. If you combine all these people, you come up with 2 billion people globally, a 2-billion-people economy. So how are you a minority?

As we conclude this session, my charge to you is as follows: Go beyond basic needs and pursuits. Go beyond self. Go beyond self-actualisation. In fact, self-transcend and leave a legacy. In order to do that efficaciously, you need to arm yourself with both academic excellence and social responsibility. As you aspire to do all this, remember a page in history is worth 10 volumes of logic.

I thank you.

(Malcolm X, 1965) (Ani, 1986) (Gates, 1997) (Jackson, 1972) (Newton, 1973) (Brown, 1993) (Alexander, 1998) (King, 1998) (Ture, 1992) (Brown, 1993)

42 Zimbabwe at the crossroads: The nature of the beast and the way forward

I am back in Zimbabwe, on a visit from MIT in the United States. As I get close to concluding my thought leadership tour of duty in the United States, I increase my engagement in Zimbabwe while looking forward to relocating to the continent, if not to Zimbabwe directly. Debates are raging in our country where myriad challenges are confronting the nation. There is no clarity on the nature of the Zimbabwean problems; much less, clearly structured and implementable solutions. Furthermore, there is no thought applied to the development of the requisite values and institutions. I decide to jump into the fray with the objective of addressing this paradigmatic and ideological deficit. It is 27 March 2000, and this public lecture is hosted by the Zimbabwe Economic Society in Harare. In analysing the constitutional referendum results, I accurately predict ZANU-PF's victory in the forthcoming June 2000 parliamentary elections.

Zimbabwe is at the crossroads, characterised by an economic crisis of immense proportions, rampant and debilitating corruption, unprecedented levels of poverty and unemployment, the AIDS crisis, the unresolved land question, a constitutional impasse, disrespect for the rule of law and a pending general election. This article seeks to understand the nature of these intractable problems confronting Zimbabwe and proffer solutions that can lead the country out of this social, economic and political quagmire.

It is essential to envision short- and long-term redemptive programmes and paradigms, which are predicated on a thorough grasp and appreciation of the issues at hand. The article proceeds by establishing three national objectives, explaining the rationale behind them, and then understanding the nature of Zimbabwe's problems and shaping the way forward around those three themes.

National objectives

Three imperative and exhaustive objectives can be identified for the Zimbabwean polity:

- Achieve effective and qualitative political change in the forthcoming elections;
- Transform Zimbabwe into a functional and sustainable democracy;
- Address matters of the Zimbabwean economy.

These objectives are equally critical, and they dialectically and dynamically affect each other. Consequently, they should be tackled simultaneously and taken into account at the beginning of any serious discussion about the way forward in Zimbabwe. A detailed elaboration of the objectives is in order.

1. *Achieve effective and qualitative political change in the forthcoming elections.* This objective entails that political change must have both form and content, that is, in addition to changing the political principals, the political principles, values, culture and programmes must be radically changed as well. The justified enthusiasm about change should be complemented by an equal zeal for the quality of change. The 2000 general elections should not be a missed opportunity for substantive change.
2. *Transform Zimbabwe into a functional and sustainable democracy.* This is a long-term objective that requires institutional reform (including constitutional changes), a vibrant and discerning civil society, effective and democratic political parties, competent and independent media houses, social mobilisation and civic education, depoliticisation of the armed services and demilitarisation of civilian institutions. A new political culture and value system characterised by transparency, tolerance, democracy, gender and social justice has to be developed and backed by institutional provisions.
3. *Address matters of the Zimbabwean economy.* The spectrum of issues that have led to the economic crisis includes mismanagement, incompetence, lack of capacity, fiscal indiscipline, corruption, ethnicity, political patronage, the DRC war, a misguided, ego-based foreign policy, a flawed Constitution, the absence of commitment to a coherent land policy, and lack of both creativity and innovation. Both short-term economic recovery strategies and long-term programmes should be devised to arrest the economic decline and rejuvenate the economy. The prime motivation should be to achieve the following related tasks: rein in inflation and interest rates, reduce the budget deficit, expand the tax base, grow the economy, create new jobs, emphasise exports, promote investment, expand the industrial base and thus restore macroeconomic stability. A radical paradigm shift is required from the land-based economy to the knowledge economy characterised by information

technology, electronic commerce, high technology, financial services and biotechnology. All economic programmes must take cognisance of the reality of globalisation and the implications thereof.

Effective and qualitative political change in 2000

The draft Constitution presented by the government in the historic February 2000 referendum was rejected because of both process and content arguments. In addition, people were simply saying 'NO' to arrogant misrule and unprecedented economic hardships. The referendum results were significant in that they showed that the ruling ZANU-PF party could be defeated. The myth of Mugabe's indestructibility and invincibility was shattered. Thus, the results constitute a clear psychological and propaganda victory for the opposition parties over the ruling party in the forthcoming elections. This then raises the question: How do Zimbabweans translate that referendum victory into effective and qualitative political change in the 2000 general elections?

Firstly, let us do the arithmetic and the corresponding analysis from the referendum results. The assumption here is that the ZANU-PF government did not rig the referendum. This is a generous assumption since it is common cause that they actually rigged it and lost. They simply miscalculated the amount of rigging required. This fact should be borne in mind in the coming elections and hence effective electoral monitoring is imperative. Back to the referendum arithmetic: The NO campaign received 55 per cent of the votes while the YES campaign got 45 per cent. From analysing results from each of the 120 constituencies, it is clear that 63 constituencies voted YES and 57 voted NO. A similar study of the 10 provinces shows that six of the provinces voted YES and four voted NO. The apparent discrepancy between the referendum result (55 per cent versus 45 per cent) and constituency-province results is explained by the fact that the whole country was treated as one constituency for the purposes of the referendum. Hence the heavy-turnout NO vote victory in the urban and peri-urban areas outweighed the low-turnout YES vote victory in the rural areas.

The implications of these results for the forthcoming general election (being run under the doctored Lancaster House Constitution) is that if the opposition parties do as well as they did in the referendum, they will get 57 seats. ZANU-PF will get 63 seats plus the 30 non-constituency seats, which means 93 seats. This analysis is not meant to discourage the opposition but rather to emphasise and dramatise the amount of work that needs to be done. To achieve parliamentary majority, the opposition parties have to increase their performance from that of the referendum by at least 50 per cent. On their side, they have the psychological advantage (alluded to earlier on), the economic crisis, the unfolding high-level corruption and the thorough unpopularity of ZANU-PF. Against them they have unclear (if not absent) coalition strategies, low campaign resources, insufficient capacity, incomplete platforms/programmes, harassment and intimidation from ZANU-PF and the definite possibility of rigging.

As the opposition parties strive to gain a parliamentary majority, they should pay special attention to the issue of the quality of political change, that is, the content and substance of change. It is not enough to ride on a wave of popular discontent and engage in reactive anti-Mugabe politics. What is required is proactive policy formulation intertwined with emphasis on both the quality of political programmes and calibre of candidates. It is insufficient to react to Mugabe's positions on land, war vets and the economy. In fact, the initiative should be taken away from the Mugabe regime on all issues. This can be achieved by having clear social, economic and political paradigms and programmes that are articulated and represented by quality candidates.

One challenge for the opposition can be posed as follows: How best to address issues where ZANU-PF's positions appear to be progressive, reasonable or popular? It is inadequate to simply observe that they, ZANU-PF, are just electioneering and that they do not mean what they say. The ability to separate the message from the messenger is a political skill. If an idea is good or useful, take it, spin it and repackage it. No one holds patents for political messages. Of course, the most satisfying circumstances would be when an idea or programme is a novel opposition original. This is where creativity, innovation, analytical capacity and intellectual depth are of the essence. However, it is foolhardy, unproductive and cheap politics to be against everything that has been done or propounded by the ruling party.

The land question and the liberation war legacy are two examples of areas where the initiative has to be wrestled from the Mugabe regime. The land issue will be addressed later in the section on the economy. ZANU-PF owns neither the liberation war legacy nor the war veterans. That legacy and its ex-combatants belong to Zimbabwe, and consequently to all opposition parties.

Most Zimbabweans made sacrifices and fought in the war in different ways, and no contribution is of insignificant value. There are many ex-combatants involved in the leadership and general membership of opposition parties. All opposition parties should clearly and actively defend the liberation war legacy and articulate policies that address the war veterans as an important section of Zimbabwean society. For example, rather than have blanket criticism of the allowances given to the war vets, one could argue for means testing of all assistance given to the ex-fighters. This means that only ex-fighters who are unemployed, destitute and landless should receive help. Ex-fighters who are gainfully employed, in charge of the armed forces, running the government or have successful businesses do not need any assistance. No one should be paid for liberating Zimbabwe.

If means testing is applied to all the allowances, the total expenditure on the ex-fighters can be reduced by more than 60 per cent. The fact that the chief criminals in abusing funds meant for the war vets were the undeserving elites running the armed services and the government is instructive. It is totally unwise for opposition parties to be pushing simplistic and opportunistic anti-war veteran rhetoric. Yes, there are individual war veterans, inside and outside the government structures, who are behaving like paid mercenaries and prostitutes on behalf of ZANU-PF.

However, this does not warrant surrendering the entire liberation war legacy, lock, stock and barrel, to Mugabe, who incidentally by the end of the war did not know how to shoot a pistol, return a subordinate's salute or properly wear a military uniform. ZANU-PF does not deserve the liberation war advantage that it is being given on a silver platter by the opposition. The farm invasions and their legal and political ramifications should be understood within the context of the above discussion. This is a case of ZANU-PF trying to use its two major trump cards – land and the liberation war legacy – to avoid defeat in the elections. The objective is to placate the ex-fighters (and some rural dwellers), appear progressive on land, make the country ungovernable and intimidate the rural electorate into voting ZANU-PF.

The opposition parties have a duty and obligation to expose the bankruptcy of ZANU-PF's electioneering gimmicks and enunciate their own exhaustive alternative platforms that cover land, war vets, the Constitution and the economy among other things.

By emphasising these clearly articulated, quality programmes that are buttressed by a leadership that has capacity to manage, implement and deliver, they can only increase their showing in the coming elections.

The emphasis on content and quality of change cannot damage the opposition; rather it will strengthen them and make them more viable. Moreover, it will ensure that when the opposition takes over there is neither further economic decay nor stagnation that could lead to a crisis of expectations as happened in Zambia. Even if the opposition does not win a parliamentary majority, it is important that a strong quality opposition is in place as a government in waiting.

Two general areas that define the quality agenda and its associated thesis are the transformation of Zimbabwe into a sustainable democracy and the clear resolution of matters pertaining to the crippled Zimbabwean economy. The following sections cover these subjects.

Transform Zimbabwe into a functional and sustainable democracy

Building a functional and sustainable democracy requires time and nurturing. Emphasis should be placed on both representative and participatory aspects of democracy. The starting point is effective and democratic institution building. In particular, a non-partisan and people-driven Constitution-making process should be embarked upon immediately after the 2000 general elections, irrespective of the results. The process of Constitution-making is as important as the contents of the final document. Human beings are not only defined and judged by the final product of their activities, but also by the processes they engage in as they produce the outcome.

As has already been indicated, the historic February 2000 referendum was rejected because of both process and content arguments. The ZANU-PF Constitution-making process was intensely partisan, fraught with irregularities and thoroughly undemocratic. The resulting Constitution (the content) did not reflect the people's wishes. It ostensibly entrenched an all-powerful executive presidency, did not empower Parliament, denied complete proportional representation, failed to create independent institutions that promote democracy and did not provide economic and social rights.

Some people have argued that since the document had some aspects slightly favourable to the opposition (for example, the removal of the 30 non-constituency seats and the introduction of the 50 seats based on proportional representation), it should have been adopted as a strategic move. This line of thinking misses the essence of the process argument. To dramatise this argument, even if the ZANU-PF Constitutional Commission had (by divine intervention) presented a Constitution similar to that mooted by the NCA, this document would have been equally rejected in spite of its content, and justifiably so. Therein lies the danger of a politicised, exclusive, polarising partisan process. Once the Constitution-making process was reduced to a partisan political fight by the government, the opposition was politically obliged to vote NO, while ZANU-PF and its surrogates had to vote YES. The process is just as important as the content, and a flawed process can never deliver for posterity.

A Constitution should not be drafted in a partisan way, even if it is just the perception of partisanship. Perception becomes reality. As the principal regulatory document of a nation, a Constitution should be developed for posterity by an all-inclusive, non-partisan, transparent and people-driven approach. Neither the incumbents nor their opposition should exclusively set the agenda or control the process. The rest of civil society, such as workers, churches, students and peasants, have critical roles to play. These are the principles that should inspire the drafting of a new Constitution after the general elections.

The two NCA demands for an all-stakeholder constitutional convention and a Constitutional Reform Act provide a good starting point. Whichever government assumes power after the election must ensure that a people-driven, all-stakeholder approach to developing a Constitution is maintained. The strategy of using the parliamentary route as advanced in the ZANU-PF 2000 manifesto must be denounced and fought against. Although this approach is legally provided for, given the referendum, its results and the activities prior to it, no political party has moral or political authority to produce a new Constitution for the nation even if it can garner a two-thirds majority in Parliament.

The NCA has a major obligation in the fight against the parliamentary approach. However, on its activities, a word of caution is in order. For the NCA to remain a viable, credible and effective vehicle in the Constitution-making process, it should remain a non-partisan, all-inclusive, democratic and transparent body where all political parties and civic organisations feel comfortable, respected and consequential. Political principles involved in the NCA and party politics should not sacrifice the NCA agenda in pursuit of party objectives. The NCA's mission of getting a Constitution for Zimbabwe should be completely delinked from the opposition parties' objective of dislodging ZANU-PF. This does not mean that the two tasks are incompatible or that they are in tension. Although any good Constitution will unequivocally facilitate the demise of the ZANU-PF monolithic political system, the process of making such a document should impartially involve all stakeholders, including small opposition parties and ZANU-PF. No political party should dominate or be over-represented in the NCA, as this will damage the NCA effectiveness.

In addition to a good Constitution, a functional democracy requires a vibrant civil society, independent media, viable political parties, a tolerant political culture, transparency and accountability. This entails a new social and political value system that cannot be achieved by sheer legislation. It has to be developed through social mobilisation, civic education, participation, effective information dissemination, new education curricula and economic empowerment. Legislation and institutional reform simply provide the enabling environment. Building this new culture is more challenging and requires more work than institution-building. Institutional provisions should be put in place to support the new value system. In Zimbabwe, the culture of monopolistic politics, personality cult, political intolerance, lack of transparency and accountability, autocratic tendencies, corruption, incompetence and mismanagement is pervasive and endemic throughout all social, political and economic organisations. It is a categorical imperative for those fighting for change to accept unequivocally the undeniable fact that they are all cut from the same ZANU-PF cloth. Hence, they have a duty and obligation to proactively create both a new political culture and a new value system in pursuit of a new Zimbabwe, against their natural political instincts.

In particular, opposition parties should develop a robust culture of internal democracy, transparency, accountability, member self-activity, issues-based politics, capacity building and tolerance towards dissent. A political party cannot be democratic externally (that is, in running a government or with respect to other civil society organisations) when it is not democratic internally. The openness should go beyond what ZANU-PF has experimented with. For example, in addition to an open, transparent and democratic way of selecting candidates for parliamentary elections, the same principle should be applied to presidential candidates in the year 2002.

Protracted presidential primaries would provide a platform for the distillation, refinement and clarity of election issues. They would also provide an opportunity for civic education and enhanced participatory democracy. It should be acceptable in our political culture to have three or four presidential candidates from the same party slug it out in an open national primary. In fact, a candidate who has gone through such a rigorous process and won would be a stronger, clearer and more electable candidate for their party. This celebration of open and democratic internal contests should be complemented by the maturity to accept defeat. Within parties, consensus politics, term limits, coupled with effective checks and balances for party leaders, should be cherished and legally provided for. The issue of gender justice and equity has to be addressed and reflected in party processes, leadership and programmes. All these ideas require a new political party culture that is backed by institutional provisions enshrined in party constitutions.

The various forms of the media should be the watchers and protectors of democracy. They should strive towards independence, objectivity, competence and professionalism. There is a difference between being independent and being anti-government. Similarly, being objective does not mean pro-opposition. The media must be both thorough and discerning, coupled with the ability to separate the message from the messenger. Civic bodies such as labour unions, student organisations, residents' associations and churches should promote the same values and culture that have been prescribed above for political parties. In particular, they should promote member self-activity, participation in the political economy and general civic education.

Address matters of the Zimbabwean economy

It is essential to clearly establish the causes and nature of the economic crisis that has crippled the country. The postulation and prescription of economic solutions should be underpinned by this critical understanding. The form of the economic problems is characterised by the following related symptoms: an unprecedented fuel crisis, hyperinflation, exorbitant interest rates, a huge budget deficit, a large internal debt, shortage of foreign currency, lack of national creditworthiness, unemployment, price increases, the AIDS epidemic and a collapsed healthcare system. The causes of the economic depression include mismanagement, incompetence, lack of capacity, fiscal indiscipline, corruption, political patronage, ethnicity, the DRC war, a misguided, ego-based foreign policy, the absence and lack of commitment to a coherent land policy, lack of creativity and innovation.

A major manifestation of the current economic depression is the shortage of liquid fuel (petrol, paraffin and diesel). A study of this matter is both instructive and revealing. How did the fuel crisis happen? For the past 20 years, Zimbabwe has been procuring fuel inefficiently and at expensive rates, while selling the fuel at low sub-economic levels. The procurement process through NOCZIM was fraught with high-level corruption, gross incompetence and thorough mismanagement, where superfluous commodity brokers were engaged and the tender process abused. Fuel is procured using foreign currency or through loans, but Zimbabwe has run out of foreign currency and it is no longer creditworthy. The foreign currency has been depleted primarily by the costs of Zimbabwe's involvement in the DRC war, the stand-off with the IMF, lack of investment, dependency on imports, lack of exports, a fixed exchange rate and general fiscal indiscipline. The country has lost its creditworthiness because of the preceding reasons and a misguided, ego-based foreign policy. Fuel has been, and still is being, taken to the DRC (in some cases airlifted), thus exacerbating the crisis and the strain on the fiscus. The six months' strategic reserves ran out around September 1999. Since then the country has been operating from tank to pump. The problems that led to the fuel crisis typify and represent what is wrong with the current management of the Zimbabwean economy. A comprehensive discussion of some of these issues within the context of the reality of the country's circumstances is in order.

Zimbabwe is a poor, landlocked, import-based country whose backbone is agriculture and mining. It is part of the global economy that is characterised by a unipolar power system, the hegemony of Western capitalism, globalisation and information technology. This is the reality of Zimbabwe in the year 2000 and any assessment of what is productive or not should be understood within this context. The challenge for the Zimbabwean leadership is how best to manage the foreign relations and global interactions of the country within the said framework so that maximum national benefit is attained.

A country should never have a foreign policy that rotates around the ego of one man, more so in the current global economy. Robert Mugabe's megalomania that stems from profound personal insecurity has ruined Zimbabwe's international relations, in particular with the United Kingdom and the IMF/World Bank. A few illustrative observations will suffice. Who in the entirety of Zimbabwe, other than Robert Mugabe, gives a damn whether there are gays in the Tony Blair UK government, or whether the same government consists of 'little men' who were in high school during the liberation war in Zimbabwe? Why should foreign policy be determined by such unmitigated rubbish?

It is common cause that the British, and their ally the United States, are influential in the international donor, loan and investment community. It is not wise to antagonise them over trivia. The same argument applies to our direct relations with the IMF. Zimbabwe is now a basket case that definitely needs money from the IMF. Mugabe's ego-based public posturing is not in Zimbabwe's interest. His actions are totally unpatriotic and should be condemned with the contempt that they deserve. Yes, the Bretton Woods institutions (IMF and World Bank) have their problems with respect to our interests; hence an uncritical endorsement of their prescriptions is not advised.

However, at the moment the IMF is, for all intents and purposes, the gatekeeper for all other investors and sources of money into the country. No one is going to come in as long as the IMF stays away. That is the nature of the beast. One has to come to terms with it. In fact, with Zimbabwe's participation in the DRC war, all sources of funds into the country feel as if they are sponsoring and paying for that war.

What is prudent is to take the IMF programme, grow the economy, expand the industrial base and work towards independence from such programmes. One should not even think about doing it the Malaysian way. They had US$20 billion in reserves while Zimbabwe has a negative balance. The IMF literally stopped the African Development Bank and South Africa from giving loans to Zimbabwe. Even the government's proposed 18-month Millennium Economic Recovery Programme will not work. While it has interesting strategies and proposals, its major weakness is that it assumes that the programme can be implemented without the IMF and World Bank.

Zimbabwe has been reduced to a dire case that requires the participation of the IMF. Baseless pride and inflated egos will only damage the country further. Yes, national sovereignty and dignity are key parameters in foreign policy formulation. They should never be sacrificed nor surrendered to international forces. The problem is that Zimbabwe is not being isolated and persecuted for taking principled foreign policy positions or for supporting just causes in the world. The country is paying for the misplaced ego of one man.

The economy: What should be done?

Given the state of the Zimbabwean economy, it is important to have both short-term recovery strategies and long-term economic solutions. The country needs a clear agro-industrial policy that is backed by a solid commitment to manufacturing and investment.

Both monetary and fiscal policies have to be carefully crafted to re-establish macroeconomic stability. On the monetary side strategies to rein in inflation and interest rates such as inflation targeting and interest rates banding should be implemented. This should be coupled with a social contract between the three main stakeholders: government, industry and labour. This arrangement requires political will and commitment (the type that has been missing from the ZANU-PF regime). For example, if the target is that inflation should not go above 15 per cent, the government will pledge not to increase its expenditure by more than 15 per cent, labour will not demand wage increases that are higher than 15 per cent, and industry won't put up prices by more than 15 per cent.

The question then becomes: What has to be done in the economy to achieve these targets? On the fiscal side, government expenditure has to be slashed. In particular, our troops in the DRC war must be pulled out immediately. The army should be heavily trimmed into lean and professional units. The oversized Cabinet must be reduced by 70 per cent and their benefits and salaries cut by a similar percentage. The number of foreign missions and trips should be reduced dramatically, leaving only those facilitating critical activities. The allowances for such missions and trips should be cut by 60 per cent. It has to be accepted that the Zimbabwean civil service is bloated and inefficient. It needs radical reform, streamlining and reduction. Reform must target management capacity building, implementation capacity enhancement, skills competency, incentive-altering structures, modernisation of operations, and improved labour productivity. For retrenched civil servants, severance packages should be provided coupled with assistance and retraining into self-employment, the informal or private sectors.

At all times, there should always be efficient liaison between those responsible for monetary policy (the Reserve Bank) and those in charge of fiscal policy (the Ministry of Finance), that is, effective macroeconomic policy co-ordination is critical.

To boost macroeconomic stability, the Reserve Bank of Zimbabwe must be converted into an independent central bank with a non-political appointee governor whose tenure and activities are independent of politicians. This arrangement must be provided for in the Constitution. One major objective of fiscal and monetary policy co-ordination should be to reduce the debilitating and crippling budget deficit to a manageable level. The ideal should be to strive for a balanced budget and even push for a legal requirement to buttress this ideal. The Zimbabwe government has a huge internal debt that has to be resolved as a matter of urgency. Although Zimbabweans are among the most highly taxed people in the world, they enjoy very few quality services. One area where the government can raise more revenue is by expanding the tax base without necessarily raising taxes. This can be achieved by improving tax-collection mechanisms, taxing the informal sector, creating more jobs and attracting more investment.

The role of the government in the economy has to be openly debated. In addition to providing the regulatory framework, setting the terms of reference and providing certain national services (armed services, civil service, infrastructure, education and health), what else is its function in the economy? Given the history of Zimbabwe and that of the world there is still a strong case for social justice, equitable distribution of wealth, levelling of the economic playing field and economic empowerment of disadvantaged groups. A government must play a serious role in addressing these matters. In particular, the provision of affordable education, healthcare and housing to the majority of Zimbabweans is a clear obligation. The government must facilitate and defend workers' rights, the living wage principle, academic freedom and the transparent equitable redistribution of both land and wealth. However, the bottom line is that wealth must be created before it is distributed. High productivity and extensive wealth creation are chief characteristics of a strong economy. Consequently, entrepreneurship, competition, market forces, innovation and the profit motivc have their place.

Nonetheless, society and the individual should not be slaves to these forces, nor should they be solely driven by them. Rather, these aspects of the market economy should be used to serve society and improve the material conditions of the generality of the people. It is within this context that privatisation, black empowerment, land redistribution, labour laws and the general management and control of the economy should be discussed.

An uncritical, all-embracing attitude towards privatisation as the *sine qua non* for Zimbabwe's survival is mistaken. Privatisation policy must answer the why, when and how questions. Primarily, only unproductive and loss-making enterprises should be targeted, and associated social costs such as job losses must be addressed by providing retrenchment packages, retraining and self-employment facilitation. When an unprofitable and debt-ridden company has been identified for privatisation, it is not financially prudent to sell it in that state. Before privatisation, the company equity must be boosted, performance enhanced and the company debt transferred to central government. In this way, the parastatal is sold as a successful enterprise and more revenue is raised. Indigenous Zimbabweans, including organised groups of workers, must get special preference in buying these companies. However, this should be done in an open and transparent way, and not based on political patronage.

A third of the money raised from privatisation should be used for private sector infrastructure investment (eg roads, power, water and telecommunications) so that an enabling environment that woos more private sector investment into the rural areas is created. Another third should be used to pay off the national debt, in particular the domestic component. The rest of the money should be spent on the provision of social services (health, education and housing).

The AIDS epidemic has ravaged the country with social and economic consequences of crisis proportion. This has been compounded by a collapsed healthcare system. The government must spend more on healthcare resources, manpower, infrastructure and education. Official openness about HIV and AIDS, supported by social campaigns and civic education, should be used to demystify the disease, remove the stigma surrounding it and raise national awareness. In this way, new infections can be prevented while existing cases are dutifully managed. The improvement of the quality of life of Zimbabweans and the availability of health facilities, drugs, information, testing equipment and the commensurate manpower can be used to reduce the number of patients who die from ordinarily manageable attributable and opportunistic infections.

On the liquid fuel crisis, the questions and lessons that should be addressed and drawn are the following: What can be done in the short run, what is the long-term solution, and how can a crisis of that immensity be prevented from ever occurring in strategic areas such as the fuel, power and water industries? The National Oil Company of Zimbabwe (NOCZIM) should be shut down and a regulatory special purpose vehicle put in its place. In addition to the government, private companies should then be allowed to procure their own fuel within that regulated framework. The central organising principle should be achieving efficient, economic and sustainable fuel procurement, while protecting the citizens from both shortages and unaffordable fuel prices. Functional six-month strategic reserves should be redesigned and re-established. Proactive and preventive studies and measures should be carried out in other strategic industries in order to avoid similar disasters in the future.

The land question remains largely unresolved, and this is a major concern for the following reasons: Zimbabwe has an agrarian-based economy, land constituted the basis of the liberation war and 70 per cent of the population consists of peasant farmers. The legitimacy and immortality of the case for land redistribution should never be compromised. However, the challenge is reconciling this clear obligation with notions of the sanctity of private property, national sovereignty, history of land transfer and the collateral value of land. The land question is too important a matter to be clouded by partisan electioneering.

ZANU-PF's lack of both a coherent policy for, and commitment to, equitable redistribution of land, with a view to alleviate poverty while sustaining productivity, is self-evident. They have had 20 years of inactivity and failure. The land that they acquired was given to their elites (the recent infamous list of the 99-year leaseholders is instructive), and their attempts at resettlement schemes in the 1980s were a total failure. Some critical matters are not being sufficiently raised and resolved in the national debate about land. There are resources, infrastructural provisions and skills that are required for effective settlement: Agricultural equipment, seeds, roads, water, electricity, literacy and agricultural training. Any meaningful land policy should clearly articulate government means and mechanisms of providing these requirements. Individual financial assistance can be provided through the establishment of a land bank. The issues of title deeds, tenure systems, land type, suitable crops and settler selection criteria have to be dealt with.

Gender justice should be a key value in the land redistribution programme. Women are the main agricultural workers and producers but they don't own land, the products of their labour, or the implements they use. Hence, empowerment of women and gender justice should be central values in the land debate.

Although the land question is of critical importance in the pursuit of economic justice and freedom in Zimbabwe, it must be acknowledged that land is finite and not expandable. It cannot be cut out and parcelled out to every citizen. There has to be a radical paradigm shift from the land-based economy to the knowledge economy characterised by information technology, electronic commerce, high technology, financial services, biotechnology, manufacturing, mechatronics and automation. This is where Zimbabwe's future lies in the global economy.

The information superhighway provides an opportunity for us to run where others walked. For example, for a person in Binga to be connected to the internet, and thus to the global economy's information superhighway, what is required there is power, telecommunications and a computer. Once one is on the information superhighway, the economic and educational activities/opportunities are endless. One such economic activity is developing software for international companies while residing in Zimbabwe. Based on this principle, many US companies are currently contracting much of their software development to India, generating a lot of employment and foreign currency for India. The same can be done in Zimbabwe.

Other information technology-based activities that could be engaged in include: electronic commerce, electronic business, trading, financial markets, financial services and engineering design. Furthermore, high technology, in the form of advanced manufacturing, mechatronics and robotics and the new advances in biotechnology, are closely linked to, and dependent on, information technology. The challenge is how to marry Zimbabwean needs with cutting-edge Western technology.

Unfortunately, Zimbabwe is actually going against and viciously fighting the knowledge economy, as evidenced by the anti-technology legislation that was passed in Parliament on 8 March 2000 and signed into law by Mugabe, in the form of the Postal and Telecommunications Act. This Act empowers the President to monitor and intercept communications via cellular phones, electronic mail and landlines. It should be emphasised that autocratic rule is not compatible with the knowledge economy.

Another approach that ties in with the philosophy and benefits of the knowledge economy is the notion of export-based investment and foreign direct investment. In this arrangement, international companies from say Japan, the United States and Germany will come into Zimbabwe and set up their manufacturing plants, build products like cellular phones, DVD players and computers, and sell them back to Europe, the Americas and Asia, thus creating jobs in Zimbabwe, bringing foreign currency and making useful products available in the country at cheaper prices. Additional benefits include the expansion of the industrial, tax and export bases of the economy. For the companies, the motivation would be our lower labour costs, highly skilled human resources, cheaper raw materials, good infrastructure and tax incentives. These companies can start with simple assembling of products from parts, and then move on to carrying out their research and development in Zimbabwe.

Yes, it has been argued that countries must identify and concentrate on their core competencies, as these define the competitive advantage of a nation. While this conventional wisdom has its place, in the global economy it is essential for countries to expand their core competencies in order to be competitive and survive.

There is no such thing as one type of technology for the poor countries and another type for the rich ones. Technology is technology, period. In fact, some of the most advanced Western technologies – such as cellular phones, laptops and solar energy – lend themselves so well to poor countries like Zimbabwe. With the rapid advances in technology all one would need to be on the internet in Binga would be a cellular phone and a laptop that are both powered by solar cells. It is within this context and vision that the paradigm shift to the knowledge economy is robustly defended.

Corruption is endemic and pervasive in all of Zimbabwean society. All the grand economic ideas and programmes proffered above will be ineffectual and at best sub-optimal in a society that is characterised by unchecked rampant corruption. Corruption constitutes a systemic problem that demands systemic solutions. Addressing symptoms of the problem and creating scapegoats won't work. For example, the unfolding corruption scandals involving NOCZIM, GMB, CBZ and Harare City Council are instructive. Who in their right mind would even believe for a second that permanent secretaries, executives and agents could embezzle millions of dollars over such long periods of time without the Cabinet ministers being in the picture and taking part of the loot? Having said that, who in Zimbabwe is so blind, deaf and dumb as to believe that all this looting and plundering by Mugabe's ministers, surrogates and cronies could take place without his direct participation? Mugabe, by accepting that his henchmen have looted the national coffers, has explicitly indicted himself. It is common cause that he is the de facto Minister of Defence and Minister of Finance, in this one-man regime. He is as culpable as those already charged. For the police to have any credibility at all, they must arrest and charge him. Otherwise, the whole exercise of arrests is tantamount to disingenuous public posturing meant for the gullible in the coming elections.

There is neither sincerity nor commitment to anti-corruption strategies and values in the ZANU-PF government. Institutional designs and mechanisms should be put in place to combat and control corruption. These should take the form of vertical and horizontal institutions. A totally new political and social culture that has been described in this document is critical. A good Constitution provides some institutional safeguards that can be used to control behaviour and punish violators.

Conclusion

Zimbabwe is really at a crossroads, and it is important that its people appreciate the nature of the problems and solve them in a structured and systematic way. It is important to note that the three national objectives established in this article affect each other. One cannot be fully achieved without the other two. Progress on one leads to progress on the other two. For example, a good Constitution with checks and balances would never have allowed Zimbabwe's participation in the DRC war (thus saving us foreign currency and fuel); nor the current lawlessness where court orders are defied and high-level corruption is superficially addressed. A functional institutional framework that is characterised by a sustainable democratic system and culture promotes macroeconomic stability, is enabling for investment and increases economic activities. Successful and gainfully employed people can build better institutions and participate more actively in a democracy. A starving peasant or a hungry unemployed youth cannot happily discuss functional separation of powers nor appreciate the need for an independent central bank.

(Fanon, 1963) (Porter, 1998) (Biko, 1979) (Soto, 2003)

Conclusion: Towards a shared Zimbabwean Dream

This book is the first of three volumes that constitute a personal journey of ideas, thoughts and perspectives about both leadership literacy and practice, from 1983 to 2017. During this period, Zimbabweans have tirelessly worked to achieve the 'Zimbabwean Dream' – peace, equality, stability, inclusive democracy and shared economic prosperity. Thought leadership – *intellectual influence through innovative and pioneering thinking* – is essential in the pursuit of this aspirational Promised Land. We must be open to plurality in terms of this dream. There are many competing dreams of what Zimbabwe should be and these include alternative versions represented by different social, political and business groupings. Naturally, these dreams evolve, shift or mutate over time. It is therefore both important and imperative that plurality is accommodated, and the resultant complexities and contradictions acknowledged and resolved. In fact, these competing dreams and contradictions have been reflected in this book.

Admittedly, most nations have similar aspirations about the peace, equality, stability, inclusive democracy and shared economic prosperity that we seek in Zimbabwe. The question which arises is: 'What is quintessentially Zimbabwean about our dream? What are the unique formulation and expression of these ambitions that we envisage?' For a quintessentially Zimbabwean Dream, we have to identify, articulate and embed in our psyche, practices and culture, a few unique aspirations, and assiduously construct the uniquely Zimbabwean identity and shared future that might constitute and reflect the distinctive Zimbabwean Dream, which would be the basis for nation building. Consequently, we can posit that the Zimbabwean Dream must have two components: the collectively desired destination of our country – *a shared national vision*, and a shared national identity – *the national brand*.

In order to achieve these two related objectives, there are two sets of questions to be answered. The first set is as follows: *'What is the state of our society, the economy and politics? What do we want to achieve as a people or country? Where do we want our society, politics and the economy to be in a bounded time frame?'* When we answer these questions, we will have established an understanding of the vision aspect of the dream. The second set of questions is as follows: *'What is our national identity? Who are we? What are we known for? What do we want to be known for? How would we unlock economic value from what we want to be known for?'* When we address these questions, we get an appreciation of the national brand aspect of the dream.

In order to address the first set of challenges and establish a vision for Zimbabwe, we need to work on establishing a time-bound picture of where we want Zimbabwe to be – the Promised Land. We must then answer the question of how we can achieve this vision. This is the strategy – our game plan. We must have clarity on how we are going to move out of our current socio-economic challenges and progress to the desired destination, the quintessentially Zimbabwean vision. Once the strategy is clear we need to develop implementation plans, matrices and timelines in order to operationalise the strategy. Execution is key, but, more importantly, the speed of execution and sustained political will are what will determine success or failure. This is how we should work towards an overarching vision for the country. Developing a coherent national strategy and successfully implementing it will be the two hardest tasks in the journey to a new reality – The Promised Land.

For example, we could aspire to make Zimbabwe a globally competitive economy, a prosperous nation with a high quality of life for our people by 2040. Ostensibly, we can then conceive three supporting pillars for this vision. The first pillar should be about the economy, while the second focuses on society, and the third pillar deals with our politics. For the economic pillar, we could say, for example, that the vision is to maintain a sustained economic growth of 10 per cent per annum over the next 30 years. In addition, we could also think in terms of the major impact projects we have to execute to achieve our economic vision. On the social pillar, we could say that we want to achieve a just and cohesive society enjoying equitable development in a clean and secure environment. Politically, we could aspire to an issue-based, people-centred, results-orientated, accountable and inclusive political democratic system. Running across these three pillars will be cross-cutting supporting frameworks – values, value system, culture, spirituality and institutions.

This is how we can begin to think about a uniquely Zimbabwean Dream by addressing one critical aspect – the vision. Now, the bigger and tougher problem then becomes, *'How do you achieve these three pillars?'* You need three inter-dependent and mutually reinforcing strategic plans and their corresponding implementation frameworks. Each implementation matrix must clearly address such issues as timelines, funding, milestones, critical success factors, workstream ownership and speed of execution.

However, there is still a major challenge. Is the vision shared by all industry and business stakeholders, all of civil society, the diaspora, the war veterans, the securocrats, rural folk and urban communities? Is it shared by all political parties in the country? Is it shared by the churches? Is it shared by the farmers? In short, is the vision shared by all the people of Zimbabwe? Indeed, these are daunting questions. There must be a deliberate and collective effort to create buy-in and ownership by the generality of the people of Zimbabwe. This has to be a process, a journey of building consensus. We must apply our minds as to who will facilitate this noble process of creating buy-in and ownership, and think about the nature of the facilitating platform. Accordingly, the question of trust becomes crucial. There has been a growing trust deficit, and hollowing out of mutual respect, among opposition parties, the ruling party, civil society, business, state institutions and the generality of the populace over the years. All this must be addressed if we are to obtain a shared national vision.

As a country, we must collectively agree on the desired destination of our society, economy and politics. In crafting that vision, there will be concessions, compromises and trade-offs among stakeholders. There will be different interpretations about how to achieve it. We can differ on the methodologies, modalities and time frames of attaining the vision, but we should not question the vision. Directional correctness must be shared. With a shared overarching national vision, we are halfway towards our uniquely Zimbabwean Dream.

The second set of questions also has to be addressed for us to have the complete and comprehensive Zimbabwean Dream. The issues around country identity and reputation are vast and many. There is a need to improve our country's reputation through policies, leadership, vision, strategy and execution. We cannot do it with mere slogans or marketing campaigns. We must build Zimbabwe's reputation in order to improve the country's global competitiveness and attractiveness. The overarching objective is establishing a competitive brand for Zimbabwe, an identity that unlocks economic value in six areas: tourism, investment and immigration, trade and exports, governance and culture (including sports and the arts). We must aspire to be both competitive and attractive in these six areas. This is the essence of establishing a competitive and attractive reputation and identity for Zimbabwe – nation branding. National reputation management is a key element in the pursuit of economic development. This is the second piece of the Zimbabwean Dream puzzle. However, just like with the national vision, we have to work on buy-in and ownership for the national brand. Every Zimbabwean must embrace the national identity and be a brand ambassador. Similarly, there will be concerns about who will facilitate consensus building, the nature of the facilitating platform, and the rebuilding of trust among all stakeholders.

It is important to note that the national vision and national brand are inter-dependent. You cannot have a national vision without a national brand.

Without a competitive and attractive reputation or identity, your national vision will be neither credible nor achievable. Similarly, you cannot have a national brand without a national vision. Your brand will not be sustainable and no economic value will be unlocked from the identity.

These consuming and seemingly intractable ideas on how to achieve a quintessentially and uniquely Zimbabwean Dream will be addressed in the second and third volumes of this *Autobiography of Thought Leadership*.

(Porter, 1998) (Nkrumah, 1965) (Anholt, 2007) (Peters, 2003) (Parahalad, 2004)

Bibliography

Alexander, F. (1998). *Got Your Back: Protecting Tupac in the World of Gangsta Rap*. Los Angeles: Blackslide.

Anderson, J. (1997). *Che Guevara: A Revolutionary Life*. New York: Bantam Books.

Anderson, T. (1976). *Introduction to Political Science*. New York: McGraw.

Anholt, S. (2007). *Competitive Identity: The New Brand Management for Nations, Cities and Regions*. London: Palgrave Macmillan.

Ani, M. (1986). *An African-Centred Critique of European Cultural Thought and Behavior.* New York: Africa World Press.

Bernal, M. (1987). *Black Athena: The Afroasiatic Roots of Classical Civilization*. New Brunswick: Rutgers University Press.

Biko, S. (1979). *Black Consciousness in South Africa; Biko's Last Public Statement and Political Testament*. New York: Random House.

Browder, A. (1992). *Nile Valley Contributions to Civilization*. New York: Institute of Karmic Guidance.

Brown, E. (1993). *A Taste of Power: A Black Woman's Story.* New York: Anchor.

Chung, F. (1985). *Socialism, Education and Development*. Harare: ZPH.

De Soto, H. (2003). *The Mystery of Capital: Why Capitalism Triumphs in the West and Fails Everywhere Else*. Michigan: Basic Books.

Diop, C. (1955). *Civilization or Barbarism*. New York: Penguin.

D'Souza, D. (1996). *The End of Racism*. London: Penguin Press.

Fanon, F. (1963). *The Wretched of the Earth*. London: Grove Press.

Gandhi, M. (1927). *Gandhi: An Autobiography: The Story of My Experiments With Truth*. London: Beacon Press.

Gates, H. L. (1997). *Thirteen Ways of Looking at a Black Man*. New York: Random House.

Gingrich, N. (1997). *Contract With America*. Washington: Taylor.

Guevara, E. C. (1961). *Guerrilla Warfare*. New York: Monthly Review Press.

Harvey, E. (2002). *Kgalema Motlanthe*. Johannesburg: Jacana.

Henrik-Clarke, J. (1993). *Who Betrayed the African World Revolution? And Other Speeches*. New York: Africa World Press.

Jackson, G. (1972). *Blood in My Eye*. Los Angeles: Black Classic Press.

James, G. (1992). *Stolen Legacy: Greek Philosophy is Stolen Egyptian Philosophy*. New York: Africa World Press.

King, M. (1998). *The Autobiography of Martin Luther King, Jr.* Atlanta: Warner Books.

Lenin, V. (1961). *What Is To Be Done?* Moscow: Publishing House.

Malcolm X (1965). *The Autobiography of Malcolm X*. New York: Grove Press.

Mandela, N. (1994). *Long Walk to Freedom*. Johannesburg: Macdonald Purnell.

Marx, K. E. (1969). *Communist Manifesto*. Moscow: Progress Publishers.

Mutambara, A. (1998). *Decentralized Estimation and Control for Multisensor Systems*. New York: CRC Press.

Mutambara, A. (1999). *Design and Analysis of Control Systems*. New York: CRC Press.

Newton, H. (1973). *Revolutionary Suicide*. New York: Randon House.

Nkomo, J. (2001). *The Story of My Life*. Harare: Sapes.

Nkrumah, K. (1965). *Neo-Colonialism, The Last Stage of Imperialism*. London: Thomas Nelson and Sons.

Nyerere, J. (1983). *Our Leadership and the Destiny of Tanzania*. Harare: ZPH.

Parahalad, P. (2004). *The Fortune at the Bottom of the Pyramid*. Philadelphia: Wharton Publishing School.

Peters, T. (2003). *Re-Imagine! Business Excellence in a Disruptive Age*. New York: DK Publishing.

Porter, M. (1998). *The Competitive Advantage of Nations*. Boston: Free Press.

Powell, C. (2003). *My American Journey*. Boston: Random House.

Seale, B. (1991). *Seize the Time: The Story of the Black Panther Party and Huey P. Newton*. New York: Black Classic Press.

Tekere, E. (2007). *A Lifetime of Struggle*. Harare: Sapes Books.

Tse-Tung, M. (1967). *Selected Works of Mao Tse-Tung*. Beijing: Foreign Language Press.

Ture, K. (1992). *Black Power: The Politics of Liberation*. New York: Vintage Books.

Ushewokunze, H. (1984). *An Agenda for Zimbabwe*. Harare: ZPH.

Index